PUBLIC INTERNATIONAL LAW

IN A NUTSHELL

THIRD EDITION

By

THOMAS BUERGENTHAL
Judge, International Court of Justice
Lobingier Professor of Comparative Law and
Jurisprudence, Emeritus
The George Washington University

SEAN D. MURPHY
Associate Professor of Law
The George Washington University

WEST
GROUP

A THOMSON COMPANY

Mat #13377898

Nutshell Series, In a Nutshell, the Nutshell Logo and the West Group symbol are registered trademarks used herein under license.

COPYRIGHT © 1985, 1990 WEST PUBLISHING CO.
COPYRIGHT © 2002 By WEST GROUP
     610 Opperman Drive
     P.O. Box 64526
     St. Paul, MN 55164–0526
     1–800–328–9352

All rights reserved
Printed in the United States of America

ISBN 0–314–21158–6

TEXT IS PRINTED ON 10% POST
CONSUMER RECYCLED PAPER

1st Reprint — 2003

PREFACE TO THE THIRD EDITION

This third edition of the Nutshell on Public International Law is designed to introduce the lawyer and the law student to the basic doctrines, institutions, and methodology of modern public international law. It is also intended as a text capable of supplementing and helping with the conceptual integration of the teaching materials on international law in use in the United States.

In a short volume of this type, the risk is great that, in the effort to consolidate and to be brief, material will be distorted or oversimplified. We have sought to reduce that risk by providing references to cases, secondary sources, and other materials where the reader can find more detailed information and nuances on the points covered. At the same time, in this edition we have sought to expand the breadth of coverage by addressing certain specialized areas of international law not dealt with in the prior editions (international environmental law and the law of the sea), as well as more detailed coverage of certain issues previously addressed (the law applicable to the recognition of states and to the use of force). In the final chapter, we provide extensive information on techniques for researching international law, with particular attention to the resources now available on the Internet.

As was noted in the first edition, what to cover and what to omit ultimately is a matter of personal judgment and preference, as well as of available space. Our decision regarding content and coverage was guided in part by what we deem to be important for understanding the basic elements of contemporary international law, recognizing full well that much more remains to be said about the topics we have covered and that a great deal of material has not been considered at all. We hope that this book will stimulate the reader to pursue the further study of international law. Given the world we live in, public international law is a subject whose basic institutions and concepts need to be understood by the legal profession as a whole.

THOMAS BUERGENTHAL
SEAN D. MURPHY

August 2002

ACKNOWLEDGMENTS

We would like to express our profound appreciation to Professor Harold G. Maier, who served as coauthor on the first two editions and whose influence continues to be felt within these pages. We would also like to express our strong gratitude to our research assistants for the many valuable contributions they made to this book. Judge Buergenthal wishes to give special thanks to Margaret Satterthwaite, Esq. for her important help. He is also profoundly indebted to his secretary, Mrs. Danielle Okandeji-Touffet, whose professionalism and patience made important contributions to this edition of the book. Professor Murphy wishes to thank Anna Conley, Matthew Haws, and Janet Sarver for their extraordinary assistance, and to thank George Washington University Law School Dean Michael K. Young for his support.

Judge Buergenthal wishes to express his very special thanks to his wife, Marjorie J. (Peggy) Buergenthal, for her understanding, support and help with this and the previous editions of the book. Professor Murphy expresses his special appreciation to his wife, Julie, and dedicates his work on this book to perhaps the next generation of international law scholars, Jack, Lisa, and Anna Murphy.

THOMAS BUERGENTHAL
SEAN D. MURPHY

August 2002

OUTLINE

Chapter 2. Sources of International Law

Chapter 3. States and International Organizations

**Chapter 4. International Dispute Settle-
ment**

Chapter 6.   Rights of Individuals

A.   Law of the U.N. Charter

C. International humanitarian law

A. Procedural issues

B. Substantive aspects

Chapter 7. Foreign Relations Law in the United States

Chapter 8. Jurisdiction

Chapter 9.   Immunities From Jurisdiction

Chapter 10. Law of the Sea

Chapter 11. International Environmental Law

Chapter 12.   Use of Force and Arms Control

Chapter 13.   International Legal Research

TABLE OF CASES

References are to Pages

TABLE OF CASES

TABLE OF CASES

*

TABLE OF ABBREVIATIONS

Am. J. Int'l L.	American Journal of International Law
Am. U.J. Int'l L. & Pol'y	American University Journal of International Law and Policy
Am. U.L. Rev.	American University Law Review
ATCA	Alien Tort Claims Act
Austl. Y.B. Int'l L.	Australian Yearbook of International Law
Brit. Y.B. Int'l L.	British Yearbook of International Law
Cardozo L. Rev.	Cardozo Law Review
C.F.R.	Code of Federal Regulations
Colum. J. Transnat'l. L.	Columbia Journal of Transnational Law
Colum. L. Rev.	Columbia Law Review
C.M.L.R.	Common Market Law Reports
Cong. Rec.	Congressional Record
ESC Res.	United Nations Economic and Social Council Resolution
E.C.R.	European Court Reporter
Eur. J. Int'l L.	European Journal of International Law
F.2d	Federal Reporter 1932–1992
F.3d	Federal Reporter 1993–present

FSIA	Foreign Sovereign Immunities Act
F. Supp.	Federal Supplement 1932–1960
F. Supp.2d	Federal Supplement 1960–present
Fed. Cl.	Federal Claims Reporter
Fed. Reg.	Federal Register
G.A.O.R.	United Nations General Assembly Official Records
G.A. Res.	United Nations General Assembly Resolution
Geo. Wash. J. Int'l L. & Econ.	George Washington Journal of International Law and Economics
Harv. Int'l L.J.	Harvard International Law Journal
Harv. L. Rev.	Harvard Law Review
Heidelberg J. Int'l	Heidelberg Journal of International Law
H.R.	House of Representatives Bill
Hum. Rights L.J.	Human Rights Law Journal
Hum. Rights Q.	Human Rights Quarterly
I.C.C.	International Criminal Court
ICCPR	International Covenant on Civil and Political Rights
ICESCR	International Covenant on Economic and Social Rights
I.C.J.	International Court of Justice (Reports of Judgments, Advisory Opinions and Orders)
ICTY	International Criminal Tribunal for the former Yugoslavia
I.L.M.	International Legal Materials
I.L.R.	International Law Reports
Inter-Am. Court H.R.	Inter-American Court of Human Rights
Int'l & Comp. L.Q.	International and Comparative Law Quarterly

TABLE OF ABBREVIATIONS

PUBLIC INTERNATIONAL LAW

IN A NUTSHELL

THIRD EDITION

*

CHAPTER 1

APPLICATION AND RELEVANCE OF INTERNATIONAL LAW

I. INTRODUCTION

This chapter introduces the reader to the basic principles of modern public international law. It provides an overview of the historical and theoretical context within which that law has developed and discusses the functions international law performs. Examples of the application of international law on the national and international plane are also provided.

II. PROBLEMS OF DEFINITION

§ 1–1. Traditional definition. International law used to be defined as the law that governs relations between states. Under the traditional definition, only states were subjects of international law; that is, only states were deemed to have rights and obligations that international law recognized. Whatever benefits or burdens international law conferred or imposed on other entities or individuals were considered to be purely derivative, flowing to these so-called "objects" of international law by virtue of their relations to or dependence upon a state.

1

§ 1–2. States under international law. When international lawyers speak of "states", they mean sovereign or nation-states. To qualify as a state under international law, an entity must have a territory, a population, a government and the capacity to engage in diplomatic or foreign relations. States in federal unions, provinces or cantons usually lack the last attribute, which is a vital element of sovereignty. *See generally* 1 *Oppenheim's International Law* 121–23 (R. Jennings & A. Watts, eds. 1992).

§ 1–3. Modern definition. Contemporary international law, although still considered to be principally the law governing relations between states, is no longer deemed to be exclusively limited to those relations. It has a wide reach and is more properly defined as law that deals "with the conduct of states and of international organizations and with their relations *inter se*, as well as with some of their relations with persons, whether natural or juridical." American Law Institute, *Restatement of the Foreign Relations Law of the United States (Third)* § 101 (1987).

§ 1–4. Modern subjects. Today intergovernmental international organizations, and even individuals, albeit to a more limited extent, are and can be the subjects of rights and obligations under international law. The United Nations and various specialized international or regional organizations such as, for example, the International Labor Organization and the Council of Europe, enjoy the legal capacity to enter into treaty relations, governed by and binding under international law, with states and other international organizations. *See Advisory*

Opinion on Reparation for Injuries Suffered in the Service of the United Nations, 1949 I.C.J. 174 (Apr. 11); *Advisory Opinion on Legality of the Use by a State of Nuclear Weapons in Armed Conflict*, 1996 I.C.J. 66 at 75 (July 8); *see also infra* ch. 3. The direct responsibility of individuals for serious international crimes, such as crimes against humanity and war crimes, and the development of the international law on human rights, indicate furthermore that, in certain circumstances, individuals have rights and obligations under international law that are not derivative in the traditional sense. *See infra* ch. 6.

III.   INTERNATIONAL AND NATIONAL APPLICATION

§ 1–5. Applications distinguished. The fact that international law governs inter-state relations does not mean that it is irrelevant on the national legal plane or that it is not applied there. The manner in which international law is applied on the national and on the international plane differs, however, even though the substantive rules as such may be the same. When studying international law, it is useful, therefore, to be aware of the differences between the national and the international application of international law.

§ 1–6. International application. On the international plane, international law is invoked and applied on a daily basis by states and by intergovernmental organizations. With minor exceptions, it is the only law that applies to the conduct of states and international organizations in their relations with one another. Here international law is a distinct legal system, comparable in its scope and function to a national legal system.

§ 1–7. National application. On the national plane, international law is not a legal system. When we say in the United States, for example, that international law is "the law of the land," we are in fact saying that it is a part or branch of our legal system, in very much the same way that the law of torts or contracts is part of our legal system. We refer to the law of torts in a case or situation involving issues that can be characterized as being governed by principles of tort law. In much the same way, we refer to international law when the facts of the case or situation demand it. Here international law is invoked in national litigation and other contexts by individuals, private and public entities, and government agencies whenever resort to it appears to be relevant in this context. The question of whether the individual invoking international law in a U.S. court, for example, has rights or obligations under international law on the international plane (that is, whether he/she is a subject of international law) is for the most part irrelevant. The relevant question here is whether this or that rule of international law is, as a matter of U.S. law, appropriate to the resolution of the controversy before the court. Viewed from this national perspective, the individual is the subject of rights and obligations which have their source in international law to the same extent that the individual is the subject of national legal rights and obligations.

§ 1–8. Some examples. Let us assume that international law requires states in peacetime to grant foreign merchant ships innocent passage through their territorial waters. Let us assume further that a merchant ship flying the flag of State X and belonging to Mr. Barco, a national of State X, is seized by the coast guard of State Y in its territorial waters in violation of the above mentioned international law rule. On the international plane, the resulting dispute would be between State X and State Y. This would be so because the right to innocent passage by merchant ships, and the obligation to permit the exercise of that right, are rights and obligations appertaining only to the subjects of international law—the states. The seizure of Mr. Barco's ship would be deemed to be a breach of an obligation owed by State Y to State X, the state of the ship's nationality. That nationality entitles State X to assert a claim against State Y. Under general international law, an injury to a state's national is deemed to be an injury to the state. *See Mavrommatis Palestine Concessions* (Gr. v. U.K.), 1924 P.C.I.J. (ser. A) No. 2 (Aug. 30).

Now let us assume that instead of proceeding through State X in the manner indicated above, Mr. Barco files a suit in the courts of State Y, seeking both the release of his ship and damages. If international law is the law of the land in State Y—which it is in different guises in most, if not all, states comprising the community of nations—Mr. Barco would have the right to invoke the relevant rule of international law to assert the illegality of the seizure of his ship. Here he would claim the violation of a right enjoyed by him under international law in much the same way that he would rely on a rule of the national law of torts or property if someone had deprived him of the use of his property in a business transaction in State Y. Whether the case concerns the law of torts or property or international law, its outcome in State Y will depend upon the legal and factual soundness of the claim under the relevant national law, both substantive and procedural, of State Y.

On the international plane, the context for the application of the international law rule relating to innocent passage of ships through territorial waters in peacetime is the international legal system. That is to say, here all issues bearing on the case, for example, whether the rule takes precedence or not over other rules, etc., would be determined by international law. On the national plane, the context for the application of the rule is the national legal system and constitutional framework. And while it is true, as a general proposition, that a national court would seek to determine the content of a rule of international law in much the same way as an international court, the same controversy might well be resolved differently by each of them because in one case the judicial context is the national legal system with its specialized rules of procedure and possibly competing principles of substantive law, and in the other it is the international legal system. That is why it is so important, when dealing with international law questions and materials, to inquire whether the context is the national or international plane, or both.

§ 1–9. Supremacy of international law. The rights and obligations which a state has under international law are, on the international plane, superior to any rights or duties it may have under its national law. Thus, for example, if a state is a party to a treaty that is valid and binding under international law, its non-performance cannot be excused as a matter of international law on the ground that the treaty was declared unconstitutional by the state's supreme court. With minor exceptions not here relevant, the unconstitutionality of the treaty is a purely national law issue. *See* Vienna Convention on the Law of Treaties, May 23, 1969, arts. 27 & 46, 1155 U.N.T.S. 331, 8 I.L.M. 679. Although it might prevent the state from giving effect to the treaty, its failure to perform would nevertheless constitute a breach of international law. *See, e.g., LaGrand Case* (Ger. v. U.S.), 2001 I.C.J. (June 27), *reprinted in* 40 I.L.M. 1069 (2001). In practice, this type of problem tends to be resolved by renegotiation of the treaty or, in rare instances, by the payment of compensation.

Conceptually, the inability of a state for national constitutional reasons to perform a treaty obligation valid under international law resembles national situations in which one party to a contract is unable or unwilling to comply with its contractual obligations and is liable for the consequences of its breach. Moreover, whether the decision of a state not to comply with a treaty is compelled by its supreme court or by a decision of its president, for example, is equally irrelevant under international law. National constitutional law does not on the international plane supersede international law, even though it may take precedence over international law on the national plane, which is the case in most states.

IV.   RELEVANCE AND FUNCTION OF INTERNATIONAL LAW

§ 1–10.   Uses of international law. International law is routinely applied by international tribunals as well as by national courts. But international law is not relevant solely in judicial proceedings. States rely on it in their diplomatic relations, in their negotiations, and in their policymaking. States defend their actions and policies (both to other states and to their own national constituents) by reference to international law and challenge the conduct of other states in reliance on it. To the extent that international law is perceived as "law" by the international community, it imposes restraints on the behavior of states and affects their decision-making process. Although there may be considerable disagreement in a particular case about the nature, scope or applicability of a given rule of international law, states rarely admit to violating international law and hardly ever assert the right to do so.

§ 1–11.   International law as law. The conduct of states is conditioned by many factors; international law is only one of them. Sometimes it is determinative, many times it is not. Yet whoever seeks to understand or predict how states will act in a given situation, or whoever has to counsel states on how they should act consistent with their national self-interest, needs to take into account applicable principles of international law. A state may be prepared to violate international law in order to achieve a given political objective. But in calculating the short-and long-term political costs of such action, the state's policymakers will have to address questions relating to the nature and function of that law, as well as the legal and political consequences of being labeled a law-breaker.

The dramatic violations of international law, principally those involving the threat or use of force, which attract worldwide attention, should not blind us to the fact that the vast body of international law which regulates international commerce, communication, transportation, and day-to-day diplomatic and consular relations, to mention but a few areas, is applied and observed as routinely as is national law. For lawyers working in these fields, whether as legal advisers to governments, to international organizations or to corporations, or as judges, legislators, policymakers, or arbitrators, international law is law in a very real, practical sense. They have to know how to find and analyze it, in what context to apply it, and where and how to enforce it.

§ 1–12. Application and enforcement. Questions about enforcement arise the moment international law is mentioned. In addressing these questions, it is important to ask whether we are talking about enforcement on the national or on the international plane. On the national plane, international law tends to be enforced by courts and administrative agencies in much the same manner as any other national law. The answer is more complex when we turn to the international plane.

As a rule, international courts do not have compulsory or automatic jurisdiction to deal with all international legal disputes that might be ripe for adjudication. The authority of these courts to hear a given dispute depends upon the acceptance of their jurisdiction by the parties to the dispute. *See infra* ch. 4. There are, as a consequence, many international legal disputes that cannot be adjudicated because one or the other of the parties to the dispute refuses to accept the jurisdiction of a court.

But courts are not the only institutions for the resolution of disputes between states. Many international disputes that cannot be submitted to formal international adjudication, can and have been settled by other methods, such as negotiation, mediation, good offices or arbitration, which all involve the application of international law. *See infra* ch. 4. Here international law performs a function similar to that which national law performs in the settlement of disputes that do not reach the courts.

Furthermore, numerous methods and organizations exist today, whether of a political, quasi-judicial, or diplomatic character—the United Nations, regional organizations, diplomatic conferences, multilateral commissions, etc.—where international law plays a role, together with other factors, in resolving conflicts and in fashioning solutions to societal problems of all types. Law plays a comparable role on the national plane. Here too, as on the international plane, its impact outside the formal judicial setting may, at different times and in different contexts, be of marginal significance, quite important or determinative in shaping political compromises or dealing with the problems confronting a given society.

§ 1–13. Enforcement and compliance. The mechanisms available on the international plane for the enforcement of a judgment rendered by international courts differ from those that may be available on the national plane. *See infra* ch. 4. International tribunals that adjudicate disputes between states do not have a sheriff or police force who can be ordered to enforce a judgment. But even on the national plane, judgments are enforced or executed differently depending upon whether the judgment was rendered against a private party or against the government. While the property of private parties may be attached to execute judgments against them, such a remedy is usually not available against governmental entities. Moreover, the enforcement powers of national courts are more symbolic than real when the confrontation is between them and the government. Governments comply with national court decisions not because the courts have the actual police or military power to force compliance. The extent of compliance tends, rather, to be a function of the political legitimacy and moral credibility that sustain the entire fabric of governmental authority and produce the expectation that law will be obeyed.

The situation is not all that different on the international plane. It is true, nevertheless, that the absence of a formal centralized lawmaking authority, coupled with the debilitating jurisdictional defects of international courts, weaken the expectation of compliance in comparison with the situation that exists on the national plane. These considerations need to be balanced against the risk that non-complying governments open themselves up to costly retaliatory measures by other governments. The likelihood of such retaliation, whether it be political or economic, is an element that has an important impact on compliance by states with their international obligations. Moreover, even the strongest states have long-term and short-term political and economic interests in an international order in which conflicts are resolved in accordance with generally accepted rules, in a manner that is reasonably predictable, and that reduces the likelihood of resort to force.

V.   HISTORICAL OVERVIEW

§ 1–14.   **Origins of the modern system.** International law or the law of nations, as it used to be called, came into its own as a separate legal system or discipline with the emergence of the modern nation-state in the 16th and 17th centuries. Of course, practices such as the exchange of diplomatic emissaries, the conclusion of peace treaties, etc., and some of the rules applicable to them can be traced back far into antiquity. *See* D. Bederman, *International Law in Antiquity* (2001). But it was not until modern times that the rules governing relations between states came to be seen as a distinct body of law. Many of these rules were derived either from Roman law or Canon law, which drew heavily on principles of natural law. These two sources of law also formed the basis of much of the national law of the nation-states that came into

being in Europe as the Medieval period drew to a
close with the dawn of the Renaissance. Roman law
and Canon law exerted great influence on the European statesmen and legal scholars of the period who
created and systematized what became modern international law. *See generally* A. Nussbaum, *A Con-
cise History of the Law of Nations* (rev. ed. 1962).

§ **1–15. Major early writers and theories**.
Hugo Grotius (1583–1645), a Dutch scholar and
diplomat, is known as the "father" of modern international law. His major work, *De Jure Belli Ac
Pacis* (1625), is one of the earliest attempts to
provide a systematic overview of the international
law of war and peace. Among Grotius' other important works is *Mare Liberum* (1609), a forceful brief
on behalf of the doctrine of freedom of the seas,
which in due course came to be accepted as a basic
principle of international law.

Grotius was preceded by a number of writers
whose important contributions to the development
of international law should be noted. Leading
among these are the Italian Alberico Gentili (1552–
1608), a professor of Roman law at Oxford University, who wrote *De Jure Belli* (1598), and the Spanish
theologian, Francisco de Vitoria (1480–1546), who,
in his lectures on the Spanish conquests in the New
World, was among the first to assert the universal
character and applicability of international law.

Of importance among the early writers on international law who followed Grotius is the German
scholar, Samuel Pufendorf (1632–1694). In his *De
Jure Naturae Gentium* (1672), Pufendorf espoused
the view that natural law was the source or basis of

international law. An individual whose influence rivaled that of Grotius for a considerable period of time was the Swiss diplomat, Emmerich de Vattel (1714–1767). His principal work, *The Law of Nations* (1758), a practical guide to international law for diplomats, was widely cited and relied upon by governments well into the 19th century. *See* F. Ruddy, *International Law in the Enlightenment* (1975).

While Pufendorf and Vattel advanced the view that natural law was the true source of international law, the English legal scholar, Richard Zouche (1590–1660), was one of the early positivists. Partisans of positivism looked to state practice as the source of international law, seeking the basis of this law in the consent of the states—its subjects. Both schools of thought found some support in Grotius' writings, because his theories about international law relied on natural law and on custom established by the practice of states. These two schools dominated the philosophical discourse about the nature of international law into the early decades of the 20th century. Positivism gradually emerged as the dominant theory, leading to the acceptance of the view that international law as law depended upon the sovereign consent of the states comprising the international community. The requisite consent had to be sought in the practice of states deemed by them to have the force of law. *See infra* § 2–3.

§ 1–16. Historical milestones. A number of events or historical milestones mark the development of modern international law. Among these are the Peace of Westphalia, the Congress of Vienna, the establishment of the League of Nations and the adoption of the Charter of the United Nations.

The Peace of Westphalia ended the Thirty Years' War (1618–1648) and established a treaty-based system or framework for peace and cooperation in Europe, that endured for more than a hundred years. It provided, *inter alia,* for the coexistence in certain parts of Europe of Catholicism and Protestantism, thus planting early seeds of religious freedom in Europe. The foundations for multi-state diplomatic congresses and negotiations were laid at the conferences that produced the two basic treaties comprising the Peace of Westphalia. These agreements also proclaimed the doctrine of *pacta sunt servanda* (treaties are to be observed)—a fundamental principle of international law—and established a machinery for the settlement of disputes arising between the signatories.

The Final Act of the Congress of Vienna (1815) formally ended the Napoleonic Wars and fashioned a sophisticated multilateral system of political and economic cooperation in Europe. The major aspects of this system survived until the outbreak of the First World War. The Congress adopted the first comprehensive set of rules governing diplomatic protocol, it formally condemned the slave trade, and it established the principle of free and unimpeded navigation on international rivers traversing the region. The Congress laid the foundation for the recognition of the neutrality of Switzerland and its guarantee by the principal European powers. Attached to the Final Act, furthermore, were various multilateral and bilateral agreements which, together with the treaties that emerged from and followed upon the Peace of Westphalia, provided Europe with a substantial body of international law and contributed in a very significant manner to the development of modern international law.

The League of Nations came into being in 1920 with the entry into force of its Covenant. The Covenant formed an integral part of the Treaty of Versailles, which ended World War I. Although the failure of the League of Nations to prevent World War II is a well-known historical fact, it is important to remember that the League constituted the first serious effort by states to create a permanent inter-governmental institutional framework for the resolution of political disputes and the preservation of peace. It was the League that established the Permanent Court of International Justice, the first such international tribunal open to all states. The machinery created by the League for the protection of the rights of minorities in eastern and southeastern Europe and for the supervision of certain non-self-governing territories (Mandates) constituted the first international attempt to establish international institutions for the protection of human rights. The League contributed in numerous other ways to the development and codification of international law. Moreover, the modern law of international organizations came into being with the establishment of the League of Nations and the legal precedents it set. *See infra* ch. 3.

The United Nations, which was founded in 1945, is discussed in detail in Chapter 3. Here it needs to be emphasized only that the mere existence of the United Nations, whatever its institutional and political weaknesses, constitutes a further advance in the efforts of the international community to make international law a more effective tool for the preservation of international peace and the improvement of the human condition throughout the world. The United Nations' legal and political achievements, if measured by the job that remains to be done, are limited at best; but its contributions gain greatly in significance if judged in relation to the accomplishments of the international law and organizations that preceded the United Nations. Whether international law and organizations can in today's world make a truly significant contribution to the solution of the problems facing mankind remains the most critical issue for international lawyers everywhere. It should be the fundamental theme that animates and permeates the study of international law.

CHAPTER 2

SOURCES OF INTERNATIONAL LAW

I. INTRODUCTION

The formal sources of national law are the constitution, if a state has one, legislative and administrative enactments and, where the doctrine of binding precedent (*stare decisis*) prevails, decisions of judicial tribunals (case law). Thus, if a U.S. lawyer were to be asked, "how do you know that this rule is the law?", he or she would point to one of these sources. Another way of looking at sources of law is to ask, "how is law made?" The answer, on the national plane, is to point to the constitutional, legislative, administrative or judicial process from which law emanates, and to certain generally accepted legal principles.

The situation is more complicated with regard to international law. Viewed in terms of law-making, international law is a primitive legal system. The international community lacks a constitution that can be viewed as a fundamental source of law. There exists no institution comparable to a national legislature with power to promulgate laws of general applicability, nor administrative agencies to produce regulations. Moreover, the International Court of Justice (I.C.J.) (discussed *infra* ch. 4) lacks plenary jurisdiction over disputes arising under international law, and the decisions of the Court are legally binding only on the parties to the dispute. They have no precedential value in a formal sense because *stare decisis* is not a rule of international law. *See* I.C.J. Statute, art. 59.

How then do we know whether a given rule is international law? This question can be answered only by reference to the sources of international law and by analyzing the manner in which international law is made or how it becomes law binding on the international plane. This chapter deals with this question as well as with issues relating to the manner in which the existence or non-existence of a rule of international law may be proved. *See generally* 1 *Oppenheim's International Law* 22 et seq. (R. Jennings & A. Watts eds., 1992).

II. PRIMARY SOURCES

§ 2–1. Article 38(1) of the I.C.J. Statute. This provision is generally considered to be the most authoritative enumeration of the sources of international law. It reads as follows:

The Court, whose function is to decide in accordance with international law such disputes as are submitted to it, shall apply:

a. international conventions, whether general or particular, establishing rules expressly recognized by the contesting states;

b.   international custom, as evidence of a general practice accepted as law;

c.   the general principles of law recognized by civilized nations;

d.   . . . judicial decisions and the teachings of the most highly qualified publicists of the various nations, as subsidiary means for the determination of rules of law.

§ 2–2. Meaning of Article 38 of the I.C.J. Statute. Article 38 was included in the I.C.J. Statute to describe the nature of the international law that the Court was to apply. Article 38(1) indicates that international law consists of or has its basis in international conventions (treaties), international custom, and general principles of law. It follows that a rule cannot be deemed to be international law unless it is derived from one of these three sources. *See* American Law Institute, *Restatement of the Foreign Relations Law of the United States (Third)* § 102(1) (1987) (*Restatement (Third)*).

"Judicial decisions" and the "teachings" of the publicists are not sources of law as such; they are "subsidiary means" for finding what the law is. International lawyers look to these authorities as evidence to determine whether a given norm can be deemed to have been accepted as a rule of international law. *See The Paquete Habana*, 175 U.S. 677 (1900); *Restatement (Third)* § 102, rptrs. note 1.

Article 38(1) is silent on the question of whether the three primary sources it lists have the same hierarchic value, that is, whether treaties take precedence over custom and custom over general principles of law. Although there is some disagreement on the subject, in practice it would appear that an international court, faced with a dispute between two states, would give precedence to a specific treaty provision binding on the parties over a conflicting rule of customary international law, provided the latter did not have the status of a peremptory or fundamental norm of international law (*jus cogens*) which a treaty may not nullify. *See* Vienna Convention on the Law of Treaties, May 23, 1969, art. 53, 1155 U.N.T.S. 331, 8 I.L.M. 679 (VCLT); *see also infra* § 5–13. By the same token, a rule of customary international law would be given preference over a general principle of law. Thus, there is a vague parallel between legislation, common law and legal principles in a national setting, on the one hand, and treaties, custom and general principles in an international context, on the other.

§ 2–3. **Customary international law**. Under I.C.J. Statute Article 38(1)(b), "a general practice accepted as law" is an international custom. The *Restatement (Third)* § 102(2) provides a more meaningful and functionally sounder definition: "customary international law results from a general and consistent practice of states followed by them from a sense of legal obligation." Hence, a rule or principle, reflected in the practice or conduct of states, must be accepted by them, expressly or tacitly, as being legally binding on the international plane in order to be considered a rule of international law.

Customary international law develops from the practice of states. To international lawyers, "the practice of states" means official governmental conduct reflected in a variety of acts, including official statements at international conferences and in diplomatic exchanges, formal instructions to diplomatic agents, national court decisions, legislative measures or other actions taken by governments to deal with matters of international concern. Inaction can also be deemed a form of state practice. On this point, see *Advisory Opinion on Legality of the Threat or Use of Nuclear Weapons*, 1994 I.C.J. 226, para. 67 (July 8).

A practice does not become a rule of customary international law merely because it is widely followed. It must, in addition, be deemed by states to be obligatory as a matter of law. This test will not be satisfied if the practice is followed out of courtesy or if states believe that they are legally free to depart from it at any time. The practice must comply with the *"opinio juris"* requirement (short for the Latin *opinio juris sive necessitatis*—a conviction that the rule is obligatory) to transform it into customary international law.

Although the *opinio juris* requirement may be implied from the fact that a rule has been generally and consistently followed over a long period of time, it is much more difficult to know how widely accepted a practice must be to meet the test. That it does not have to be universal seems to be clear. Equally undisputed is the conclusion that, in general, the practice must be one that is accepted by the world's major powers and by states directly affected by it. There must also not be a significant number of states that have consistently rejected it. Beyond that, it is difficult to be more specific. It should not be forgotten, however, that there exists a vast body of customary international law whose legal status is not disputed. Problems of proof arise primarily in areas of the law affected by ideological disputes or technological advances. *See, e.g., North Sea Continental Shelf Cases* (F.R.G. v. Den.; F.R.G. v. Neth.), 1969 I.C.J. 3 (Feb. 20); *Continental Shelf* (Libya/Malta), 1985 I.C.J. 13 (June 3).

Since international law is consensual in nature and since a practice does not have to be universally accepted to become a rule of customary international law, it follows that a state which has consistently rejected a practice before it became law, will not be bound by it. Although this is not a frequent occurrence, states may "contract out" of customary international law during its formative stage by persistently objecting to it. *Cf. Fisheries Case* (U.K. v. Nor.), 1951 I.C.J. 116 (Dec. 18). But once a practice has acquired the status of law, it is obligatory for all states that have not objected to it.

There is some disagreement over whether newly independent states are bound by all rules of international law in force at the time they become subjects of international law. The *Restatement (Third)* § 102, cmt. d, answers the question in the affirmative. *See generally* M. Virally, *The Sources of International Law*, in *Manual of Public International Law* 132, 137–39 (M. Sorensen ed., 1968).

§ 2–4. Conventional international law. In its enumeration of the sources of international law, Article 38(1)(a) of the I.C.J. Statute speaks of "international conventions, whether general or particular, establishing rules expressly recognized by the contesting states." The reference here is to international agreements or treaties, both bilateral and multilateral. (For the law of treaties, see *infra* ch. 5.) Although a bilateral treaty between State A and State B would be a source of law in a dispute between them concerning an issue governed by the treaty, it is not a source of international law for the international community in general.

Some treaties, however, can give rise to or be a source of customary international law. The *Restatement (Third)* § 102(3) makes that point in the following terms: "[i]nternational agreements create law for the states parties thereto and may lead to the creation of customary international law when such agreements are intended for adherence by states generally and are in fact widely accepted." These treaties can perform a function comparable to legislation on the national plane. Resort to this type of international law-making has increased in recent years, in part because customary international law usually develops much too slowly to meet the contemporary needs of the international community for new law. In a formal sense, as the *Restatement (Third)* points out, these legislative or law-making treaties bind only the states parties to them. But if a very large number of states informally accepts the provisions of the treaties as law even without becoming parties to them, to that extent they can be viewed as an independent source of international law for those states as well. Examples of such treaties are the VCLT, the Vienna Convention on Diplomatic Relations, Apr. 18, 1961, 23 U.S.T. 3227, 500 U.N.T.S. 95, and the Convention on the Prevention and Punishment of the Crime of Genocide, Dec. 9, 1948, 78 U.N.T.S. 277, as well as various provisions of the U.N. Charter. *See generally* I. Brownlie, *Principles of Public International Law* 11–15 (5th ed. 1998).

It is not always easy to distinguish these "legislative treaties" from agreements that are thought to be declaratory of preexisting customary international law. In one sense, the latter are merely evidence of what a group of states considers customary international law to be. The fewer the states that ratify the treaty or agree with the characterization, the less the treaty will be viewed as reflecting customary international law. On the other hand, if very many states adhere to the treaty or otherwise accept it as stating what the law is, the question whether it is declaratory of customary law loses significance. *See generally* R. Higgins, *Problems and Process: International Law and How We Use It* 28 (1994). At some point, the agreement will come to be viewed as an independent source of general international law. The VCLT would appear to have gone through these law-making stages.

§ 2–5. General principles of law. Among the sources of international law listed in Article 38(1) are "the general principles of law recognized by civilized nations." Today we speak of general principles of law recognized by or common to the world's major legal systems. Historically, general principles of law played an important role in the evolution of international law. The rules derived from them were often the only norms available and acceptable to states to regulate their international relations. They were accepted as a source of law on the theory that where states have universally applied similar principles in their national law, their consent to be bound by those same principles on the international plane could be inferred. The legal rules governing the responsibility of states for injuries to aliens were at one time based almost exclusively on that source.

Modern international law relies less on general principles of law as a source of law. This is so in part because of the extraordinary growth of treaties and international institutions as a means of regulating interstate relations, and in part because many of the norms that were originally derived from general principles have over time become customary international law. The process of law-making by so-called "legislative treaties" has also reduced the need for general principles of law to fill substantive lacunae in the international legal system. That is why the *Restatement (Third)* quite soundly characterizes general principles as a "secondary source of international law." *Restatement (Third)* § 102, cmt. l.

General principles are still used to fill gaps, primarily for procedural matters and problems of international judicial administration. An international tribunal might resort to general principles, for example, to rule that the doctrine of *res judicata* or laches is part of international law, or that international judges have to conduct themselves in a manner that does not cast doubt on their impartiality or independence. For a review of some illustrative cases that rely on general principles, see M. Shaw, *International Law* 77–82 (4th ed. 1997).

§ 2–6. Character of modern international law. The discussion in the preceding sections indicates that modern international law consists principally of conventional and customary international law. The fact that legislative treaties now play an important role in the law-making process is beginning to transform international law into a more dynamic legal system. The development of customary international law is, on the whole, more cumbersome and consequently less suited for the fast pace of modern life. General principles perform an ever more marginal role as a source of law.

III. SECONDARY SOURCES OR EVIDENCE

§ 2–7. Evidence of international law. Article 38(1)(d) lists judicial decisions and the views of duly qualified publicists "as subsidiary means for the determination of rules of law." This provision is generally understood to mean that the existence of a rule of international law may be proved by reference to the above mentioned "subsidiary means." *Restatement (Third)* § 103. These sources are cited by international lawyers as authoritative evidence that a given proposition is or is not international law.

Although judicial decisions and the teachings of publicists appear to be treated in Article 38 as being of equal weight, this seems not to be true in practice. Certain judicial decisions enjoy much greater status as legal authority than the views of the publicists. Thus, I.C.J. decisions are by far the most authoritative of these "subsidiary means" on the international plane. For example, if the I.C.J. concludes that a given proposition has become a rule of customary international law, that holding, while not binding precedent in theory, is "the law" for all practical purposes. It would be extremely difficult, if not impossible, to refute such a holding on the international plane. Similarly, decisions of other modern international tribunals, particularly permanent ones, *see infra* ch. 4, are deemed to be highly authoritative. Much less importance attaches to decisions of national courts applying international law. What weight they will be given depends on the prestige and perceived impartiality of the national court, on whether the decision is in conflict with decisions of international courts, and on the forum where the decision is being cited. A decision of the U.S. Supreme Court interpreting international law is conclusive in the United States, despite a contrary opinion even of the I.C.J.; but in Belgium, for example, the U.S. decision will most certainly be less authoritative than a decision of an international arbitral tribunal. The result would probably be the same in a U.S. court, if it had to choose between a decision of the Belgian Supreme Court and that of an international tribunal.

The meaning of the phrase, "teachings of the most highly qualified publicists," must also be clarified. The reference is not only to individual publicists or writers, although that is what was probably meant at one time. Today it includes entities such as the International Law Commission (I.L.C.), which was established by the United Nations to encourage "the progressive development of international law and its codification." U.N. Charter, art. 13(1)(a); *see infra* § 3–15. The I.L.C. is composed of distinguished international lawyers from all regions of the world. On the international plane, its conclusions would undoubtedly be considered more authoritative than the judicial opinions of national courts, for example. The "teachings" of prestigious private scholarly institutions having a membership consisting of lawyers from all major legal systems of the world, such as, for example, the Institut de Droit International, would also be accorded greater respect than some types of judicial opinions. Note too that international lawyers trained in states whose legal systems follow the civil law tradition are more likely to give greater weight to scholarly writings than are common law lawyers, who tend to view judicial decisions as more authoritative. In a U.S. court, furthermore, the *Restatement (Third)* would likely be given greater weight as evidence of international law than many types of foreign and international judicial opinions.

In recent decades, resolutions and similar acts of intergovernmental international organizations have acquired a very significant status both as sources and as evidence of international law. Some of these resolutions are legally binding on the member states of the organizations. That is true, for example, with regard to some U.N. Security Council resolutions. *See* U.N. Charter, arts. 24–25; *Advisory Opinion on Legal Consequences for States of the Continued Presence of South Africa in Namibia (South-West Africa) Notwithstanding Security Council Resolution 276 (1970)*, 1971 I.C.J. 16, at 40–41 (June 21). It is also true of various legislative measures promulgated by the International Civil Aviation Organization. *See* T. Buergenthal, *Law-Making in the International Civil Aviation Organization* 57 (1969). The binding character of these enactments is provided for in the treaties establishing the organizations. The resolutions in question consequently are a form of treaty law and, to that extent, a source of law. *See* J. Charney, *Universal International Law*, 87 Am. J. Int'l L. 529 (1993).

The vast majority of resolutions of international organizations are not, however, formally binding in character. This is true, for example, of resolutions of the U.N. General Assembly. *See infra* § 3–14. Some of these resolutions (declarations, recommendations, etc.) can and do become authoritative evidence of international law. *See Restatement (Third)* § 103, cmt. c. To understand how acts of international organizations acquire this status, it is important to recall that customary international law evolves through state practice to which states conform out of a sense of legal obligation. How states vote and what they say in international organizations is a form of state practice. Its significance in the law-making process depends upon the extent to which this state practice is consistent with the contemporaneous conduct and pronouncements of states in other contexts. Thus, for example, if a U.N. General Assembly resolution declares a given principle to be a rule of international law, that pronouncement does not make it the law, but it is some evidence on the subject. If the resolution is adopted unanimously or by an overwhelming majority, which includes the major powers of the world, and if it is repeated in subsequent resolutions over a period of time, and relied upon by states in other contexts, it may well reach the stage where its character as being declaratory of international law becomes conclusive. When that stage is reached is difficult to determine, but that these resolutions play an important part in the international law-making process can no longer be doubted. The following pronouncement of the International Court of Justice is particularly relevant on this entire subject:

> The Court notes that General Assembly resolutions, even if they are not binding, may sometimes have normative value. They can, in certain circumstances, provide evidence important for establishing the existence of a rule or the emergence of an *opinio juris*. To establish whether this is true of a given General Assembly resolution, it is necessary to look at its content and the conditions of its adoption; it is also necessary to see whether an *opinio juris* exists as to its normative

character. Or a series of resolutions may show the gradual evolution of the *opinio juris* required for the establishment of a new rule.

Advisory Opinion on Legality of the Threat or Use of Nuclear Weapons, 1996 I.C.J. 226, para. 70 (July 8).

Of course, not very many measures adopted by international organizations acquire normative status. The resolutions or declarations in question usually have to proclaim one or more principles and identify them either as preexisting international law or as rules that states in general should comply with as a matter of law. These acts might be characterized as "legislative" resolutions that are not all that dissimilar in their content or purpose from the "legislative treaties" discussed *supra* § 2–4. Resolutions dealing with human rights, decolonization, outer space, ocean resources, environmental issues, use of force, etc., are at times formulated to perform that purpose. *See, e.g.*, *Military and Paramilitary Activities in and against Nicaragua* (Nicar. v. U.S.), 1986 I.C.J. 14, at 100–1 (June 27); *Advisory Opinion on Western Sahara*, 1975 I.C.J. 12, at 23–33 (Oct. 16). It is not uncommon in some of these areas for the "legislative" declarations to be followed up by a formal treaty open to accession by the international community in general. On this subject generally, see R. Higgins, *Problems and Process: International Law and How We Use It* 22–32 (1994).

§ 2–8. **Law-making process**. Because of the consensual character of customary and conventional international law, and because of the absence of a centralized legislative or judicial system, states play a dual role in the law-making process: they act both as legislators and as advocates or lobbyists. *See* M. McDougal, *The Hydrogen Bomb Tests and the International Law of the Sea,* 49 Am. J. Int'l L. 356–58 (1955). They are legislators or law-makers in the sense that, as we have already seen, the practice of states and the treaties which states conclude create international law. States also assert certain claims on the international plane in their diplomatic correspondence, in international courts, in international organizations, etc., through which they seek to obtain new rules of international law or to modify existing ones. Their individual assertions about what is or is not law, particularly customary law, is a form of lobbying or advocacy; it becomes law-making when these claims find the broad-based support that is required to transform them into law. Claims by governments about what is or is not law must take the law-making consequences of their actions into account.

§ **2–9. Where to find the evidence.** It is not always easy to prove the existence of a practice deemed by states to be obligatory, especially if unambiguous judicial decisions or other authoritative pronouncements relating to it are not available. To gather the necessary proof, international lawyers examine, *inter alia,* relevant government pronouncements on the subject, national judicial decisions, debates and resolutions of international organizations, minutes and final acts of diplomatic conferences. This search is frequently facilitated by the availability of digests or compilations dealing with the international law practice of individual nations. A number of private collections containing decisions of national courts on questions of international law are also available, as are compilations of decisions of international arbitral tribunals and of permanent courts. International law treatises written by renowned legal scholars in different parts of the world are usually also consulted and cited by international lawyers. The U.N. and various regional organizations as well as individual states publish official and unofficial collections of international agreements. Historical collections, especially those dealing with diplomacy, may also yield useful information concerning the existence of customary rules of international law. Increasingly, this information is available on the Internet. For an overview of the reference material mentioned in this section and for a guide to conducting international legal research, see *infra* ch.13.

CHAPTER 3

STATES AND INTERNATIONAL ORGANIZATIONS

I. INTRODUCTION

This chapter considers the principal "actors" in international law: states and international organizations created by states. First, this chapter discusses the law and practice associated with "recognizing" the creation of a new state or formation of a new government that has come to power through non-constitutional means. Second, this chapter introduces the core legal issues that arise with respect to international organizations, paying particular attention to the United Nations and the European Union. Finally, this chapter briefly notes the role of non-governmental organizations in the formation and implementation of international law.

II. STATES

§ 3–1. Recognition doctrine generally. When an extraordinary political event occurs—the emergence of a new state or the rise to power of a new government by other than routine processes—other states in the world community indicate their willingness to accept both the fact of change and the legal consequences arising from that fact by

either explicitly or implicitly "recognizing" the new
state or government.

§ **3–2. Recognition of states**. Under traditional international legal theory, an entity aspiring
to be recognized as a new state first had to meet
certain factual conditions. The aspiring entity had
to have: (1) a defined territory; (2) a permanent
population; (3) an effective government; and (4) the
capacity to enter into relations with other states.
See Inter–American Convention on the Rights and
Duties of States, Dec. 26, 1933, 49 Stat. 3097, 165
L.N.T.S. 19 ("Montevideo Convention"); *see also* T.
Grant, *Defining Statehood: The Montevideo Convention and its Discontents*, 37 Colum. J. Transnat'l L.
403 (1999).

For the most part, these conditions continue to be
taught today as the fundamental elements of statehood. With respect to the third condition, in practice the emphasis has been on the control that the
government exercises over the relevant territory, to
the exclusion of other entities. The degree of control
necessary may be a function of the manner in which
the government came to power. If the prior sovereign in the territory has consented to the creation
of a new state under a new government, then a
relatively lower degree of control by the new government may be tolerable in finding statehood. *See*
J. Crawford, *The Creation of States in International
Law* 44–45 (1979).

While the conditions for statehood are broadly
accepted in traditional international legal theory,
the issue of who gets to decide whether these conditions have been met is less clear. Some theorists

contend that an entity is *ipso facto* a state once these conditions are met, regardless of what other states do or say (the "declaratory theory of recognition"). Other theorists, however, contend that only when other states decide that such conditions have been met, and consequently acknowledge the legal capacity of the new state, is a new state actually constituted (the "constitutive theory of recognition").

§ 3–3. **Dissolution of the USSR.** The fragmentation of the Union of Soviet Socialist Republics (USSR) after 1989 is both an example of recognition practice and an illustration of modern trends in this area. In December 1989, the Congress of the USSR People's Deputies found that the July 1939 Molotov–Ribbentrop Accords, by which the USSR first occupied and then annexed the Baltic States (Estonia, Latvia, and Lithuania), were contrary to international law. On this basis, the Baltic States held referenda in early 1991 on whether to seek independence. The overwhelming response was positive, and the Baltic States then waged a successful campaign for full independence. The State Council of the Soviet Union released the Baltic States and recognized their independence on September 6, 1991. The Baltic States were then admitted to the United Nations on September 17, 1991.

Thereafter, several of the other republics of the Soviet Union held referenda on whether to secede. All (except Kazakhstan) proclaimed their independence during 1991, while Russia proclaimed itself as the successor state to the former Soviet Union. Virtually all other states recognized the republics of the former Soviet Union as new states and they were admitted as members of the United Nations. A notable aspect of this recognition was the approach taken by the European Community, which on December 16, 1991, issued a *Declaration on the "Guidelines on the Recognition of New States in Eastern Europe and in the Soviet Union"*, 31 I.L.M. 1486 (1992). In that declaration, the European Community and its member states affirmed:

> their readiness to recognise, subject to the normal standards of international practice and the political realities in each case, those new states which, following the historic changes in the region, have constituted themselves on a democratic basis, have accepted the appropriate international obligations and have committed themselves in good faith to a peaceful process and to negotiations.

The Declaration then set down general conditions requiring the new state: (1) to respect the U.N. Charter, the Helsinki Final Act, and the Charter of Paris, "especially with regard to the rule of law, democracy and human rights"; (2) to guarantee rights for ethnic and national groups and minorities; (3) to respect existing borders; (4) to accept relevant arms control commitments; and (5) to commit to settle by agreement all questions regarding state succession and regional disputes. The European Community and United States recognized the statehood of the republics of the former Soviet Union based on these principles.

Thus, while the traditional Montevideo Convention criteria still reflect the minimum requirements for the formation of a new state, in some situations the willingness of other states to recognize the new state may turn on additional requirements relating to more modern notions of human rights and democracy.

§ 3–4. Recognition of governments. Under traditional international legal theory, the establishment of a new government through normal, constitutional processes within a state does not raise questions regarding the recognition of the government. In such situations, the new government is entitled to all the rights and obligations accorded under international law. By contrast, an entity that comes to power through non-constitutional means is not automatically accorded such rights and obligations. Rather, its status as the government of the state may be in doubt until such time as it is widely recognized by other states. *See generally* M. Peterson, *Recognition of Governments: Legal Doctrine and State Practice, 1815–1995* (1997); L. Galloway, *Recognizing Foreign Governments: The Practice of the United States* (1978).

The central (and often determinative) issue for a state when deciding whether to recognize a newly formed government has been whether the new government is in "effective control" of its state (sometimes referred to as the "de facto control test"). "Effective control" has largely been measured by the degree to which the government commands the obedience of the people within the state. Although in a given case there may be extremely complicated facts concerning what factions control what portions of a territory, the "effective control" test is a relatively simple one, and allows states to proceed pragmatically in their relations with the new government.

The decision by states to recognize a new government, however, has not always been dictated simply by whether the new government passes the effective control test. For instance, capital exporting states, such as the United States, at one time found relevant whether the new government had declared its willingness to honor the international obligations of its predecessor, including debt obligations. Further, states often refused to recognize a government's authority over territory that the government had acquired through aggression. States have also found relevant the political nature of the new government, including the degree to which it is democratic.

The notion of states "recognizing" a new government of a state, however, is anathema to those states that see it as an interference in national affairs. The 1930 Estrada Doctrine, named for the Mexican Foreign Secretary Genaro Estrada, stands for the proposition that the manner in which a new government comes to power is wholly a matter of national concern. *See* P. Jessup, *The Estrada Doctrine*, 25 Am. J. Int'l L. 719 (1931). As such, states should not seek to influence the outcome of an internal power struggle by granting or withholding recognition. The Estrada Doctrine is attractive because many states view it as politically difficult to announce publicly whether or not they "recognize" a new government, and would prefer simply to open diplomatic channels or otherwise develop relations with the new government without issuing a pronouncement that could be construed as approval of the new government. In such instances, determination of the legal effects of the new relationship is often left to national courts, which must pass upon the legal rights and obligations of the new government in the absence of a clear statement of recognition.

Establishing diplomatic relations with a new government is not required as a part of the recognition process, although they usually go hand in hand. Breaking diplomatic relations merely signifies that one state declines to deal with another's government; it does not vitiate the recognition of that government.

§ 3–5. Recognition in U.S. practice. In the United States, the power to recognize foreign governments is inferred from the express grant to the President of the power to "receive Ambassadors and other public Ministers." *U.S. Const.* art. II, § 3; *see* L. Henkin, *Foreign Affairs and the United States Constitution* 38 (2d ed. 1996). Moreover, the Supreme Court has consistently stated that whether a government should be recognized is a political question whose determination is within the exclusive prerogative of the executive branch. *See Banco Nacional de Cuba v. Sabbatino*, 376 U.S. 398, 410 (1964); *National City Bank of New York v. China*, 348 U.S. 356, 358 (1955); *Guaranty Trust Co. v. United States*, 304 U.S. 126, 137–8 (1938).

Rights of recognized governments in the United States include the rights (1) to bring a law suit in U.S. court; (2) to claim sovereign immunity in U.S. courts and to receive diplomatic protection to the same extent as other recognized governments; and (3) to have access to the state's U.S. bank deposits and other property. Courts will not deny a recognized government the rights that it would normally have under United States law solely because diplomatic relations with it have been broken. *See Banco Nacional de Cuba v. Sabbatino*, 376 U.S. 398, 410 (1964).

III.   INTERNATIONAL ORGANIZATIONS GENERALLY

§ 3–6.   Nature of international organizations. While they can appear in a variety of forms, public international organizations—also known as intergovernmental organizations—typically are: (1) institutions established by a treaty—sometimes denominated as a "charter"—which serves as the "constitution" of the organization; (2) composed of members that are states or international organizations; (3) regulated by international law; and (4) endowed with a legal personality, and thus generally can engage in contracts, and can sue and be sued in national courts subject to certain immunities. *See Advisory Opinion on Reparation for Injuries Suffered in the Service of the United Nations*, 1949 I.C.J. 174 (Apr. 11). An international organization normally has various "organs" that collectively undertake the work of the organization. One standard organ is composed of all the member states of the organization, which may meet on an annual basis. Yet other organs may exist consisting of a sub-set of the member states; such an organ may meet more frequently and be charged with handling specific matters set forth in the treaty. All international organizations have some kind of permanent secretariat or institutional structure, which carries on the day-to-day functions of the organization, and is often headed by a secretary-general. *See generally* H. Schermers & N. Blokker, *International Institutional Law: Unity Within Diversity* (3d ed. 1995).

§ **3-7. Operational legal issues**. There are a wide range of legal issues that may arise concerning the operations of an international organization. Membership issues concern the conditions under which states may be admitted to, withdraw from, or be expelled from the organization, as well as the conditions under which a member state's rights or privileges may be suspended. Voting issues arise with respect to actions taken by the various organs; in some instances, a unanimous or consensus vote may be required, while in other instances a supermajority or simple majority vote may be sufficient. Some institutions provide greater weight to the votes of certain states or blocs of states. Lawyers may be called upon to assess whether organs are acting outside of the powers accorded to them by the organization's charter, in which case the *ultra vires* act might not be regarded as lawful. When the organization is sued (usually in national courts), issues arise regarding the organization's immunity from suit, which may be governed by the organization's charter or by a "headquarters agreement" concluded between the organization and its host state. Important issues may arise regarding the finances of the organization, such as how the organization's budget is adopted, how dues are apportioned among the members, and what sanctions (if any) exist for the failure to pay dues. *See generally* C. Amerasinghe, *Principles of the Institutional Law of International Organizations* (1996); P. Sands & P. Klein, *Bowett's Law of International Institutions* (5th ed. 2001).

§ 3–8.   Historical background. International organizations have a relatively recent history. The earliest ones date from the second half of the 19th century, among them, the International Telegraphic Union (1865) and the Universal Postal Union (1874). The League of Nations, the International Labor Organization and a number of other smaller organizations were created after World War I. The United Nations and the majority of functional and regional international organizations in existence today came into being after World War II. The dramatic growth in the number of international organizations is the result of an ever-increasing acceptance by governments of the international dimensions of the political, economic and social problems they face and of the need for international cooperation in resolving them. The powers, functions, and structure of contemporary international organizations reflect the tension that exists between the reality of international interdependence and the reluctance of governments to relinquish some of their governmental authority to these organizations. *See* D. Armstrong, L. Lloyd & J. Redmond, *From Versailles to Maastricht: International Organisation in the Twentieth Century* (1996).

IV.   UNITED NATIONS

§ 3–9.   U.N. Charter. The United Nations
came into being with the entry into force on October 24, 1945 of the U.N. Charter, which is a multilateral treaty that also serves as the United Nation's "constitution". At the time of its founding, the United Nations had a membership of 51 states. Since then the membership has grown to some 190 states, which constitutes virtually all the independent states of the world. *See generally United Nations Legal Order* (O. Schachter & C. Joyner eds., 1995) (two volumes); *The Charter of the United Nations: A Commentary* (B. Simma ed., 1994).

§ 3–10.   Nature and function. The United Nations is a universal organization both in terms of its membership and the purposes it is designed to advance. It is an organization charged with peacekeeping responsibilities; with the development of friendly relations among nations; with the achievement of international cooperation in solving international problems of an economic, social, cultural and humanitarian character; and with the promotion of human rights and fundamental freedoms for all human beings without discrimination. U.N. Charter, art. 1. In discharging these functions, the United Nations is enjoined from intervening in matters which are "essentially within the domestic jurisdiction" of any state, except when acting through the Security Council to address threats to the peace. U.N. Charter, art. 2(7). The meaning and significance of this prohibition has been extensively debated by legal scholars and diplomats. Article 2(7) has not, however, proved to be a serious obstacle to U.N. action despite the fact that it has been frequently invoked in U.N. debates. *See, e.g.*, R. Higgins, *The Development of International Law Through the Political Organs of the United Nations* 64–76, 82–130 (1963).

§ 3–11. International constitutional supremacy. The U.N. Charter contains a supremacy clause which provides that "[i]n the event of a conflict between the obligations of the Members of the United Nations under the present Charter and their obligations under any other international agreement, their obligations under the present Charter shall prevail." U.N. Charter, art. 103. This provision places the U.N. Charter at the apex in the hierarchy of international law norms, giving it a status on the international plane roughly comparable to that of a national constitution in national law.

§ 3–12.   U.N. organs. The principal organs of the United Nations are the General Assembly, the Security Council, the Economic and Social Council, the International Court of Justice, and the Secretariat. (The Trusteeship Council suspended operations in 1994 after the independence of Palau, the last remaining U.N. trust territory.) Some of these bodies have numerous subsidiary organs.

The General Assembly is the only U.N. organ in which all member states have the right to be represented and to vote. The Assembly has plenary powers in the sense that it "may discuss any questions or any matters within the scope of the ... Charter." U.N. Charter, art. 10.

The Security Council has "primary responsibility for the maintenance of international peace and security." U.N. Charter, art. 24(1). It consists of fifteen member states, five of them permanent members (China, France, Russia, the United Kingdom, and the United States). The remaining members are elected to two-year terms in accordance with a formula that is designed to ensure an equitable geographic representation.

The Economic and Social Council (ECOSOC) consists of fifty-four member states elected by the General Assembly to three-year terms. To discharge its responsibilities in the economic, social and humanitarian areas, ECOSOC has established a large number of subsidiary organs with specialized competence in those fields. Among these are regional economic commissions and bodies, the U.N. Commission on Human Rights, and the U.N. Environment Program.

The Charter stipulates that the Secretariat "shall comprise a Secretary–General and such staff as the Organization may require." U.N. Charter, art. 97. The Secretary–General is elected to a five-year term by the General Assembly upon the recommendation of the Security Council. Since that recommendation is subject to the veto power, the Secretary–General can be elected only with the acquiescence of the five permanent members of the Security Council. Besides being the chief administrative officer of the United Nations, the Secretary–General has the power under Article 99 of the Charter to "bring to the attention of the Security Council any matter which in his opinion may threaten the maintenance of international peace and security."

The International Court of Justice is the principal judicial organ of the United Nations. U.N. Charter, art. 92. Its functions are described in greater detail in Chapter 4.

§ 3–13. Voting procedures. Voting procedures in the General Assembly differ from those in the Security Council. Article 18 of the U.N. Charter, which applies to the General Assembly, distinguishes between "important questions" and "other questions." Resolutions involving "important questions" require a two-thirds majority of the members present and voting, while those dealing with "other questions" require only a majority vote. Besides expressly identifying some categories of questions as "important," the Charter provides that the Assembly may, by a majority vote, determine additional categories of questions to which the two-thirds majority rule shall apply. U.N. Charter, art. 18(3).

The rules governing voting in the Security Council distinguish between "procedural matters" and "all other matters." Resolutions on matters that are not "procedural" in character require nine affirmative votes, including "the concurring votes of the permanent members." U.N. Charter, art. 27(3). Under this rule, each of the five permanent members may veto the adoption of any resolution that is not "procedural." The Charter neither defines the meaning of "procedural matters" nor identifies the categories of matters that are non-procedural. Security Council practice indicates, however, that disagreements concerning whether a resolution is or is not subject to the veto power can be authoritatively resolved only by a vote which requires the concurring votes of the permanent members. This practice results in the so-called "double veto" procedure. It permits each permanent member to use its first veto to prevent the characterization of a resolution as "procedural" and the second veto to defeat the resolution itself. Abstentions by permanent members are not, however, deemed to constitute a veto. The mere absence of a permanent member will also not prevent the adoption of a Security Council resolution.

§ 3–14. Binding character of U.N. resolutions. The power of the General Assembly to adopt binding resolutions is extremely limited. Some of its decisions on budgetary matters are obligatory; so too are its instructions concerning the internal operations of the United Nations. All other General Assembly resolutions are non-binding. They have the status of recommendations which the member states have no formal legal obligation to obey. U.N. Charter, arts. 10 & 14.

The powers of the Security Council under U.N. Charter arts. 24–25 and Chapter VII are more extensive. Using the authority granted under Chapter VII, the Security Council may enact resolutions that are binding upon U.N. member states after a determination that there exists a "threat to the peace, breach of the peace, or act of aggression." These "peace enforcement" measures may involve the imposition of comprehensive economic sanctions on a state for its wrongful conduct, such as occurred when Iraq invaded Kuwait in 1990. *See* S.C. Res. 661 (1990); *see also Advisory Opinion on the Legal*

Consequences for States of the Continued Presence of South Africa in Namibia (South West Africa) Notwithstanding Security Council Resolution 276 (1970), 1971 I.C.J. 16, at 52–53 (June 21). For more on Security Council "peace enforcement" measures, see *infra* ch. 12.

§ 3–15.   Law-making and legislative activities. In addition to the imposition of sanctions and the authorization to use military force, the Security Council has used Chapter VII to pursue various innovative initiatives, such as the creation of international criminal tribunals for the former Yugoslavia and for Rwanda, the establishment of a U.N. Compensation Commission for damage caused by Iraq's invasion, and the formation of boundary demarcation or arms inspection commissions. These bodies are capable of generating decisions that have important legal effects on states and on persons. Some have charged that, by engaging in these activities, the Security Council has exceeded the powers originally envisaged for it. Further, some assert that, if the Security Council is to be used in this manner, it should be restructured so as to be more representative of the global community. *See, e.g.*, *The United Nations at Age Fifty: A Legal Perspective* (C. Tomuschat ed., 1995).

The subject matter jurisdiction of the Security Council and its power to adopt binding resolutions are, in principle, limited to matters which concern international peace and security. This means that the Security Council has no general law-making authority. The General Assembly, by contrast, has broad subject matter jurisdiction but lacks formal legislative authority because its resolutions do not have the force of law. The General Assembly does play a very important role, however, in the process by which international law is made and develops. *See supra* § 2–7 ; *see also* R. Gorman, *Great Debates at the United Nations: An Encyclopedia of Fifty Key Issues, 1945–2000* (2001).

Article 13(1)(a) of the U.N. Charter requires the General Assembly "to initiate studies and make recommendations ... encouraging the progressive development of international law and its codification." The General Assembly has discharged this responsibility in various ways. In 1947, it established the International Law Commission. This body, composed of distinguished international lawyers, has drafted a number of important multilateral conventions that are now in force, including the Vienna Convention on the Law of Treaties, May 23, 1969, art. 53, 1155 U.N.T.S. 331, 8 I.L.M. 679, and the Vienna Convention on Diplomatic Relations, Apr. 18, 1961, 23 U.S.T. 3227, 500 U.N.T.S. 95. *See* J. Morton, *The International Law Commission of the United Nations* (2000). The General Assembly has also adopted and opened for signature many major international treaties, such as the two International Covenants on human rights. Much of the existing international legislation relating to the law of the sea, the international environment, and space law originated with the General Assembly or with diplomatic conferences that were convened by it. These codification efforts by the General Assembly have contributed significantly to the growth and modernization of international law.

Some resolutions of the General Assembly have also come to be accepted as declaratory of customary international law. For example, the Universal Declaration of Human Rights, which was adopted by the General Assembly in the form of a resolution, is often cited as evidence of customary international law regarding human rights. Although the normative effect of U.N. resolutions is a highly controversial topic, few authorities dispute the fact that these resolutions have played and will continue to play an important role in the international lawmaking process. At the very least, widely supported and repeatedly reaffirmed U.N. resolutions reflect and articulate accepted principles on the basis of which international legal rules can and do develop. Hence, the statement that U.N. General Assembly resolutions are not binding, although true in a formal sense, contributes little to an understanding of the significant effect some of these resolutions may have on the development of international law. *See supra* § 2–7.

V.   U.N. SPECIALIZED AGENCIES

§ 3–16.   Definition. Despite their name, the so-called specialized agencies of the United Nations are neither organs nor subsidiary organs of the United Nations. They are autonomous international organizations having an institutional affiliation with the United Nations. That affiliation is provided for in Article 57 of the U.N. Charter, which stipulates that "the various specialized agencies, established by intergovernmental agreement and having wide international responsibilities ... in economic, social, cultural, educational, health, and related fields, shall be brought into relationship with the United Nations...."

§ **3–17. Organizations having specialized agency status.** More than a dozen international organizations have obtained specialized agency status by concluding the necessary agreements with the United Nations. *See* U.N. Charter, art. 63. Some of these organizations predate the United Nations itself, among them the International Telecommunications Union (ITU), the Universal Postal Union (UPU), and the International Labor Organization (ILO). Other well-known specialized agencies are the United Nations Educational, Scientific and Cultural Organization (UNESCO), the International Civil Aviation Organization (ICAO), the World Health Organization (WHO), and the Food and Agriculture Organization (FAO). The two major international financial institutions—the World Bank and the International Monetary Fund (IMF)—also have specialized agency status.

§ **3–18. Member states.** The membership roster of the specialized agencies is not necessarily identical to that of the United Nations. Not all U.N. member states belong to every specialized agency. This is particularly true of the IMF and the World Bank. On the other hand, all states of the world are members of the UPU. Although a few organizations have cultivated a certain exclusivity, most specialized agencies strive for universal membership, though they may not have achieved it.

§ 3–19. **Legislative activities**. The specialized agencies are responsible for a large body of international legislation which greatly facilitates international commerce, transportation and communication. This is true, in particular, of the air navigation codes adopted by ICAO, the health regulations promulgated by WHO, the international standards established by the World Meteorological Organization (WMO), and the postal rules and regulations of the UPU. ILO has been responsible for a large number of treaties dealing with the protection of the rights and safety of workers around the world. These are but a few of the many examples that demonstrate the important legal contributions that the specialized agencies are making. *See generally* D. Williams, *The Specialized Agencies and the United Nations: The System in Crisis* (1987).

VI.   REGIONAL ORGANIZATIONS

§ 3–20. **General description**. Regional and subregional intergovernmental organizations constitute another important group of international institutions. They, too, are created by international agreements, which specify their functions and institutional structure. On the whole, the legal and institutional framework of these organizations resembles that of other intergovernmental organizations. However, they differ from the latter principally in that their mandate is to deal with regional problems, either generally or in regard to specific matters. *See* U.N. Charter, ch. VIII; *see also* J. Hawdon, *Emerging Organizational Forms: The Proliferation of Regional Intergovernmental Organizations in the Modern World–System* (1996).

§ **3–21. Basic characteristics**. There exist a large number of regional and subregional institutions in all parts of the world. Their mandate, political significance and law-making powers vary substantially. A few enjoy extensive legislative or so-called supranational authority. This is true of the European Community, discussed in part VII of this Chapter. Other regional and subregional organizations have the power to adopt only non-binding recommendations and/or draft treaties. The majority has some, albeit not very extensive, law-making authority. Some of them play a very important role in their regions, others are of only marginal significance, and a few exist on paper only.

§ **3–22. Major regional organizations**. Among the principal regional organizations are the African Union (previously known as the Organization of African Unity or OAU), the Organization of American States (OAS), the Council of Europe, the Arab League, and the Association of South East Asian Nations (ASEAN). The oldest of these is the OAS, which is based in Washington, D.C. and, as of 2002, consists of thirty-five member states. Although it was established in its present form in 1948 with the entry into force of its Charter, the OAS traces its origins to the Union of American Republics which, together with its permanent secretariat—the Pan American Union—came into being during the first decade of the 20th century. *See* G. Connell–Smith, *The Inter–American System* 37–76 (1966); *see also* <http://www.oas.org>. The Council of Europe was created in 1949 to help rebuild political institutions in a Europe devastated by war. The Council of Europe is based in Strasbourg, France and, as of mid-2002, has forty-four member states. *See* <http://www.coe.int>. The African Union was established as the OAU in 1963 in Addis Ababa, Ethiopia. As of 2002, the African Union consists of fifty-three African states. *See* <http://www.oau-oua.org>. In the sections that follow some of the functions and characteristics of the OAS, African Union, and Council of Europe will be examined.

§ 3–23. **Membership requirements**. African Union membership is open to any African State. Constitutive Act of the African Union, July 11, 2000, art. 29. By contrast, until 1988, the OAS excluded from membership states that were embroiled in territorial disputes with OAS member states pending the resolution of the disputes. This requirement kept Guyana and Belize out of the OAS. Today, membership in the OAS is open to all independent American States. However, in 1992, the OAS adopted a procedure for suspending the rights of a member state when its democratically constituted government has been overthrown by force. *See S. Treaty Doc. No.* 103–22 (1994). Likewise, Article 30 of the Constitutive Act of the African Union provides that governments "who shall come to power through unconstitutional means shall not be allowed to participate in the activities of the Union." Unlike the OAU and the OAS, the Council of Europe restricts its membership to states committed to the rule of law and the enjoyment of human rights. Statute of the Council of Europe, May 5, 1949, art. 3, 87 U.N.T.S. 103, 106. This requirement barred Spain, Portugal, and the Soviet bloc states from becoming member states until they established democratic regimes.

§ **3–24. Institutional structure**. The OAS, African Union, and Council of Europe all have organs comprised of the heads of state or the foreign ministers of the member states and all have a permanent secretariat or commission headed by a secretary-general or chairman. The institutional structure of the Council of Europe and the African Union differs from that of the OAS in one important respect: they have parliaments. While the parliament of the African Union as of mid–2002 was not yet functioning, the Council of Europe Parliamentary Assembly consists of elected representatives of the national parliaments of the member states. In fact, the Council of Europe was the first intergovernmental organization to establish such an institution, although various other regional and subregional organizations have now adopted similar organs. The Council of Europe also has an organ called the Congress of Local and Regional Authorities. Although these two organs lack genuine legislative power—they are principally deliberative bodies—their existence opens the policymaking process of the Council of Europe to influence by individuals who would not normally represent their governments diplomatically.

§ **3–25. Functions and achievements**. The principal purpose of these three regional organizations is to promote cooperation between the states of their regions in a variety of different fields. *See* OAS Charter, arts. 1–2; Constitutive Act of the African Union, art. 3; Statute of the Council of Europe, art. 1. In this regard, the OAU/African Union has placed great emphasis on political cooperation; the Council of Europe has concentrated more on human rights, legal, social, and cultural issues; and the OAS has sought to make its influence felt both in political and legal areas, and in the field of human rights. The Council of Europe has been particularly successful in drawing up and obtaining the ratification by member states of a large number of treaties designed to facilitate commercial, cultural, scientific and educational interaction and cooperation within its region. These are reproduced in the multi-volume treaty series of the Council of Europe entitled *European Conventions and Agreements* (1949–). There exist a large number of inter-American treaties on similar subjects, but the OAS has been less successful than the Council of Europe in obtaining their widespread acceptance and implementation. As a younger organization, the OAU/African Union has had less opportunity to develop inter-African law, but is responsible for the adoption of the Treaty Establishing the African Economic Community, June 3, 1991 (the Abuja Treaty). On the role played by these organizations—and the institutions they have established—in the field of human rights, see *infra* ch. 6.

VII.   SUPRANATIONAL ORGANIZATIONS

§ 3–26.   **Meaning of supranationality**. An international organization with "supranational powers" is generally regarded as one that has the power to bind its member states by its decisions. As such, they have more governmental authority and law-making power in relation to their member states than do traditional international organizations. One key indicator of supranationality is the authority of the organization to make its law directly applicable and enforceable within the territory of the member states without further execution by the national governments.

§ 3–27. Supranationality and the European Union. The concept of supranationality acquired real significance with the adoption in 1951 of the Treaty establishing the European Coal and Steel Community (ECSC). The ECSC was followed by the adoption in 1957 of treaties establishing its two sister organizations—the European Economic Community (EEC) and the European Atomic Energy Community (Euratom). Together, these three institutions became known as the "European Communities." The treaties establishing the European Communities have been revised several times through the Single European Act (1985), the Treaty on European Union or "Maastricht Treaty" (1992), and the Treaty of Amsterdam (1997). *See generally* J. Hanlon, *European Community Law* (2d ed. 2000); P. Mathijsen, *A Guide to European Union Law* (6th ed. 1995); *see also* <http://europa.eu.int>.

§ 3–28. Mandate of the European Union. Under the Maastricht Treaty, a "three pillar" European Union was established. *Pillar One* incorporates the three founding communities, which are now called the "European Community" (EC). The original communities were established to bring about the economic integration of the national economies of the member states by doing away with all trade barriers *inter se* and by adopting a common economic policy, including customs duties, in relation to non-member states. To achieve these objectives, the member states delegate to the European Community sweeping powers to regulate broad sectors of their economies, embracing the movement of goods, services, labor, transportation, etc. Although the ultimate goal of this economic integration—complete political union—remains unfulfilled, the European Community has in large measure succeeded in its efforts to forge an economic union or common market. A European Central Bank, located in Frankfurt am Main, Germany, began operations in 1998, charged with defining and implementing EC monetary policy. In 2002, eleven EU member states replaced their national currencies with Euro notes and coins, concluding a three-year transition to a European currency.

Pillar Two established the Common Foreign and Security Policy, which makes it possible for the European Union to take joint action in foreign and security affairs when the members agree to do so. *Pillar Three* created the Justice and Home Affairs Policy, which deals with asylum, immigration, judicial cooperation in civil and criminal matters, drug trafficking, fraud, and customs and police cooperation against terrorism. These two pillars operate by intergovernmental cooperation, rather than by the EC institutions associated with *Pillar One*.

As of 2002, the European Union consists of the following fifteen member states: Austria, Belgium, Denmark, Finland, France, Germany, Greece, Ireland, Italy, Luxembourg, the Netherlands, Portugal, Spain, Sweden, and the United Kingdom. Thirteen additional states are candidates for joining the European Union. To ease such accessions, EU member states adopted in December 2000 the Treaty of Nice which, once it enters into force, will further amend existing EU treaties, and permit qualified majority voting rather than unanimous voting on a range of issues.

§ 3–29. **EC institutional structure**. There are four principal institutions of the European Community: the Council of the European Union, the European Commission, the European Parliament, and the European Court of Justice. The *Council* is the main EC decision-making body and meets in Brussels and Luxembourg. The Council consists of one representative from each member government. These representatives are politically responsible to their national parliament and to the nationals they represent. The *Commission*, which is located in Brussels, makes recommendations to, and implements the measures decided on by, the Council and the Parliament. The Commission has twenty members, including a president and two vice-presidents. The members are appointed by the member states acting in concert. In practice, each member state has the right to designate at least one commissioner; the remaining members are filled by nationals of the largest member states. Whereas the Council members are government representatives, the Commissioners are Community officials. They serve in their personal capacities and as such are not permitted to receive instructions from their governments. The *Parliament* has its seat in Strasbourg, France. It consists of 626 representatives, elected every five years in direct popular elections that are held in the member states. While at one time the Parliament had a limited role, it now exercises some democratic control over all the Community institutions (in particular the Commission), shares some legislative power with the Council, and plays a decisive role in the adoption of the budget. *See generally Democratizing the European Union* (C. Hoskyns & M. Newman eds., 2000). The *Court of Justice* sits in Luxembourg and consists of fifteen judges who are designated by the member states acting in concert. For a description of the role of the Court, see *infra* § 4–30.

§ **3–30. EC law-making**. In general—such as on matters concerning completion of the internal market, the environment or consumer protection— Community legislation is adopted jointly by the Council and Parliament under a co-decision procedure. Since the Treaty of Amsterdam entered into force in 1999, the field of application of this procedure has been extended to cover new areas, such as non-discrimination, free movement and residence, and combating social exclusion. On certain other issues, the Council adopts the legislation after the Parliament is only consulted. The Commission proposes legislation to the Council and the Parliament, administers and implements Community policies, enforces Community law (jointly with the Court of Justice), speaks for the European Community, and negotiates international agreements, mainly those relating to trade and cooperation.

§ **3–31. EC law and national law**. Certain provisions of the Community treaties and various legislative measures of the Community are directly applicable law within the member states, superseding national law in case of conflict. To that extent, the law of the Community has a status within the member states comparable to federal law in the United States.

However, the *type* of act taken by the EU institutions will determine its exact legal effect. *Regulations* are directly applicable and binding in all EU member states without the need for any national implementing legislation. *Directives* bind member states as to the objectives to be achieved within a certain time-limit, but leave to national authorities the choice of form and means to be used. Directives have to be implemented in national legislation, but only in accordance with the procedures of the individual member states. *Decisions* are binding upon those to whom they are addressed, whether a state, company, or person (thus, decisions do not require national implementing legislation). *Recommendations* and *opinions* are not binding.

The Court of Justice of the European Community has repeatedly affirmed the supremacy of Community law over national law and its direct applicability on the national legal plane. *See, e.g., Case 6/64, Costa v. ENEL*, 1964 E.C.R. 1141, 3 C.M.L.R. 425 (1964). This conclusion is based on two theories: the institutional theory, that the member states transferred sovereignty to the European Community in designated fields and thus gave up power to act inconsistently with Community norms; or the political theory, that the member states agreed to limit their sovereignty in favor of the Community, thus making any single unilateral act ineffective if contrary to Community norms.

The European Court of Justice supervises the uniform interpretation and application of Community law. It does so in cases brought to it by the

European Community institutions, the member states and private enterprises, as well as in opinions rendered at the request of national tribunals called upon to apply Community law. The European Community treaties enable and, in certain instances, require these courts to obtain an authoritative ruling from the Court of Justice concerning Community law questions arising in cases being tried by them.

The breadth of European Community law, combined with its direct and independent applicability on national law, distinguishes it from the law of traditional international organizations. The legislative process of the European Community is also substantially more independent of the will of the member states than is the legislative process of international organizations, which, as a rule, is under the exclusive control of governments. Viewed from this perspective, supranational organizations, as exemplified by the European Community, represent a more advanced and more effective form of international cooperation than do traditional international organizations.

VIII.   NON–STATE ACTORS

§ 3–32.   **Non-governmental organizations**. In addition to states and international organizations, there is a third type of organization relevant to international law known as private or non-governmental international organizations (NGOs). *See, e.g.,* U.N. Charter, art. 71. Well-known NGOs include Amnesty International, Greenpeace International, the International Law Association, and the International Committee of the Red Cross. These institutions are created under and governed by national, rather than international, law, but they can play important roles in the promotion of international law and in its observance. *See* P. Spiro, *New Global Potentates: Nongovernmental Organizations and the "Unregulated" Marketplace*, 18 Cardozo L. Rev. 957 (1996).

NGOs can be important voices for raising public awareness about transnational problems. Further, they often engage in transnational lobbying campaigns to influence how governments address transnational problems. NGOs increasingly participate as observers in multilateral treaty negotiations, where they may comment on draft treaty text and otherwise seek to influence the views of states. *See generally "The Conscience of the World": The Influence of Non–Governmental Organisations in the UN System* (P. Willetts ed., 1996).

CHAPTER 4

INTERNATIONAL DISPUTE SETTLEMENT

I. INTRODUCTION

This chapter deals with the traditional non-judicial, quasi-judicial and judicial institutions and methods that are used by the international community to resolve disputes between states. The procedures established under the U.N. Charter to prevent such disputes from leading to the use of force are discussed in Chapter 12. Here we describe the methods international law has developed for the peaceful resolution of international disputes. *See generally* J. Collier & V. Lowe, *The Settlement of Disputes in International Law* (1999).

Article 33(1) of the U.N. Charter provides a useful list of the methods used to deal with international disputes. The article reads as follows:

The parties to any dispute, the continuance of which is likely to endanger the maintenance of international peace and security, shall, first of all, seek a solution by negotiation, enquiry, mediation, conciliation, arbitration, judicial settlement, resort to regional agencies or arrangements, or other peaceful means of their own choice.

In addition to reviewing the dispute settlement methods enumerated in Article 33(1) of the U.N. Charter, this Chapter also describes the jurisdiction and functions of the major international courts in existence today. For a comprehensive overview, see J. Merrills, *International Dispute Settlement* (3d ed. 1998); *see also* C. Romano, *The Proliferation of International Judicial Bodies: The Pieces of the Puzzle*, 31 N.Y.U.J. Int'l L. & Pol. 709 (1999); J. Charney, *The Impact on the International Legal System of the Growth of International Courts and Tribunals*, 31 N.Y.U.J. Int'l L. & Pol. 697 (1999).

II.   NON–JUDICIAL METHODS

§ 4–1.   Introduction. The traditional non-judicial methods for the resolution of international disputes are negotiation, inquiry, mediation and conciliation. Depending upon the dispute, its context and the attitude of the parties to it, one or more and sometimes all of these methods may come into play. In short, they are not necessarily distinct or exclusive techniques for the resolution of a conflict. Each of these methods has national institutional counterparts which function in much the same way.

§ 4–2.   Negotiation. Bilateral and multilateral negotiation to resolve differences between two or more states or between groups of states may be carried out by diplomatic correspondence, or by face-to-face encounters between permanent diplomatic envoys or specially designated negotiators. Negotiation is the traditional and most commonly employed method. It tends to be the first stage in a process that may require resort to other, more formal, dispute-resolution methods. Prior negotiation is often also required as a condition precedent to the exercise of jurisdiction by international courts.

§ 4–3. Inquiry. The reference of a dispute to a process of inquiry involves the designation of a group of individuals or an institution to act as an impartial fact-finding or investigatory body. This method can be extremely effective under certain circumstances. An inquiry undertaken with the consent of the parties that results in an unambiguous finding of fact is more likely than not to lead to the resolution of the dispute when the disagreement between the parties involves only issues of fact.

§ 4–4. Mediation or good offices. This technique consists of third-party efforts to assist the parties to a dispute to resolve their disagreements through negotiation. The role of mediator is to bring the parties together, to serve as intermediary between them, to propose solutions and to explore opportunities for settlement. Today these techniques take on many different forms. Mediators may serve as a bridge between contending states whose representatives may or may not speak to each other—the Middle East shuttle diplomacy provides a good example. Mediators may sit in on negotiations, chair meetings, suggest solutions, cajole, etc.

§ 4–5. Conciliation. This is a more formal process than the other dispute resolution techniques described above. It requires an agreement by the parties to the dispute referring the controversy to a group of individuals or to an institution which will receive the views of the parties and then issue a report containing recommendations for resolution of the disputes. The parties do not obligate themselves to accept the recommendations, but the existence of a report tends to make it more difficult for the parties to disregard it or to reject the recommendations, particularly if they wish to avoid the appearance of acting in an arbitrary manner.

§ **4–6. Negotiation, mediation, conciliation combined**. There exist today numerous international institutions and mechanisms that consist of a combination of negotiation, fact-finding, mediation and conciliation. Institutions that have been established to resolve disputes concerning claims of human rights violations are but one example of this phenomenon. They normally consist of a committee or commission created by a treaty, which also contains a catalog of the protected rights. Disputes concerning violations of these rights may be referred by the states parties to the committee or commission. That body then initiates a formal process which moves from negotiations and fact-finding to efforts to bring about a friendly settlement, followed by a report containing conclusions and, if a friendly settlement is not reached, recommendations. *See, e.g.*, International Convention on the Elimination of All Forms of Racial Discrimination, Dec. 21, 1965, arts. 11–13, 660 U.N.T.S. 195, 5 I.L.M. 352; International Covenant on Civil and Political Rights, Dec. 16, 1966, arts. 41–42, 999 U.N.T.S. 171. In some of these treaties, provisions are even made for adjudication, which is resorted to as a final step in the dispute-settlement process. This possibility exists, for example, under the European and American Conventions on human rights.

For an overview, see T. Buergenthal, D. Shelton & D. Stewart, *International Human Rights in a Nutshell* chs. 3 & 4 (3d ed., 2002). A much more complex machinery for the resolution of disputes, which draws on all the aforementioned techniques in a variety of different contexts and combinations, has been established by the Law of the Sea Convention. *See infra* § 10–13. The U.N. Charter itself envisages a dispute resolution process in which the Security Council and the General Assembly play different roles in activating resort to the various methods listed in Article 33 of the Charter. *See* U.N. Charter, chs. VI & VII; *see also infra* § 12–3.

III.   QUASI–JUDICIAL METHODS

§ 4–7.   Arbitration and adjudication distinguished. International arbitration and adjudication by international courts differ from the dispute-resolution techniques discussed in the preceding section in one very important respect: arbitral and judicial decisions are binding on the parties. At the same time, there are important differences between international arbitration and judicial dispute settlement. An arbitral tribunal or panel is not a permanent judicial body. *See generally International Arbitration: Past and Prospects* (A. Soons ed., 1990); C. Gray & B. Kingsbury, *Developments in Dispute Settlement: International Arbitration since 1945*, 63 Brit. Y.B. Int'l L. 97 (1992). Its composition, as well as its jurisdiction and the rules of procedure it applies, must be agreed upon by the parties. (The agreement in which all of these matters are settled is known as a *compromis*.) Judicial dispute settlement, by contrast, normally takes place in the context of a permanent court, which has a fixed composition and operates under preexisting jurisdictional standards and rules of procedure, not ones established *ad hoc* by the parties appearing before the court.

§ **4–8. International arbitral clauses**. In practice, at least three types of international arbitral agreements can be identified. The first consists of an arbitration clause that is included in a treaty, be it bilateral or multilateral, that deals with one or more other substantive matters. The function of this clause is to provide a method for the resolution of disputes that might arise in the interpretation or application of that particular treaty. It is not uncommon to find such a clause in bilateral commercial treaties (for example, bilateral investment treaties or BITS) or in international civil aviation agreements.

The second type of arbitral agreement consists of treaties whose sole function is to establish a method for the resolution and arbitration of whatever disputes or categories of disputes might arise between the parties in the future. The best known agreements of this type are the 1899 Hague Convention for the Pacific Settlement of International Disputes, as revised by the 1907 Hague Convention, and the 1928 General Act for the Pacific Settlement of International Disputes, which was amended in 1949. The Hague Conventions established the Permanent Court of Arbitration which, despite its name, is not a court but an institution for the facilitation of international arbitration. It maintains a roster of arbitrators, drawn from lists of four individuals presented by each of the states parties as being qualified to serve on arbitral panels or tribunals. The Permanent Court of Arbitration continues to be used by states to decide disputes between them. *See The Permanent Court of Arbitration: International Arbitration and Dispute Resolution* (P. Hamilton et al. eds., 1999).

In the third category are arbitral agreements that are concluded after a dispute arises and which the parties have not been able to settle by other means. An example of such an agreement was the decision of the United States and Iran to arbitrate certain outstanding claims, which led to the establishment of the Iran–U.S. Claims Tribunal. *See* Declaration Concerning the Settlement of Claims, Jan. 19, 1981, U.S.-Iran, 10 I.L.M. 230 (1981). This Tribunal has been in existence since 1981. *See* C. Brower & J. Brueschke, *The Iran–United States Claims Tribunal* (1998); G. Aldrich, *The Jurisprudence of the Iran–United States Claims Tribunal* (1996).

§ 4–9. Consent to arbitrate. It is a basic principle of international law that states cannot be required to arbitrate a dispute unless they have given their consent thereto, either before or after the dispute has arisen. The first two types of arbitral agreements, mentioned *supra* § 4–8, often contain provisions permitting either party to the dispute to require the other party to arbitrate. But where this is not true, the subsequent consent of both parties will be needed for arbitration to take place. In the third type, the consent to arbitrate is contained in the *compromis*.

§ **4–10.** *Compromis*. This instrument is an agreement that contains provisions for the establishment and operation of the arbitral panel. It will identify the issues that are to be decided, specify the rules of procedure to be followed, and state the undertaking of the parties to abide by and implement the award. Since the *compromis* is a binding international agreement, a party's failure to abide by the award would constitute a separate breach of international law. States comply with the vast majority of international arbitral awards.

§ **4–11. Nature and composition of arbitral tribunals**. Arbitral tribunals are established either to deal with a specific dispute or to decide a variety of claims. In some instances, so-called *ad hoc* international arbitral tribunals have continued to function for decades. Normally, arbitral tribunals are composed of three members. Each party to the dispute may name one member, with the third member to be designated by agreement of the parties or, failing such agreement, by the President of the International Court of Justice or some other person of international stature. If the parties are unable to agree on the third member and the arbitral agreement does not contain an alternative method for his or her selection, there may be no way to implement the agreement to arbitrate because international courts have no general power under international law to impose an arbitrator. While arbitral tribunals vary in size—the Iran–U.S. Claims Tribunal, for example, consists of nine members—the tripartite structure described above is usually maintained.

§ 4–12. Arbitral award. Unless the agreement provides otherwise, arbitral awards are binding on the parties to the dispute and are not subject to appeal. The validity of arbitral awards may be challenged in a national court, however, in certain special circumstances. The most commonly accepted bases for such a challenge, codified in the U.N. Model Rules on Arbitral Procedure, are that the tribunal has exceeded its powers; that there was corruption on the part of a member of the tribunal; that there was a failure to state the reasons for the award or a serious departure from a fundamental rule of procedure; or that the undertaking to arbitrate or the *compromis* is a nullity. *See* U.N. Model Rules on Arbitral Procedure, 13 U.N. G.A.O.R. Supp. No. 9, at 5–8, art. 35 (1958). On this subject, see *Arbitral Award of 31 July 1989* (Guinea–Bissau v. Sen.), 1991 I.C.J. 53 (Nov. 12); American Law Institute, *Restatement of the Foreign Relations Law of the United States (Third)* § 904 (1987).

§ 4–13. Applicable law and sources of law. Arbitral tribunals apply international law unless the parties specify that some other law should be applied. Up until the early 20th century, international case law consisted principally of decisions of arbitral tribunals and judgments of national courts applying international law. (The Central American Court of Justice rendered only a handful of decisions during its brief existence between 1908 and 1918, and the Permanent Court of International Justice was not established until 1920. *See infra* pt. IV.)

Although the authority of the older arbitral decisions has diminished with time, and some have been characterized by new states as relics of colonialism and imperialism, they remain a valuable secondary source of law. The legal authority of contemporary arbitral decisions is much greater, of course. In the absence of a decision by the International Court of Justice or one of the other permanent courts, these decisions are the best quasi-judicial evidence of international law. *See, e.g.,* J. Merrills, *The Contribution of the Permanent Court of Arbitration to International Law and the Settlement of Disputes by Peaceful Means*, in *The Permanent Court of Arbitration: International Arbitration and Dispute Resolution* 3 (P. Hamilton et al. eds., 1999).

§ **4–14. International arbitration and the individual**. Narrowly defined, international arbitration is a method for the adjudication on the international plane of disputes between states. Nevertheless, the facts giving rise to such disputes often involve claims by nationals of one state against another state. Here the states are said to be "espousing" the claims of their nationals. Over the years, international arbitral tribunals have developed a whole body of international law, both procedural and substantive, bearing on the various legal issues that arise in the litigation of such claims. *See infra* ch. 6, pt. III. Much of that law, particularly its procedural and jurisdictional components, has found its way into the constitutions and rules of procedures of existing international courts.

More broadly defined, international arbitration can include arbitration between a state and a person (including a corporation), at least where the

arbitral tribunal is governed by international law
and procedures in resolving the dispute. For example, if a U.S. corporation invests in a major infra-
structure project in a developing state (such as
building oil refineries), the corporation will likely
insist upon an agreement with that state setting
forth the terms of the investment. The corporation,
however, will not want that agreement to be subject
solely to the national law and courts of the state,
since the state might seek to manipulate its law and
courts to serve its own interests. Consequently, the
corporation might further insist upon a compromis-
sory clause in the agreement stating that, if a
dispute arises, it shall be resolved in accordance
with international law by international arbitration
at a major institution, such as the International
Chamber of Commerce in Paris or the International
Centre for Settlement of Investment Disputes (IC-
SID) in Washington, D.C. If a dispute arises, the
corporation has the right to demand resolution at
the chosen international forum. Further, if the corporation obtains an award in its favor, and the state
refuses to pay the award, the corporation may be
able to enforce the award in numerous jurisdictions
worldwide through use of certain enforcement conventions, such as the New York Convention on the
Recognition and Enforcement of Foreign Arbitral
Awards, 21 U.S.T. 2517 (implemented in U.S. law at
9 U.S.C. §§ 201–08 (1994)) or the Inter–American
Convention on International Commercial Arbitration, Jan. 30, 1975, 14 I.L.M. 336 (implemented in
U.S. law at 9 U.S.C. §§ 301–07 (1994)). Most of the

decisions of the Iran–U.S. Claims Tribunal (mentioned *supra* §§ 4–8, 4–11) involved disputes between U.S. nationals and the government of Iran. While successful U.S. nationals were paid out of a security account in the Netherlands, in cases where Iran prevailed but the U.S. national refused to pay, Iran successfully enforced its awards in U.S. courts through resort to the New York Convention. *See, e.g., Iran v. Gould*, 887 F.2d 1357 (9th Cir.1989).

IV.   JUDICIAL METHODS

§ 4–15. Introduction. International courts, that is, permanent international judicial institutions, are a relatively recent phenomenon of international life. The Central American Court of Justice (1908–1918) was the first such court. It did not survive the periodic upheavals dividing the five Central American republics (Costa Rica, El Salvador, Guatemala, Honduras, and Nicaragua) which established it. This tribunal holds a special place in the history of international courts, not only because it was the first, but also because under its charter individuals had standing to institute proceedings against governments. For the history and practice of the Central American Court of Justice, see M. Hudson, *Central American Court of Justice*, 26 Am. J. Int'l L. 26 (1932). Today there exist a number of permanent international courts, including the International Court of Justice (I.C.J.) and various specialized regional courts, which will be discussed below.

Under international law, states cannot be required to submit disputes to an international court unless they have consented to its jurisdiction. Thus, the threshold question for an international court hearing a case always is the issue of whether its jurisdiction has been accepted by the states parties to the dispute. States are free, as a rule, to accept jurisdiction either before a dispute has arisen or thereafter, to limit their acceptance to certain types of disputes, and to attach various conditions to the acceptance. Jurisdictional issues consequently always loom large in the work of international courts.

A. International Court of Justice

§ **4–16. Historical development**. The I.C.J. is the successor to the Permanent Court of International Justice (P.C.I.J.), which was established in 1920 under the auspices of the League of Nations. The P.C.I.J. stopped functioning in 1939 because of the Second World War, although it was not formally dissolved until 1946. That court rendered some 30 judgments, 27 advisory opinions, and various interlocutory orders. These decisions continue to be cited as authority by international lawyers and courts.

The I.C.J., which is the principal judicial organ of the United Nations, came into being in 1945. Its Statute or constitution, modelled on that of the P.C.I.J., is annexed to and forms an integral part of the U.N. Charter. All U.N. member states are *ipso facto* parties to the Statute of the Court. States that are not U.N. members may adhere to the Statute under conditions that the United Nations has prescribed. *See* U.N. Charter, arts. 92–94; *see generally* S. Rosenne, *The Law and Practice of the International Courts, 1920–1996* (1997) (four volumes).

§ 4–17. Composition and institutional structure. The I.C.J. consists of 15 judges, no two of whom may be nationals of the same state. The judges are elected by the U.N. General Assembly and the Security Council and must receive an absolute majority of the votes in both bodies. The regular term of the judges is nine years; they may be reelected. There is no formal rule allocating a seat on the Court to each permanent member of the Security Council, although this is done in practice. When none of the I.C.J. judges possess the nationality of a state party to a case before the Court, that State is allowed to appoint a person to serve as a judge *ad hoc* for the duration of the case.

The Court has two distinct types of jurisdiction: contentious jurisdiction and advisory jurisdiction. Different rules and procedures apply to each.

1.   Contentious Jurisdiction

§ 4–18.   Bases of contentious jurisdiction. The contentious jurisdiction of the I.C.J. applies only to disputes between states which have accepted that jurisdiction. The Court lacks contentious jurisdiction to deal with disputes involving individuals or entities that are not states. I.C.J. Statute, art. 34(1).

In discussing the Court's jurisdiction, it is important not to equate adherence by a state to the Court's Statute with acceptance of its jurisdiction. The doors of the Court are open to a state which is a party to its Statute—that is what adherence to the Statute signifies. But whether the Court may hear a case filed by a state party to the Statute against another state party depends upon whether both have in addition accepted the tribunal's jurisdiction.

Article 36 of the Statute deals with the Court's contentious jurisdiction. There are basically three ways in which states can submit to the jurisdiction of the I.C.J. First, under Article 36(1), they can accept the Court's jurisdiction on an *ad hoc* basis for the adjudication of an existing dispute. For example, the United States and Canada jointly agreed to bring to the Court a dispute over their maritime boundary. *See Delimitation of the Maritime Boundary of the Gulf of Maine Area*, 1984 I.C.J. 246 (Oct. 12).

Second, also under Article 36(1), states can adhere to a treaty, be it bilateral or multilateral, in which the Court's jurisdiction is accepted for cases relating to the interpretation or application of the treaty or for any other disputes that might arise. Provisions of this type may be limited to specific disputes or be general in character. For example, the Convention on the Prevention and Punishment of the Crime of Genocide, Dec. 9, 1948, 78 U.N.T.S. 277 (Genocide Convention), sets forth various obligations of states with respect to preventing and punishing genocide, but it further provides in Article IX that disputes arising under the convention between parties shall be submitted to the I.C.J. at the request of one of the parties. Thus, if a state party to the Genocide Convention believes that another state party is violating the convention, resort to the I.C.J. is one option for resolving the dispute.

However, it is always important to determine whether a state filed a reservation to the provision on dispute resolution when ratifying the convention. The United States ratified the Genocide Convention in 1988, but it stated that before any dispute could be submitted to the Court under Article IX, "the specific consent of the United States is required in each case." *See* 28 I.L.M. 782 (1989). When Yugoslavia in 1999 sought to sue the United States under the Genocide Convention (for acts associated with the NATO intervention relating to Kosovo), the I.C.J. found that—in light of the U.S. reservation—there was no jurisdiction under the Genocide Convention. On this basis, the Court dismissed the case. *See Legality of Use of Force* (Yugo. v. U.S.), 1999 I.C.J. 916 (June 2).

Third, under Article 36(2), which is known as the "optional clause," the states parties to the Statute may by means of a unilateral declaration undertake that "they recognize as compulsory *ipso facto* and without special agreement, in relation to any other state accepting the same obligation, the jurisdiction of the Court in all legal disputes . . ." involving issues of law or fact governed by rules of international law. The Court lacks jurisdiction to hear cases that are governed by national law rather than international law. I.C.J. Statute, art. 38(1). *See generally* M. Fitzmaurice, *The Optional Clause System and the Law of Treaties: Issues of Interpretation in Recent Jurisprudence of the International Court of Justice*, 20 Austl. Y.I.L. 127 (1999); J. Merrills, *The*

Optional Clause Revisited, 64 Brit. Y.B. Int'l L. 197 (1993).

§ **4–19. Reciprocity**. Under Article 36(2), a state's unilateral declaration accepting the Court's jurisdiction is applicable "in relation to any other state accepting the same obligation." By filing this declaration, a state accepts the Court's jurisdiction on the basis of reciprocity and, consequently, is required to respond only if sued by a state that has made a similar declaration.

Moreover, whatever jurisdictional defenses the appellant state might have been able to assert against the respondent under its declaration, if the roles were reversed, are open to the respondent because of reciprocity. As the I.C.J. has explained in the leading case on the subject, "since two unilateral declarations are involved, such jurisdiction is conferred upon the Court only to the extent to which the two Declarations [of France and Norway] coincide in conferring it." *Certain Norwegian Loans* (Fr. v. Nor.), 1957 I.C.J. 9, at 23–24 (July 6); *see Aerial Incident of 10 August 1999* (Pak. v. India), 2000 I.C.J. 12 (June 21). *But see Military and Paramilitary Activities in and against Nicaragua* (Nicar. v. U.S.), 1984 I.C.J. 392, 417–19 (Nov. 26).

The reciprocity principle has special significance because a majority of the sixty-odd states which have accepted the Court's jurisdiction under Article 36(2) have done so with various reservations. The Court's jurisdiction is consequently narrowed in any case in which one of the parties to the dispute has a reservation, because the party that has not made the reservation may nevertheless invoke it against the other party. *See Interhandel Case* (Switz. v. U.S.), 1959 I.C.J. 6, at 23 (Mar. 21). For example, in the *Norwegian Loans* case, France filed the action against Norway, but had accepted the Court's jurisdiction under Article 36(2) with a reservation providing that "this declaration does not apply to differences relating to matters which are essentially within the national jurisdiction as understood by the government of the French Republic." The Norwegian declaration contained no reservation. Under the principle of reciprocity, which was expressly reiterated in the Norwegian declaration, Norway was permitted to "except from the compulsory jurisdiction of the Court disputes understood by Norway to be essentially within its national jurisdiction." *Certain Norwegian Loans* (Fr. v. Nor.), 1957 I.C.J. 9, at 23–24 (July 6). Most commentators agree that the result would have been the same even if the Norwegian declaration had merely repeated the text of Article 36(2), without reiterating that its acceptance was "on condition of reciprocity."

The question whether a state, which accepts the Court's jurisdiction "unconditionally," will be deemed to have waived reciprocity under Article 36(2), has been answered in the negative by a majority of commentators. They suggest that the stipulation in Article 36(3) of the Statute that Article 36(2) declarations "may be made unconditionally or on condition of reciprocity on the part of several or certain states, or for a certain time," was not designed to affect the principle of reciprocity proclaimed in Article 36(2). Instead, it was inserted to enable states to condition the entry into force of their declaration upon the acceptance of the Court's jurisdiction by certain other states. It would appear, therefore, that a state which has accepted the Court's jurisdiction under Article 36(2) and declared it to be "unconditional" would be entitled to invoke the reservation of any state that filed an action against it. *Cf. Military and Paramilitary Activities in and Against Nicaragua* (Nicar. v. U.S.), 1984 I.C.J. 392 (Nov. 26).

§ 4–20.　U.S. Article 36(2) declaration. The United States accepted the Court's jurisdiction under Article 36(2) in 1946. It did so with a number of reservations, however. Most important was the so-called "Connally Amendment," named for the Texas Senator who proposed it. Similar to the French reservation noted above, the U.S. reservation excluded from the jurisdiction of the Court "disputes with regard to matters which are essentially within the domestic jurisdiction of the United States of America as determined by the United States of America." The purpose of this so-called "self-judging" clause was to ensure that the United States and not the I.C.J. would decide, as a practical matter, whether a dispute is "domestic" in character and consequently outside the Court's jurisdiction. Given the principle of reciprocity, this reservation had the effect of entitling any state the United States wished to sue to invoke the reservation against the United States, requiring the Court to dismiss the suit. *See* L. Gross, *Bulgaria Invokes the Connally Amendment*, 56 Am. J. Int'l L. 357 (1962).

It has been argued from time to time that the Connally Amendment and similar self-judging clauses are invalid because they violate Article 36(6) of the Statute of the Court, which provides that "in the event of a dispute as to whether the Court has jurisdiction, the matter shall be settled by the decision of the Court." The I.C.J. has not addressed this issue, although it had the opportunity to do so in a number of cases. Judge Hersch Lauterpacht, an eminent I.C.J. judge, considered the question in the *Norwegian Loans* case, *supra*, at 101–02, and in the *Interhandel* case, *supra*, at 95. He concluded that such self-judging clauses violate the Statute. A similar view was expressed by Judge Schwebel in *Military and Paramilitary Activities in and against Nicaragua* (Nicar. v. U.S.), 1984 I.C.J. 392, 601–02 (Nov. 26) (dissenting opinion of Judge Schwebel). Likewise, Judge Vereshchetin commented in the *Fisheries Jurisdiction* case that "self-judging" is not allowed, since the Court has the competence to determine its own jurisdiction. *See Fisheries Jurisdiction* (Spain v. Can.), 1998 I.C.J. 432, 575 (Dec. 4) (dissenting opinion of Judge Vereshchetin).

§ **4–21. Withdrawal of U.S. declaration**. The debate over the wisdom of the Connally Amendment became academic for the United States when it gave notice in 1985 of its decision to terminate U.S. acceptance of the jurisdiction of the I.C.J. under Article 36(2) of its Statute. This termination became effective in 1986 and was prompted by the U.S. Government's dissatisfaction with the U.S.–Nicaragua litigation. *See United States: Department of State Letter and Statement concerning Termination of Acceptance of I.C.J. Compulsory Jurisdiction,* 24 I.L.M. 1742 (1985).

The withdrawal by the United States of its acceptance of the Court's jurisdiction under Article 36(2) does not affect the Court's jurisdiction over the United States under Article 36(1). The United States is a party to many treaties that confer jurisdiction on the Court under that provision of its Statute, enabling the United States to sue and be sued thereunder. *See, e.g., LaGrand Case* (Ger. v. U.S.), 2001 I.C.J. (June 27), *reprinted in* 40 I.L.M. 1069 (2001) (involving a dispute brought against the United States under the Optional Protocol Concerning Compulsory Settlement of Disputes to the Vienna Convention on Consular Relations, Apr. 24, 1963, 21 U.S.T. 325, 596 U.N.T.S. 487).

A state's ability to withdraw or modify its Article 36(2) declaration, however, may be limited by the terms of the declaration. In its 1946 acceptance of the Court's jurisdiction under Article 36(2), the United States provided "that this declaration shall remain in force for a period of five years and thereafter until the expiration of six months after notice may be given to terminate this declaration." The declaration remained in force in its 1946 form until 1984, when the United States sought to amend it as follows:

The aforesaid [1946] declarations shall not apply to disputes with any Central American state arising out of or related to events in Central America, any of which disputes shall be settled in such a manner as the parties to them may agree.

§ 4–22 *JUDICIAL METHODS* 87

> Notwithstanding the terms of the aforesaid declaration, this proviso shall take effect immediately and shall remain in force for two years. . . .

With this amendment, the United States sought to anticipate Nicaragua's decision to file suit against the United States in the I.C.J. and to prevent the Court from assuming jurisdiction in the case. The I.C.J. upheld Nicaragua's contention that the United States was bound by the six-months notice requirement contained in the 1946 declaration, despite the fact that Nicaragua's reservation contained no notice provision and could have been withdrawn at any time. Justifying its refusal to permit the United States to rely on the principle of reciprocity, the Court ruled that the "notion of reciprocity is concerned with the scope and substance of the commitments entered into, including reservations, and not with the formal conditions of their creation, duration or extinction." *Military and Paramilitary Activities in and against Nicaragua* (Nicar. v. U.S.), 1984 I.C.J. 392, 419 at para. 62 (Nov. 26).

§ 4–22. National security considerations. Issues of national security are usually perceived to be the most sensitive and, thus, least likely to be submitted to international adjudication. For example, in recent decades several states have modified their acceptance of the compulsory jurisdiction of the I.C.J. to exclude matters related to national security or self-defense. The United States, which had not made such a modification to its Article 36(2) declaration, cited these considerations, *inter* *alia,* as reasons for its withdrawal from the *Nicaragua* case after the Court ruled against it on the jurisdictional issue. *See U.S. Statement of January 8, 1985,* 24 I.L.M. 246 (1985). Similar considerations explain the French position in the *Nuclear Test Cases* (Austl. v. Fr.; N.Z. v. Fr.), 1973 I.C.J. 99, 135 (June 22); 1974 I.C.J. 253, 257 (Dec. 20). In the *Nicaragua* case, the I.C.J. rejected the view that disputes involving issues of national security or self-defense were *ipso facto* not suitable for adjudication by the Court or inadmissible. *See Military and Paramilitary Activities in and Against Nicaragua* (Nicar. v. U.S.), 1984 I.C.J. 392, 433–37 (Nov. 26). The Court amplified on this view in its subsequent judgment in the *Nicaragua* case, which it decided against the United States on the merits. *See Military and Paramilitary Activities in and against Nicaragua* (Nicar. v. U.S.), 1986 I.C.J. 14 (June 27). For different assessments of this case, see *Appraisal of the ICJ's Decision: Nicaragua v. United States (Merits),* 81 Am. J. Int'l L. 77 (1987).

§ 4–23. Effect and enforcement of judgments. Judgments rendered by the I.C.J. in contentious cases are binding on the parties thereto. I.C.J. Statute, art. 59. They are also deemed to be "final and without appeal." I.C.J. Statute, art. 60. The Statute of the Court, however, does not specify how its judgments are to be enforced. That subject is governed by Article 94 of the U.N. Charter. In Article 94(1), each U.N. member state "undertakes to comply with the decision of the International Court of Justice in any case to which it is a party." A state which fails to abide by the Court's judgment would thus violate the U.N. Charter. This point is reinforced by Article 94(2), which permits a party in a case to appeal non-compliance to the U.N. Security Council, "which may, if it deems necessary, make recommendations or decide upon measures to be taken to give effect to the judgment." It should be emphasized that the Security Council "may" but need not take any action. Moreover, if it acts, it may do so by means of a recommendation or decision; only the latter is binding. The failure of a member state to comply with a Security Council decision may in certain circumstances give rise to enforcement measures. *See* U.N. Charter, arts. 39, 41, 42. Since the veto power of the permanent members applies to enforcement measures, such action will only be taken in cases in which these states are prepared to cooperate. For a U.S. veto of a Security Council resolution on the subject, see 25 I.L.M. 1337, 1352–65 (1986).

§ **4–24. Provisional measures**. Under Article 41 of its Statute, the Court has jurisdiction to issue so-called provisional measures (temporary injunctions) when necessary "to preserve the respective rights of either party." The Statute of the P.C.I.J. contained a comparable provision. Until recently, however, neither the I.C.J. nor its predecessor had addressed the question of the binding character of provisional measures, and the answer to it was disputed in the literature. Finally, in 2001, the Court provided the answer in the *LaGrand Case* (Ger. v. U.S.), 2001 I.C.J. (June 27), *reprinted in* 40 I.L.M. 1069 (2001), where it held that provisional measures were binding.

2. *Advisory Jurisdiction*

§ **4–25. Scope of advisory jurisdiction**. The advisory jurisdiction of the I.C.J. may be invoked only by U.N. organs and by the specialized agencies of the United Nations. *See* I.C.J. Statute, art. 65(1). States and individuals have no standing to request advisory opinions. Article 96(1) of the U.N. Charter expressly authorizes the U.N. General Assembly and the Security Council to seek advisory opinions "on any legal question". Other U.N. organs and specialized agencies may do so with the approval of the General Assembly and only concerning "legal questions arising within the scope of their activities". *See* U.N. Charter, art. 96(2). The Assembly has given this authorization not only to the principal organs listed in Article 7 of the U.N. Charter, but also to various subsidiary organs. As for the authority of the specialized agencies to request advisory opinions, the requisite approval is, as a rule, contained in their cooperative agreements with the United Nations. *See* K. Keith, *The Extent of the Advisory Jurisdiction of the International Court of Justice* 36–41 (1971). On the conditions that limit the right of the specialized agencies to request advisory opinions, see *Advisory Opinion on Legality of the Use by a State of Nuclear Weapons in Armed Conflict*, 1996 I.C.J. 66 (July 8).

§ **4–26. Legal character**. Advisory opinions are by definition non-binding. Whether the requesting institution will be guided by or accept as obligatory the Court's ruling is a matter that is governed by the institution's internal law. In the United Nations, it is customary for the requesting organ to vote on whether to accept the opinion. Some international agreements provide that the advisory opinion requested by an organization is binding on the organization and the states parties. *See* M. Pomerance, *The Advisory Function of the International*

Court in the League and U.N. Eras 388–90 (1973). The non-binding character of advisory opinions should not be confused with their juridical authority, the legitimating effect they may have on the conduct of states and organizations, or with their value as precedent in a legal system in which there is a scarcity of judicial pronouncements. In practice, advisory opinions are relied upon and cited as legal authority as frequently as judgments rendered in contentious cases. Since the doctrine of *stare decisis* (binding precedent) is not a doctrine of international law and since it does not apply to contentious decisions of the I.C.J., the Court's advisory opinions have in theory no less precedential value than judgments rendered in contentious cases. The fact that the latter are binding on the parties to the case and that the former are not does not affect their value as legal precedent in future controversies involving other parties.

B. Other major international courts

§ 4–27. Introduction. In addition to the I.C.J., which is the world's only permanent international court of general jurisdiction, there exists a number of other international and regional courts with specialized jurisdiction. The most important of these include the International Tribunal for the Law of the Sea, the international criminal tribunals for the former Yugoslavia and for Rwanda, the Court of Justice of the European Community, the European Court of Human Rights, and the Inter–American Court of Human Rights. Two additional courts are in the process of being established—the permanent International Criminal Court and the African Court of Human and Peoples' Rights. On the consequences for the development of international law of the proliferation of international courts, see J. Charney, *Is International Law Threatened by Multiple International Tribunals?*, 271 R.C.A.D.I. 102 (1999); Symposium, *The Proliferation of International Tribunals: Piecing Together the Puzzle*, N.Y.U. J. Int'l L. & Pol. 679 et seq. (1999); T. Buergenthal, *Proliferation of International Courts and Tribunals: Is It Good or Bad?*, 14 Leiden J. Int'l L. 267 (2001).

§ 4–28. International Tribunal for the Law of the Sea. This Tribunal (ITLOS) was established in accordance with the provisions of Annex VI of the Law of the Sea Convention (LOSC), which entered into force on November 16, 1994. *See S. Treaty Doc.* 103–39 (1994); *see also infra* ch. 10. The ITLOS was formally constituted in 1996, the year the 21 judges comprising it were first elected by the states parties to the LOSC. It has its seat in Hamburg, Germany.

The ITLOS has jurisdiction to interpret the LOSC. That jurisdiction is not exclusive, however, since with regard to many disputes likely to arise under the LOSC the states parties to it are free to select alternative dispute resolution institutions or methods provided for in the LOSC. These include the I.C.J., a general arbitral tribunal established pursuant to Annex VII of the LOSC, or a specialized arbitral tribunal with expertise, *inter alia*, in certain areas, including fisheries, environmental protection, and marine scientific research. *See infra* § 10–13.

The Tribunal does have exclusive jurisdiction, however, with regard to the special procedure provided for under the LOSC for the release of vessels detained for alleged violations of the Convention. To date this jurisdiction has been invoked on a number of occasions and thus far constitutes the greatest part of the ITLOS's judicial practice. For sources on the Tribunal's practice, see *infra* § 13–18. Another area of the ITLOS's exclusive jurisdiction relates to disputes concerning deep sea-bed mining issues. This jurisdiction is to be exercised by the Tribunal's Deep Sea–Bed Chamber, consisting of 11 of its judges. The deep sea-bed mining regime provided for by the LOSC remains to be fully implemented. *See infra* § 10–7. The Tribunal also has jurisdiction to enter provisional measures in a case being submitted to an arbitral tribunal pursuant to the above-mentioned provisions of the LOSC whenever such measures are deemed required by the urgency of the situation. For an example of such provisional measures, see *Bluefin Tuna Cases* (N.Z. v. Japan; Austl. v. Japan), ITLOS Nos. 3 & 4 (Aug. 27, 1999), 38 I.L.M. 1624 (1999) (this dispute is described *infra* § 10–13). On the ITLOS generally, see T. Treves, *The Law of the Sea Tribunal: Its Status and Scope of Jurisdiction after November 16, 1994*, 55 Heidelberg J. Int'l L. 421(1995); T. Mensah, *The Dispute Settlement Regime of the 1982 United Nations Convention on the Law of the Sea*, 2 Max Planck Y.B.U.N.L. 306 (1998).

§ 4–29. *Ad hoc* international criminal tribunals. In 1993 the U.N. Security Council, acting under Chapter VII of the U.N. Charter, which gives it the power to adopt binding resolutions in situations determined to constitute a threat to the peace, breach of the peace or act of aggression, established the International Criminal Tribunal for the former Yugoslavia (ICTY) to try violations of international humanitarian law committed in Yugoslavia since 1991. *See* S.C. Res. 827 (1993). A year later, the Security Council created the International Criminal Tribunal for Rwanda (ICTR), conferring on it jurisdiction to try individuals responsible for serious violations of international humanitarian law committed in 1994 in the territory of Rwanda, as well as Rwandan nationals responsible for genocide and other such violations committed in the territory of neighboring states. *See* S.C. Res. 955 (1994).

The ICTY has its seat in The Hague, Netherlands. The ICTY consists of 16 full-time judges. This number was expanded in 2001 with the election of a pool of 27 *ad litem* judges to be drawn upon by the Tribunal when the need arises. The ICTR has its principal seat in Arusha, Tanzania (there is a prosecutor's office in Kigali, Rwanda), and consists of 14 judges. The judges of the ICTY and ICTR are elected by the U.N. General Assembly for a term of four years and may be reelected. Both Tribunals work in trial chambers of three judges. The Appeals Chamber of the ICTY performs the same function for the ICTR. The two Tribunals also share the same Chief Prosecutor, which helps in coordinating the prosecutorial standards of the two tribunals.

The two Tribunals have similar subject-matter jurisdiction. The "serious violations of international humanitarian law" to which Article 1 of the Statute of the ICTY refers are deemed to include the following crimes: grave breaches of the Geneva Conventions of 1949, violations of the laws and customs of war, genocide, and crimes against humanity. The jurisdiction of the ICTR embraces crimes against humanity, genocide and violations of common Article 3 of the Geneva Conventions and of Additional Protocol II thereto. Unlike the ICTY, the ICTR was not given jurisdiction over grave breaches of the Geneva Conventions or violations of the laws and customs of war because of the internal character of the Rwanda conflict. Since their establishment, both Tribunals have rendered important judgments that are making significant contributions to the development of international humanitarian law. For the practice of the ICTY and ICTR, see J. Jones, *The Practice of the International Criminal Tribunals for the Former Yugoslavia and Rwanda* (2d ed. 2000); D. Stroh, *State Cooperation with the International Criminal Tribunals for the Former Yugoslavia and for Rwanda*, 5 Max Planck Y.B.U.N.L. 249 (2001); J. Ackerman & E. O'Sullivan, *Practice and Procedure of the International Criminal Court for the Former Yugoslavia* (2000); S. Murphy, *Progress and Jurisprudence of the International Criminal Tribunal for the Former Yugoslavia*, 93 Am. J. Int'l L. 57 (1999); P. Magnarella, *Justice in Africa: Rwanda's Genocide, Its Courts and the UN Criminal Tribunal* (2000); J. Alvarez, *Crimes of State, Crimes of Hate: Lessons from Rwanda*, 24 Yale J. Int'l L. 365 (1999). For sources on the work of the Tribunals, see *infra* ch. 13–17.

§ 4–30. Court of Justice of the European Community. This Court, which renders more than 150 judgments annually, is the judicial organ of the European Community. *See supra* ch. 3, pt. VII. The Court has its seat in Luxembourg and was established in 1952 after entry into force of the treaty establishing the European Coal and Steel Community. Its jurisdiction was expanded in 1958 when the European Economic Community and the European Atomic Energy Community were created. The separate Community treaties confer similar, but not identical, powers on the Court of Justice. These treaties, as amended, now spell out the jurisdiction of the Court of Justice. *See supra* §§ 3–27, 3–28.

In 1992, to reduce the case load of the Court, the European Community established a Court of First Instance. It has jurisdiction over claims against the Community by its employees. Here, the Court of First Instance performs functions comparable to those of international administrative tribunals. It also has limited jurisdiction to deal with some anti-competition claims.

The Court of Justice's principal function is the interpretation and application of the constitutive instruments of the Community and of the legislative measures emanating from the bodies established by them. *See supra* §§ 3–30, 3–31. The jurisdiction of the Court extends to disputes involving the member states and the authorities of the Community. Private enterprises and individuals may also refer certain types of cases to the Court. Moreover, the national courts of the member states may, and in some circumstances must, request the Court to provide them with rulings interpreting questions of Community law arising in national litigation. The authority to render these rulings was conferred on the Court to ensure the uniform interpretation of Community law by the courts of all member states. In this sense it roughly parallels the federal question jurisdiction of the U.S. Supreme Court. *See generally* K. Lasok, *The European Court of Justice: Practice and Procedure* (2d ed. 1994); W. Mattli & A. Slaughter, *Revisiting the European Court of Justice*, 52 Int'l Org. 177(1998); N. Fennelly, *Preserving the Legal Coherence within the New Treaty: The European Court of Justice after the Treaty of Amsterdam*, 5 Maastricht J. Eur. & Comp. L. 185 (1998).

§ 4–31. European Court of Human Rights. The European Court of Human Rights was established in 1959. It is the judicial organ of the European Convention for the Protection of Human Rights and Fundamental Freedoms, Nov. 4, 1950, 312 U.N.T.S. 221 (European Convention). That treaty was concluded within the institutional framework of the Council of Europe, the 44–member European regional intergovernmental organization which has its seat in Strasbourg, France. *See supra* ch. 3, pt. VI; *infra* ch. VI, pt. II(B)(1). The jurisdiction of the Court extends to the interpretation and application of the European Convention and its various additional protocols. *See generally* T. Buergenthal, D. Shelton & D. Stewart, *International Human Rights in a Nutshell*, ch. 3 (3d ed. 2002).

Protocol No. 11 to the European Convention, which entered into force in 1998, restructured the protective system established by the European Convention. Today the Court has jurisdiction to deal with cases referred to it by the states parties to the Convention and by individuals claiming to be victims of a violation of the human rights guaranteed in that treaty or one of its protocols. Prior to the entry into force of Protocol No. 11, which abolished the European Commission of Human Rights, all cases had to be dealt with by the Commission before they could be referred to the Court. The Court consists of 43 judges, a number equal to the current number of states parties to the European Convention. They are elected to six-year terms by the Parliamentary Assembly of the Council of Europe. The Court sits in chambers of seven judges and in a Grand Chamber of 17 judges. The plenary Court deals with administrative matters only. Many of the functions previously discharged by the Commission, including questions relating to the admissibility of cases, are now decided by different chambers of the Court.

The membership of the Council of Europe almost doubled with the end of the Cold War and the demise of the Soviet Union. Most of the Warsaw Pact states and many former Soviet Republics joined the Council of Europe and ratified the Convention. *See* V. Djerić, *Admission to Membership of the Council of Europe and Legal Significance of Commitments Entered into by New Member States*, 60 Heidelberg J. Int'l L.605 (2000). In matters of human rights the Court has become for all practical purposes the constitutional court of Europe. The impact of its judgments on the law of the states parties to the Convention and on the manner in which they protect human rights has increased dramatically over the years. On the Convention and Court generally, see A. Drzemczewski, *The European Human Rights Convention: Protocol 11—Entry into Force and First Year of Application*, 21 Hum. Rts. L.J. 1 (2000); P. van Dijk & G. van Hoof, *Theory and Practice of the European Convention on Human Rights* (3d ed. 1998); J. Merrills, *The Development of International Law by the European Court of Human Rights* (1988).

§ 4–32. Inter–American Court of Human Rights. The seven-judge Inter-American Court of Human Rights was established in 1979. It has its seat in San José, Costa Rica. The Court is the judicial organ of the American Convention on Human Rights, Nov. 22, 1969, 9 I.L.M. 673 (American Convention), which entered into force in 1978. *See infra* ch. VI, pt. II (B)(2). This treaty is modelled on the European Convention and provided for an institutional structure similar to that of its European counterpart prior to the entry into force of Protocol No. 11 to the European Convention. *See supra* § 4–31. The American Convention creates an Inter-American Commission and Court of Human Rights. Unlike its European counterpart, the Inter–American Court has extensive powers to render advisory opinions interpreting the Convention as well as other human rights treaties. The contentious jurisdiction of the Inter–American Court resembles that of the European Court. Only the Commission and the member states that have accepted the Court's jurisdiction have standing to bring cases to it; individuals lack the right to do so. Complaints filed with the Commission by private individuals may be referred to the Court by the Commission or an interested member state. Here it is noteworthy that amendments to the Court's and Commission's Rules of Procedure, which entered into force in 2001, have strengthened the position of individuals in protecting and asserting their rights in proceedings before the Commission and the Court, although individuals still lack standing to refer their cases to the Court.

The Inter–American Court dealt with only a very limited number of contentious cases in the first decade of its existence because few such cases were referred to it. During that time its practice was limited mainly to advisory opinions. Since then, however, an ever greater number of important contentious cases have been considered by the Court. Further, the Court has also rendered an increasing number of provisional measure orders. *See generally* A. Trindade, *Judicial Protection and Guarantees in Recent Case Law of the Inter–American Court of Human Rights*, in *Liber Amicorum "in Memoriam" of Judge José Mariá Ruda* 527 (C. Barea ed., 2000); C. Cerna, *The Inter–American Court of Human Rights*, in *International Courts for the Twenty First Century* 112 (M. Janis ed., 1992); S. Davidson, *The Inter–American Court of Human Rights* (1992); T. Buergenthal, D. Shelton & D. Stewart, *International Human Rights in a Nutshell* ch. 4 (2002).

§ **4–33.** **New courts.** Two new courts are in the process of being established. One new court is the permanent International Criminal Court (I.C.C.), whose Statute was adopted in Rome in

1998 at a U.N. conference and entered into force in July 2002. *See* Rome Statute of the International Criminal Court, 37 I.L.M. 999 (1998). The Rome Statute confers jurisdiction on the ICC to investigate and prosecute individuals for genocide, crimes against humanity, war crimes, and (once certain issues have been decided) the crime of aggression. The I.C.C. may only exercise its jurisdiction over an accused person when either the state where the crime was allegedly committed or the state of the accused's nationality is a party to the Court's Statute. *See generally* L. Sadat, *The International Criminal Court and the Transformation of International Law* (2002). The United States signed the Rome Statute in December 2000, but then notified the United Nations in May 2002 that it did not intend to seek ratification of the treaty. The United States expressed concerns that the Rome Statute would undermine the role of the Security Council, would provide too much power to the ICC prosecutor (possibly leading to politically-motivated prosecutions), and could lead to assertion of jurisdiction over nationals of states that have not ratified the treaty.

The other new court is the African Court of Human and Peoples' Rights, which will probably be established by 2004. The African Court will join the existing African Commission on Human and Peoples' Rights in enforcing the rights guaranteed in the African Charter on Human and Peoples' Rights, which entered into force in 1986. On the African Court, see *infra* ch. VI, pt. II(B)(3); V. Nmehielle, *The African Human Rights System* 259 (2001).

CHAPTER 5

INTERNATIONAL LAW
OF TREATIES

I. INTRODUCTION

Treaties perform a variety of functions on the international plane that in national law are performed by many different types of legal acts and instruments, including constitutions, laws of general applicability, contracts, deeds, trust agreements, corporate charters, etc. Treaties, by contrast, serve as the constitutions of international organizations, *see supra* ch. 3, they can be a source of general international law, *see supra* ch. 2, they are used to transfer territory, to regulate commercial relations, to settle disputes, to protect human rights, to guarantee investments, and so on. *See generally* P. Reuter, *Introduction to the Law of Treaties* (2d ed. 1995); A. Aust, *Modern Treaty Law and Practice* (2000).

The term "treaty", as used on the international plane, describes international agreements in general, whether they be denominated conventions, pacts, covenants, charters, protocols, etc. These different names have no legal significance; the same legal rules apply to one as to the other. The choice of this or that name may at times be prompted by the belief that a given designation implies greater or lesser solemnity or importance. But as a matter of international law, a treaty by whatever name is still a treaty. In U.S. national law, by contrast, the term "treaty" has a special meaning. It describes an international agreement that, unlike other international agreements the United States might conclude, requires the advice and consent of the Senate before the United States may become a party to it. *See infra* § 7–3.

The international law of treaties has been codified to a large extent in the Vienna Convention on the Law of Treaties, May 23, 1969, 1155 U.N.T.S. 331, 8 I.L.M. 679 (VCLT). *See generally* I. Sinclair, *The Vienna Convention on the Law of Treaties* (2d ed. 1984). The VCLT entered into force in 1980 and has been ratified by many states. Its authoritative character as law, even for states not parties to it, derives from the fact that it is now generally accepted that most of its provisions are declaratory of the customary international law of treaties. Although the United States has not become a party to the treaty, it considers that the substantive provisions of the VCLT state the international law on the subject. *See* American Law Institute, *Restatement of the Foreign Relations Law of the United States (Third)* pt. III, intro. note (1987) (*Restatement (Third)*).

II.   DEFINITION AND CONCLUSION OF TREATIES

§ 5–1. Definition. Treaties, whether bilateral or multilateral, are defined somewhat circuitously as agreements governed by international law. Since it is international law which applies to relations between and among the subjects of international law (states and intergovernmental organizations), it follows that agreements which they conclude with one another are, as a general rule, treaties. Some agreements entered into between states or international organizations may be governed, expressly or by implication, by national law and would, therefore, not be treaties but contracts. An example of such a contract would be an agreement between two states for the sale of land to construct an embassy that the parties intend to be governed by local property law. Other purely commercial arrangements (a contract for the sale of wheat or military equipment, for example) between the governments of two or more states might fall into the same category. Although there is a presumption that an agreement between two states is a treaty, that presumption may be rebutted by a showing that they intended it to be governed exclusively by national law.

The VCLT defines a treaty as "an international agreement concluded between States in written form and governed by international law ...". VCLT, art. 2(1)(a). This does not mean that an agreement between a state and an international organization or between two such organizations cannot be a treaty. VCLT, art. 3. The VCLT adopts a more restrictive definition because it was expressly made applicable only to agreements between states. International agreements involving international organizations are governed by a more recent treaty, the Vienna Convention on the Law of Treaties between States and International Organizations or between International Organizations, Mar. 21, 1986, 25 I.L.M. 543 (1986). This instrument complements the VCLT and amplifies to a significant extent the existing body of norms applicable to international agreements. Furthermore, although both of these conventions apply only to written agreements, a treaty does not have to be in writing in order to be valid and enforceable under international law. *See Legal Status of Eastern Greenland* (Den. v. Nor.), 1933 P.C.I.J. (ser. A/B) No. 53 (Apr. 5); *see also* VCLT, art. 3.

§ 5–2. Negotiation of treaties. Although the same legal rules apply to multilateral and bilateral treaties, the process by which these treaties are negotiated and concluded may differ. Bilateral treaties tend to originate in the foreign ministry of one of the two interested parties. Following discussions, usually involving the respective embassies and exchanges of diplomatic notes, one or more draft texts will be prepared by the respective legal advisers. These texts will be the subject of negotiations until an acceptable draft has emerged.

Multilateral treaties between only a few states tend to be negotiated much the same way as bilateral treaties. Treaties designed to have a large number of states parties, however, are drafted at diplomatic conferences where the participating states are represented by diplomatic delegations that include legal advisers. The conference will usually have before it various working papers or draft proposals, prepared by some states or international organizations in advance of the meeting. These documents serve as the basis for the negotiations and bargaining that ultimately result in the text of a treaty. VCLT, art. 9.

The negotiating and drafting process at these diplomatic conferences resembles that of national legislatures. Here amendments to different provisions of the working papers are presented, rapporteurs are designated, drafting committees are established, alternative texts are proposed and debated, etc. The conference records are a valuable source of information on the drafting history of the treaty. The formal results of the conference are frequently summarized in a so-called Final Act, which usually contains the text of the treaty. The Final Act can and often does serve to authenticate the text of the treaty. VCLT, art. 10. But the adoption of the Final Act is not as a rule designed to bring the agreement into force; it simply establishes that the negotiations are completed.

**§ 5–3.	Entry into force of treaties**. Bilateral treaties enter into force on the international plane when both states indicate their intention to be bound by the agreement as of a certain date. Multilateral treaties often contain a provision indicating how many states have to accept the treaty before it will be in force as between them. VCLT, art. 24.

§ 5–4. Consent to be bound by treaty.
VCLT Article 11 declares that "[t]he consent of a
State to be bound by a treaty may be expressed by
signature, exchange of instruments constituting a
treaty, ratification, acceptance, approval or accession, or by any other means if so agreed." Under
international law, any of the abovementioned methods may be utilized by a state to indicate its acceptance of the treaty. Often, of course, the treaty will
specify the method, and if it declares, for example,
that the states will be bound upon signing the
treaty, their signature will have that effect. VCLT,
art. 12.

It is more common for a treaty to provide that it
shall become binding upon ratification. VCLT, art.
14(1). On the international plane, ratification is an
act whereby a state, through its head of state,
foreign minister, or duly authorized diplomatic
agent (VCLT, art. 7) declares that it considers itself
bound by the treaty. VCLT, art. 14. The declaration
is usually contained in a so-called instrument of
ratification. These instruments are either ex-
changed between the parties or deposited with a
previously designated depositary government or organization, which performs various custodial functions relating to the treaty. VCLT, arts. 76–77.

§ 5–5. Signature followed by ratification.
If a treaty imposes a ratification requirement, it will
most likely also provide for the prior signature
thereof during a specified period of time. Thus,
ratification usually is the second step in a two-stage
process, involving signature followed by ratification.
In treaties which adopt this approach, the signature

serves principally as a method for the authentication of the text of the agreement. VCLT, art. 10. It is the states' subsequent ratification which brings the agreement into force for them; their earlier signature alone does not have that effect. By signing a treaty that is subject to ratification a state does not undertake eventually to ratify the agreement, although it does have some minimal obligations relating thereto. VCLT, art. 18; *see* J. Charme, *The Interim Obligation of Article 18 of the Vienna Convention on the Law of Treaties*, 25 Geo. Wash. J. Int'l L. & Econ. 71 (1991).

Treaties tend to provide for signature followed by ratification in order to make it possible for governments to submit them to those national authorities, usually their legislatures, that are empowered under national law to approve the state's adherence to international agreements. Most national constitutions impose some such approval requirement, particularly for treaties that will have to be given effect on the national plane. Thus, a typical sequence for the United States would be: (1) negotiation of a treaty by the President or his representative; (2) signature by the President or his representative; (3) submittal of the treaty by the President to the Senate; (4) the granting of advise and consent by the Senate; and (5) the President's deposit of the instrument of ratification. Only then is the United States bound thereunder.

Treaties which call for signature and subsequent ratification usually also have a provision permitting accession for those states that did not sign the treaty during the period it was open for signature.

Such treaties might contain a provision that reads as follows, for example: "This treaty may be ratified by all states signatories thereto. Any other state wishing to become a party to it, may do so by depositing an instrument of accession [adherence]...." Under such a clause, a signatory state becomes a party by ratification of the agreement; accession is reserved for states that were unable to or did not sign. VCLT, art. 15. Once a state becomes a party, its status is the same whether it did so by ratification, adherence, accession or any other method allowed under the treaty.

III. RESERVATIONS

§ **5–6. Definition**. Article 2(1)(d) of the VCLT defines a reservation as follows:

... a unilateral statement, however phrased or named, made by a State, when signing, ratifying, accepting, approving or acceding to a treaty, whereby it purports to exclude or to modify the legal effect of certain provisions of the treaty in their application to that State.

States sometimes sign and/or adhere to treaties with statements they label "reservations," "declarations," "understandings," "clarifications," etc. By defining a reservation as "a unilateral statement, however phrased or named," the VCLT indicates that the label selected by a state will not be determinative. The test instead is whether the unilateral statement "purports to exclude or to modify the legal effect of certain provisions of the treaty in their application to that State". VCLT, art. 2(1)(d). In that sense, a reservation is an attempt by the reserving state to amend the treaty *pro tanto* the reservation as between itself and the other states parties to it.

An "understanding" or "declaration," by contrast, is a statement in which a state declares that it understands a given provision of the treaty to mean "X", for example, without seeking the concurrence, either express or implicit, of any other state in the interpretation proposed by it. To the extent that the state does not intend the "understanding" to alter the legal effect of a treaty provision as between itself and the other states, it will not be considered a reservation. In practice, there may be considerable ambiguity at times whether a declaration is a reservation or merely a unilateral interpretation, and some foreign offices will seek clarification from the state which made the statement to avoid subsequent misunderstandings.

States often attach understandings or other declarations to their instruments of ratification because of national political or legal considerations. In states where national courts are called upon to apply and interpret international agreements, the formal interpretation of a treaty provision by their foreign offices or legislatures, however denominated, will carry great weight. And in some states, the courts will consider themselves bound to give effect to these declarations, even though they may have little legal significance on the international plane.

§ 5–7. Right to make reservations. As a general rule, states are free to adhere to a treaty with reservations. There are three exceptions to this rule: if the treaty prohibits reservations; if the treaty permits only certain types of reservations and the one being made is of a different type; or, in general, if the reservation is incompatible with the object and purpose of the treaty. VCLT, art. 19. What types of reservations are incompatible with the object and purpose of the treaty is not always an easy question to answer. In a decision bearing on this subject, the Inter–American Court of Human Rights indicated that

> a reservation which was designed to enable a State to suspend any of the non-derogable fundamental rights [guaranteed in the American Convention on Human Rights, Nov. 22, 1969, 9 I.L.M. 673 (American Convention)] must be deemed to be incompatible with the object and purpose of the [American] Convention. . . .

Advisory Opinion on Restrictions to the Death Penalty, Inter–Am. Court H.R., OC–3/83 (ser. A) No. 3, para. 61; 23 I.L.M. 320 (1984). The Court based this conclusion on the fact that the American Convention expressly barred states from suspending, even in time of war or other national emergency, the non-derogable rights referred to above. The American Convention consequently attached the greatest importance to the protection of these rights, and to permit reservations that would remove these rights from the treaty would defeat that overriding purpose. *See also Advisory Opinion on Reservations to the Convention on the Prevention and Punishment of the Crime of Genocide*, 1951 I.C.J. 15, at 23–24 (May 28).

§ **5–8. Acceptance and legal effect of reservations**. A state's attempt to join a treaty with a reservation constitutes a proposal to modify the terms of the treaty as between it and the other parties to the agreement. In the case of a bilateral treaty, the acceptance of the reservation results in an amendment of the treaty. If the treaty is multilateral, the reservation will accomplish its object only if at least some states are willing to accept it. But if some states accept the reservation and others reject it, what treaty relations, if any, have been created? What acts constitute acceptance, and can acceptance be implied? VCLT Article 20 deals with these and related questions.

First, a reservation expressly authorized by a treaty does not require acceptance. VCLT, art. 20(1); *see Advisory Opinion on the Effect of Reservations*, I–A Court H.R. (ser. A) No. 2, 22 I.L.M. 37 (1983). Second, some multilateral treaties, because of their special nature and the limited number of states that negotiated them, may indicate that a reservation requires acceptance by all parties. VCLT, art. 20(2). Third, when a treaty is the constituent instrument of an international organization, the reservation will have to be accepted by the organization. VCLT, art. 20(3).

In the circumstances described in the preceding paragraph, a state meeting the requisite requirements for the acceptance of its reservation becomes a party to the treaty. As between it and the other parties, the treaty will have been modified to the extent of the reservation. VCLT, art. 21. But what is the law in situations where reservations are neither expressly prohibited nor expressly permitted, and a state proposes to become a party with a reservation? If the reservation is not incompatible with the object and purpose of the treaty, the other states parties are free to accept or reject the reservation. VCLT, art. 20(4). If the reservation has been accepted by a state party, the treaty as modified by the reservation will be in force as between it and the reserving state. VCLT, arts. 20(4)(a) & 21(1)(a). As between a state party that objects to the reservation and the reserving state, the former has two choices. First, it may declare that it objects to the reservation and does not wish to enter into a treaty relationship with the reserving state. As between these two states, there will be no treaty relationship. Second, a party may refuse to accept the reservation but not object to entering into the treaty relationship with the reserving state. Here it will be presumed that a treaty relationship has been created. VCLT, art. 20(4)(b). However, "the provisions to which the reservation relates do not apply as between the two States to the extent of the reservation." VCLT, art. 21(3). Of course, under any of the scenarios described above, the reservation does not affect the treaty relations *inter se* the other states that became parties without a reservation. VCLT, art. 21(2).

To illustrate the application of these rules, let us assume that there is a multilateral treaty with a large number of states parties that contains no prohibition regarding reservations. Let us assume further that State A seeks to ratify with a reservation modifying Article 5 of the treaty. What will be the treaty relations of State A, if State B accepts the reservation, State C objects to it but does not object to A becoming a party, and State D objects to the reservation and does not want the treaty to enter into force between it and State A? Under the international law of treaties as codified in the VCLT, the result will be as follows: (1) between State A and B, the treaty is in force as modified by A's reservation to Article 5; (2) between State A and C, the treaty is in force, but Article 5 is inapplicable; (3) the treaty is not in force between A and D; and (4) the treaty relations between B, C, D and all other parties and their obligations *inter se* are unaffected by A's reservation. The hypothetical would become more complicated if many of the other states parties themselves also made different types of reservations. This would further multiply the bifurcation of the treaty. That is, under the rules described above, reservations can and in fact do transform a multilateral treaty into a complex network of interrelated bilateral agreements.

In recent years, the European Court of Human Rights and some U.N. human rights treaty bodies, including the U.N. Human Rights Committee, have asserted the right to disregard reservations attached to human rights treaties deemed by them to be incompatible with the object and purpose of the treaty in question, while at the same time not holding the purported ratification to be a nullity. Here the state making the reservation is deemed to have become a party to the treaty even though it ratified the treaty subject to the reservation, which is denied its intended legal effect. For a discussion of these cases and the objections voiced to them, see B. Simma, *Reservations to Human Rights Treaties– Some Recent Developments*, in *Liber Amicorum Professor Ignaz Seidl–Hohenveldern* 34 (G. Hafner et al. eds., 1998); A. Aust, *Modern Treaty Law and Practice* 119 (2000).

IV.   OBSERVANCE OF TREATIES

§ 5–9.   Pacta sunt servanda. VCLT Article 26 declares that "[e]very treaty in force is binding upon the parties to it and must be performed by them in good faith." The U.N. International Law Commission, in its commentary to this rule, characterized it as a "fundamental principle of the law of treaties." 1966 Report of the I.L.C., *reprinted in* 61 Am. J. Int'l L. 248, at 334 (1967) (I.L.C. Report). The *Restatement (Third)* § 321, cmt. a, refers to this norm as "perhaps the most important principle of international law." VCLT Article 27 makes clear, furthermore, that the obligation to perform treaties in good faith applies, as far as international law is concerned, irrespective of any conflicting national law. It provides that "[a] party may not invoke the provisions of its internal law as justification for its failure to perform a treaty." *See also* VCLT, art. 46. That, too, is an undisputed and fundamental principle of international law. *See supra* § 1–9.

§ 5–10. Territorial scope of treaties. VCLT Article 29 provides that "[u]nless a different intention appears from the treaty or is otherwise established, a treaty is binding upon each party in respect of its entire territory." Some treaties contain federal-state clauses, designed to permit federal states, which lack federal legislative jurisdiction relating to the subject-matter of the treaty, to limit their obligations under the treaty to subjects within their federal jurisdiction. As Article 29 indicates, such clauses may be permitted, but if they are not included in a treaty, a state party will not be able to deny the treaty's territorial scope even if it is a federal state, unless it makes an express reservation to that effect. The United States now regularly attaches such reservations to the human rights treaties it ratifies. *See* T. Buergenthal, D. Shelton & D. Stewart, *International Human Rights in a Nutshell* § 7–5 (2002).

§ 5–11. Interpretation of treaties. Although at one time international legal scholars were divided about the law governing the interpretation of treaties, the applicable rules are today no longer in dispute. The basic principle is proclaimed in VCLT Article 31(1), which stipulates that "[a] treaty shall be interpreted in good faith in accordance with the ordinary meaning to be given to the terms of the treaty in their context and in the light of its object and purpose." Hence, the starting point for the interpretation of an international agreement is the text, which is assumed to constitute "the authentic expression of the intentions of the parties." I.L.C. Report, at 354. For the manner in which the International Court of Justice recently applied this provision, see *LaGrand Case*, 2001 I.C.J., paras. 99

et seq. (June 22), *reprinted in* 40 I.L.M. 1069 (2001). In seeking to understand the terms used in the text, their "ordinary meaning" must serve as the guide. The VCLT recognizes, however, that "[a] special meaning shall be given to a term if it is established that the parties so intended." VCLT, art. 31(4). *See Restatement (Third)* § 325.

Article 31(2) defines the "context" as comprising, "in addition to the text, including its preamble and annexes," the following:

(a) any agreement relating to the treaty which was made between all the parties in connexion with the conclusion of the treaty;

(b) any instrument which was made by one or more parties in connexion with the conclusion of the treaty and accepted by the other parties as an instrument related to the treaty.

The basic principle here is that the treaty must be interpreted as a whole. In seeking to understand the meaning of a treaty provision, for example, it is not enough to look only at the text of the particular provision. It must be analyzed in a manner that relates the specific contents of the provision to the object and purpose of the treaty as reflected in its text and those additional instruments that are referred to in Article 31(2). The preamble can often be particularly relevant when one seeks to determine the object and purpose of the agreement.

The VCLT also recognizes that subsequent agreements between the parties regarding the interpretation or application of the treaty as well as subsequent relevant practice by them "shall be taken into account, together with the context," in interpreting a treaty. VCLT, art. 31(3). *See Territorial Dispute* (Libya/Chad), 1994 I.C.J. 6, para 53 (Feb. 13), for the elements the Court considers to constitute the "context" of a treaty being interpreted. The drafting history or so-called *travaux préparatoires* of a treaty is characterized as a "supplementary means of interpretation". VCLT, art 32. Recourse to it may be had only in two circumstances: first, to "confirm" the meaning derived from the textual analysis; second, when the textual analysis "(a) leaves the meaning ambiguous or obscure; or (b) leads to a result which is manifestly absurd or unreasonable." *Id.* In these latter two situations, recourse to the drafting history "is not to confirm, but to determine, the meaning," Aust, *supra*, at 197.

§ 5–12.   **Treaties and third states**. It is a basic principle of international treaty law that "a treaty does not create either obligations or rights for a third State without its consent." VCLT, art. 34. Under certain circumstances, however, third states can assume obligations and be granted rights under treaties to which they are not parties. The latter situation would arise, for example, if the treaty conferred third-party beneficiary status on a non-party state. VCLT, arts. 35–36. These rules should not be confused with the principle that the norms enunciated in a treaty can become binding on states that are not parties to it. That principle applies only in situations where the law codified in the treaty is or has become customary international law. VCLT, art. 38; *see supra* § 2–4.

V. INVALIDITY, TERMINATION, AND SUSPENSION OF TREATIES

§ **5–13. Invalidity of treaties**. The usual grounds which may be invoked under national law to invalidate contracts, that is, error of fact, fraud, corruption and duress, are also available under international law to invalidate treaties. VCLT, arts. 48–52. Although national law contains many provisions of law and public policy that are obligatory in the sense that individuals may not by contract enter into arrangements in conflict with such law and policy, the basic assumption in international law is almost absolute freedom of contract. In general, states are free to enter into treaties that change, as between them, otherwise applicable rules of customary international law.

The only limitation on that absolute freedom is that states may not by treaty contravene a rule of *jus cogens*, meaning a peremptory norm of general international law. *See generally* M. Ragazzi, *The Concept of International Obligations Erga Omnes* ch. 3 (1997). The VCLT defines "a peremptory norm of general international law" as follows: "a norm accepted and recognized by the international community of States as a whole as a norm from which no derogation is permitted and which can be modified only by a subsequent norm of general international law having the same character." VCLT, art. 53. The VCLT does not identify any such norms, and there is little agreement on the overall scope of this concept. It seems to be generally accepted, however, that a treaty to violate the U.N. Charter's Article 2(4) prohibition of the use of force, or to commit genocide, legalize the slave trade or engage in torture, would be void as in contravention of *jus cogens*. In dealing with torture, the International Criminal Tribunal for the former Yugoslavia declared that the prohibition against torture "has evolved into a peremptory norm or *jus cogens*, that is, a norm that enjoys a higher rank in the international hierarchy than treaty law and even 'ordinary' customary rules". *Prosecutor v. Furundzija*, 38 I.L.M. 317, para. 153 (1999). The same view was expressed by the House of Lords in *Ex Parte Pinochet Ugarte*, [1999] 2 All ER 97, 38 I.L.M. 581 (1999). Finally, it should be noted that a treaty, valid at the time of its conclusion, will become void if it conflicts with a *jus cogens* norm that has emerged subsequently. VCLT, art. 64.

§ 5–14. National law and invalidity. States sometimes attempt to avoid performing their obligations under a treaty by claiming that their consent to be bound by the treaty was invalid because it was effected in a manner that violated applicable national law. This argument will fail unless the "violation was manifest and concerned a rule of . . . [the state's] internal law of fundamental importance." VCLT, art. 46(1). The VCLT clarifies the matter further by providing that "[a] violation is manifest if it would be objectively evident to any State conducting itself in the matter in accordance with normal practice and in good faith." VCLT, art. 46(2). Here it might be asked, for example, whether the failure of the U.S. President to submit a treaty to the Senate for its advice and consent before ratifying the agreement would permit the United States to declare its consent invalid? The answer has to be no, because under U.S. law there are a number of different types of international agreements which the President may ratify with or without the Senate's advice and consent. The law on that subject is by no means clear. *See infra* § 7–3. At times, in fact, the President may decide to seek the Senate's consent when he might have chosen a different route, and vice versa. In the light of these circumstances, the violation would certainly not be manifest to a foreign state. *See Restatement (Third)* § 311, cmt. c.

§ 5–15. Termination, suspension, and breach of treaties. The mere fact that the government of a state party to a treaty has changed or has been overthrown does not, as a matter of law, terminate or result in the suspension of the treaty. The same is true if the parties to the treaty sever diplomatic or consular relations. VCLT, art. 63. Of course, a treaty may be suspended if it can be shown that it was tied specifically to the existence of a particular government or if diplomatic or consular relations are indispensable for its application.

States may withdraw from a treaty, terminate it, or suspend its operation in a manner prescribed by the treaty or with the consent of all states parties thereto. VCLT, arts. 54 & 57. Treaties usually contain provisions permitting withdrawal subject to certain notice requirements, but even where the treaty does not contain a specific clause on the subject, the right to denounce may be implied under certain circumstances. VCLT, art. 56.

It is an established principle of international law that a material breach of a treaty is a valid ground for its suspension or termination. A material breach has traditionally been defined as "the violation of a provision essential to the accomplishment of the object or purpose of the treaty." VCLT, art. 60(3)(b). The unlawful repudiation of the treaty in its entirety, of course, also constitutes a material breach. VCLT, art. 60(3)(a).

The VCLT distinguishes between the material breach of a bilateral treaty and of a multilateral one. VCLT, art. 60. In the case of the former, it declares that "[a] material breach of a bilateral treaty by one of the parties entitles the other to invoke the breach as a ground for terminating the treaty or suspending its operation in whole or in part." VCLT, art. 60(1). If a multilateral treaty has been materially breached by a party, a distinction has to be made between the rights of all other (innocent) parties to the treaty, on the one hand, and states parties specially affected by the breach. VCLT, art. 60(2). The latter have the right to suspend, but not to terminate, the operation of the treaty in whole or in part in relation to the default-ing state. VCLT, art. 60(2)(b). The former have the right to suspend or terminate the treaty altogether or only as between themselves and the defaulting party, provided the decision to do so has been arrived at by unanimous agreement of the innocent parties. VCLT, art. 60(2)(a). *See Restatement (Third)* § 335.

The rules which the VCLT prescribes for the suspension or termination of treaties because of a material breach are made expressly inapplicable "to provisions relating to the protection of the human person contained in treaties of a humanitarian character, in particular to provisions prohibiting any form of reprisals against persons protected by such treaties." VCLT, art. 60(5). Treaties of a humanitarian character include the 1949 Geneva Conventions and the 1977 Protocols thereto, for example, which deal with the treatment of prisoners of war, the protection of civilians, and wounded military personnel, etc. A material breach by one party to these treaties or of modern human rights treaties does not authorize other parties to suspend their operation in relation to the individuals the treaties seek to protect even if those individuals are nationals of the defaulting state. *See Advisory Opinion on the Effect of Reservations*, Inter–Am. Court H.R. (ser. A) No. 2, 22 I.L.M. 37 (1983) (analyzing the unique character of humanitarian and human rights treaties and the consequences they have on questions relating to the interpretation and application of treaties).

International law recognizes that impossibility of performance and a fundamental change of circumstances (*rebus sic standibus*) in certain situations may justify the termination of or the withdrawal from a treaty. Impossibility of performance may be so invoked, for example, if "the impossibility results from the permanent disappearance or destruction of an object indispensable for the execution of the treaty." VCLT, art. 61(1). This will not be a valid ground for termination or withdrawal by the party invoking it "if the impossibility is the result of a breach by that party either of an obligation under the treaty or of any other international obligation owed to any other party to the treaty." VCLT, art. 61(2).

A fundamental change of circumstances, which was not foreseen by the parties, will justify termination of or withdrawal from a treaty only if

(a) the existence of those circumstances constituted an essential basis of the consent of the parties to be bound by the treaty; and

(b) the effect of the change is radically to transform the extent of obligations still to be performed under the treaty.

VCLT, art. 62(1); *see Fisheries Jurisdiction* (U.K. v. Ice.), 1973 I.C.J. 3 (Feb. 2). But even if the above two conditions are met, this ground may not be invoked to terminate or withdraw from a treaty if the treaty establishes a territorial boundary. It may also not be resorted to if the changed circumstances resulted from a violation by the state invoking it of an international obligation under the treaty or any other international obligation owed to any of the parties to the treaty. VCLT, art. 62(2). Of course, the grounds that a state may invoke to terminate a treaty or to withdraw from it because of impossibility of performance or changed circumstances also permit the less serious remedy of suspension. *See* VCLT, arts. 61(1) & 62(3); *see generally Restatement (Third)* § 336.

The effect of war or other armed hostilities on treaties is a subject that was expressly excluded from the VCLT. VCLT, art. 73. As a practical matter, most treaties are suspended, if not terminated, in wartime. *Cf. Techt v. Hughes*, 229 N.Y. 222, 128 N.E. 185 (1920), *cert. denied*, 254 U.S. 643 (1920). This is not true, of course, with regard to treaties that are intended to be applied in wartime situations, for example, treaties relating to the law of war and humanitarian treaties. Furthermore, various human rights treaties contain provisions that prohibit the suspension even in wartime of certain of the most basic rights that the treaties guarantee. *See* International Covenant on Civil and Political Rights, Dec. 16, 1966, art. 4, 999 U.N.T.S. 171; European Convention for the Protection of Human Rights and Fundamental Freedoms, Nov. 4, 1950, art. 15, 312 U.N.T.S. 221; American Convention, art. 27.

It is important to recognize that states frequently invoke the various grounds referred to in this section in order to justify the suspension or termination of and their withdrawal from a treaty, even when there is little or no valid basis for doing so. To limit these abuses, the VCLT establishes a formal procedure that must be followed by states asserting the right to terminate or withdraw from a treaty on these grounds. VCLT, arts. 65–68.

It should also be noted that the Draft Articles on the Responsibility of States for International Wrongful Acts, adopted by the International Law Commission in 2001, *Report of the International Law Commission*, G.A.O.R. Supp. No. 10, Doc. A/56/10 (2001) (I.L.C. Draft Articles), are likely in the future to have a significant impact on the remedies applicable under the VCLT, even though the Draft Articles are not intended to supersede VCLT provisions. *See* I.L.C. Draft Articles, art. 56.

§ 5–16. **Treaties and state succession**. Questions of state succession to treaties arise, for example, when two or more independent states merge to form a single state, which happened with the unification of Germany. The same is true when entities that were not previously independent break away from a state they were part of, which was the case of the former Soviet Republics, the states that withdrew from the former Yugoslavia, the break-up of Czechoslovakia into the Czech Republic and Slovakia, and former colonies or dependent territories that gained their independence.

The questions that arise in these situations concern the fate of treaties concluded prior to these events. For example, are the newly independent states automatically parties to the treaties of the state they broke away from? When states merge or are absorbed by another state, what happens to the treaties to which they were parties before the merger or absorption? Does the subject-matter of the treaty affect the answer to some of these questions? VCLT Article 73 does not address these issues. The Vienna Convention on Succession of States in Respect of Treaties, Aug. 22, 1978, 1946 U.N.T.S. 3, 17 I.L.M. 1488, does address this issue, but thus far has entered into force for only a small number of states and is not deemed to be declaratory of customary international law. *See Restatement (Third)* § 208, rptrs. note 4. Nor has the practice of states thus far established many rules on the subject that are considered to have become customary international law.

There seems to be general agreement, however, with regard to some issues. *See Restatement (Third)* § 210. One of these is that the treaties of a state absorbed into another state are terminated while the treaties of the absorbing state become applicable to the absorbed state. The Unification Treaty between the Federal Republic of Germany and the German Democratic Republic expressly stipulated these consequences. It is also generally accepted that when a part of a state becomes a new state, the latter does not automatically succeed to the treaty rights and obligations of the state from which it broke away. Thus, the new states that emerged following the collapse of the Soviet Union did not automatically become parties to the treaties of the former Soviet Union. Here the Russian Republic was accepted both by the United Nations and states generally as the successor to the treaties to which the Soviet Union had been a party, whereas the former Soviet republics were not deemed to have remained parties to these treaties. The same was the case for the states that emerged from the former Yugoslavia. *See, e.g., 767 Third Ave. Assoc. v.*

SFRY, 218 F.3d 152 (2d Cir.2000) (finding that international law does not support a landlords' claim that the successor states to the former Yugoslavia are automatically liable to the landlords for Yugoslavia's debt). The many former colonies that gained their independence in the 1960's and 1970's were in a similar position.

However, there is one general exception to these rules. Treaties that fix territorial boundaries remain in force for the successor states or newly created entities. *See* Vienna Convention on Succession to Treaties, art. 11; *Restatement (Third)* § 210(4). On the subject of state succession to treaties, see generally M. Shaw, *International Law* 686 (4th ed. 1997); Aust, *supra*, at 305; S. Rosenne, *Automatic Treaty Succession*, in *Essays on the Law of Treaties* 97 (J. Klabbers & R. Lefeber eds., 1998).

CHAPTER 6

RIGHTS OF INDIVIDUALS

I. INTRODUCTION

This chapter deals with the international law that applies to the protection of the human rights of individuals. On this subject generally, see T. Buergenthal, D. Shelton & D. Stewart, *International Human Rights in a Nutshell* (3d ed. 2002). The law on this subject evolved from two different branches of international law: the international law of human rights and the law on the international responsibility of states for injuries to aliens. Although the substantive rights that each of these branches protects can be said to have converged in recent decades, significant procedural distinctions exist between them, depending upon the particular branch in which the rights are sought to be enforced. This chapter will therefore deal separately with the law of human rights and the law of state responsibility.

These two branches of the law differ in one major respect: the law of state responsibility protects individuals against violations of their rights only when their nationality is not that of the offending state; international human rights law protects individuals regardless of their nationality. The concept of nationality is irrelevant in human rights law because the individual is deemed to be the subject of these rights. Nationality is of vital importance, however, under the law of state responsibility, because here the injury to a national is deemed to be an injury to the state of his/her nationality. This legal fiction accommodates the traditional doctrine that individuals are not subjects of international law. *See Barcelona Traction, Light & Power Co.* (Belg. v. Spain), 1970 I.C.J. 3 (Feb. 5). Hence, if an individual is stateless or a national of the offending state, any remedy he/she might have on the international plane would have to be found in the international law of human rights and not that of state responsibility.

II.   INTERNATIONAL LAW OF HUMAN RIGHTS

§ 6–1.   Historical development. The international law of human rights evolved over the last six decades, tracing its origin to the adoption of the Charter of the United Nations. This is not to say that prior to 1945 there existed no rules that would today be deemed to be part of the international law of human rights. What did not exist prior to 1945 was a comprehensive body of law that protected the individual *qua* human being. The international law of the pre-U.N. Charter era did, however, develop various rules and institutions that today are part of the international law of human rights. *See generally* L. Sohn, *The New International Law: Protection of the Rights of the Individual Rather Than States*, 32 Am. U.L. Rev. 1, 2–6 (1982).

The doctrine of humanitarian intervention, which deals with the right of states and international organizations to come to the assistance of the nationals of a state if it subjects them to treatment that "shocks the conscience of mankind," can be traced back to Grotius. *See* S. Murphy, *Humanitarian Intervention: The United Nations in an Evolving World Order* ch. 2 (1996). International agreements to combat the slave trade originated in the early decades of the 19th century. The treaties that sealed the Peace of Westphalia (1648), *see supra* § 1–16, dealt with some aspects of religious freedom in Europe, as did the Treaty of Paris (1856) and the Treaty of Berlin (1878).

The peace treaties that ended the First World War (1914–1918) established a formal system for the protection of national, religious and linguistic minorities under the administration of the League of Nations, which applied in various parts of Central, Eastern and Southeastern Europe. The Covenant of the League of Nations created the so-called Mandate system. It applied to certain colonial territories that were placed under the protection of the League, which had the task of ensuring that the states administering these territories would promote the welfare of the native populations. *See Advisory Opinion on the Legal Consequences for States of the Continued Presence of South Africa in Namibia (South West Africa) Notwithstanding Security Council Resolution 276 (1970)*, 1971 I.C.J. 17 (June 21). During that same period, the International Labor Organization began the process of promoting international standards for the protection of workers. International efforts making some basic humanitarian norms applicable to the conduct of war gained formal multilateral recognition as early as 1864. The law applicable to the responsibility of states for the injuries to aliens, which can be traced back to the early days of modern international law, is yet another precursor of international human rights law. Although it protects only foreign nationals, it produced a body of human rights law binding on all states and universal in character. *See* American Law Institute, *Restatement of the Foreign Relations Law of the United States (Third)*, pt. VII, intro. note (1987) (*Restatement (Third)*).

A. Law of the U.N. Charter

§ 6–2. U.N. Charter. What distinguishes the human rights provisions of the U.N. Charter from earlier international agreements or from preexisting customary international law on the subject is their general scope. The pre-Charter human rights law was designed to protect certain categories of human beings or guarantee certain types of rights. The Charter imposes no such limitations. It speaks of "human rights and fundamental freedoms for all without distinction as to race, sex, language or religion" U.N. Charter, art. 55(c); *see, id.*, arts. 1(3), 13(1)(b) & 62(2).

The Charter creates two interrelated obligations. It provides, first, that the United Nations "shall promote . . . universal respect for, and observance of, human rights and fundamental freedoms for all without distinction as to race, sex, language or religion." U.N. Charter, art. 55(c). Second, it contains a pledge by U.N. member states "to take joint and separate action in cooperation with the Organization for the achievement of the purposes set forth in Article 55." U.N. Charter, art. 56. The commitment to promote human rights and fundamental freedoms was thus established as a legally binding obligation both of the United Nations and of its member states. Modern international human rights law has its source in these two provisions. They laid the conceptual foundation for the development of substantive human rights law and for making human rights a matter of international concern. *See generally* T. Buergenthal, *The Normative and Institutional Evolution of International Human Rights*, 19 Hum. Rights Q. 703 (1997).

§ 6–3. Universal Declaration of Human Rights. The U.N. Charter speaks only of "human rights and fundamental freedoms" without defining or enumerating them. The principal instrument to perform these functions is the Universal Declaration of Human Rights, G.A. Res. 217A (III) (Dec. 10, 1948) (Universal Declaration). Although adopted in the form of a non-binding resolution, the Universal Declaration over the years has come to be accepted as an authoritative interpretation or definition of the rights that the United Nations and its member states have an obligation to promote under Articles 55 and 56 of the U.N. Charter. Various commentators have argued, furthermore, that it has acquired the status of customary international law. Much more general support exists for the view that at least some of the rights proclaimed in the

Universal Declaration enjoy the status of customary international law, including freedom from systematic governmental acts and policies involving torture, slavery, murder, prolonged arbitrary detention, disappearances, racial discrimination, and other gross violations of human rights. *See, e.g., Filartiga v. Pena–Irala,* 630 F.2d 876 (2d Cir.1980); *Restatement (Third)* § 702. There is also support for the proposition that a state which pursues a governmental policy denying individuals or groups the rights proclaimed in the Declaration because of their race, sex, language or religion, violates the principle of non-discrimination that is fundamental to the human rights obligations assumed by the states parties to the U.N. Charter.

The Universal Declaration proclaims a catalog of basic civil and political rights, including the rights to life, not to be held in slavery, not to be tortured, equal protection of law, due process guarantees, freedom of speech, assembly and movement, privacy, etc. It also guarantees the right to own property as well as a number of economic, social and cultural rights, such as the rights to work, education, health care and various other social services, and to participate in the cultural life of the community. All of these rights are proclaimed in language that is general in character and lacking the specificity of a treaty or law. The Declaration does recognize, however, that states may limit the rights it proclaims by laws intended to secure "due recognition and respect for the rights and freedoms of others and of meeting the just requirements of morality, public order and the general welfare in a democratic society." Universal Declaration, art. 29(2). For the legal, political and moral impact of the Universal Declaration, see *Reflections on the Universal Declaration of Human Rights: A Fiftieth Anniversary Anthology* (B. van der Heijden & B. Tahzib–Lie eds., 1998).

§ 6–4. U.N. human rights covenants. In 1966, the U.N. General Assembly adopted the International Covenant on Civil and Political Rights, Dec. 16, 1966, 999 U.N.T.S. 171 (ICCPR); the International Covenant on Economic, Social and Cultural Rights, Dec. 16, 1966, 993 U.N.T.S. 3 (ICESCR); and the Optional Protocol to the ICCPR, Dec. 16, 1966, 999 U.N.T.S. 302. These instruments, together with a Second Optional Protocol to the ICCPR Aiming at the Abolition of the Death Penalty, 29 I.L.M. 1464, the Universal Declaration, and the human rights provisions of the U.N. Charter, comprise what is known as the "International Bill of Human Rights."

The Covenants are treaties requiring ratification. They entered into force in 1976 after ratification by thirty-five states. That number has in the meantime increased to approximately 150 states. The United States ratified the ICCPR in 1992; it is not a party to the ICESCR.

In addition to proclaiming two so-called rights of "peoples"—the right to self-determination and the right of all peoples to freely dispose of their natural wealth and resources—the ICCPR guarantees a large number of individual rights and freedoms. *See generally The International Bill of Rights* (L. Henkin ed., 1981); T. Meron, *Human Rights Law–Making in the United Nations* 83 (1986). The list includes, *inter alia,* the right to life, freedom from torture and slavery, the right to liberty and security of person, the right of detained persons to be treated humanely, the right not to be imprisoned for debt, freedom of movement, the right to a fair trial, freedom from *ex post facto* laws and penalties, the right to privacy, freedom of thought, opinion, expression, conscience and religion, freedom of assembly and association, the right to marry and found a family, the rights of the child, the right to participate in government, and equal protection of law. The right to property, proclaimed in the Universal Declaration, does not appear in either Covenant.

The ICCPR is drafted with much greater legal precision than is the Universal Declaration. The rights are qualified, moreover, by various exceptions, restrictions and limitations. A special provision, permitting the suspension of some rights in emergency situations, is also included. *See* ICCPR, art. 4.

The ICESCR amplifies the economic, social and cultural rights proclaimed in the Universal Declaration. It also guarantees the same rights of peoples established in the ICCPR. The principal difference between these two instruments, apart from the rights they ensure, is that they impose different legal obligations. The ability to guarantee many of the economic, social and cultural rights proclaimed in the ICESCR presupposes the availability of economic and other resources that not all states possess to the same extent. Few such resources are required, as a general rule, in order for states to comply with their obligations to protect civil and political rights; more often than not, they are obliged merely to abstain from acting in a manner that violates these rights. These considerations explain why the states parties to the ICESCR merely undertake to take steps "to the maximum of [their] available resources" to achieve "progressively the full realization of the rights recognized in the ... Covenant by all appropriate means, including particularly the adoption of legislative measures." ICESCR, art. 2(1). The ICCPR, by contrast, requires each state party to undertake "to respect and to ensure to all individuals within its territory and subject to its jurisdiction the rights" recognized in the ICCPR. ICCPR, art. 2(1). Here the obligation to comply is immediate, whereas the states parties to the ICESCR assume an obligation that is progressive in character and tied to the availability of resources. *See generally Economic, Social and Cultural Rights: A Textbook* (A. Eide et al. eds., 1995).

The so-called measures of implementation, that is, the international methods for the supervision of compliance by the states parties with their obligations under the respective Covenants, also differ significantly. The ICCPR, supplemented by its Optional Protocol, provides for a system that permits investigation and quasi-adjudication of individual and inter-state complaints by a committee of experts—the U.N. Human Rights Committee. It also reviews the periodic reports of the member states.

See T. Buergenthal, *The UN Human Rights Committee*, 5 Max Planck Y.B.U.N.L. 341 (2001). Although the ICESCR provides only for a system of periodic reports to be filed by states and certain specialized agencies with the U.N. Economic and Social Council, that body has now established a special Committee on Economic, Social and Cultural Rights. This committee is composed of 18 experts who are elected in their individual capacities to review the reports. *See generally* P. Alston, *The Committee on Economic, Social and Cultural Rights*, in *The United Nations and Human Rights* 473 (P. Alston ed., 1991).

§ 6–5. Other U.N. human rights instruments. The International Bill of Human Rights is supplemented by a large number of human rights treaties concluded within the framework or under the auspices of the United Nations. Most important of these are the Convention on the Prevention and Punishment of the Crime of Genocide, Dec. 9, 1948, 78 U.N.T.S. 277 (Genocide Convention); the International Convention on the Elimination of All Forms of Racial Discrimination, Dec. 21, 1965, 660 U.N.T.S. 195, 5 I.L.M. 352 (CERD); the Convention on the Elimination of All Forms of Discrimination Against Women, Dec. 18, 1979, 1249 U.N.T.S. 13; the Convention Against Torture and Other Cruel, Inhuman or Degrading Treatment, Dec. 10, 1984, 1465 U.N.T.S. 85, 23 I.L.M. 1027 (Torture Convention); and the Convention on the Rights of the Child, Nov. 20, 1989, 1577 U.N.T.S. 3, 28 I.L.M. 1448. All of these human rights treaties have entered into force and have been ratified by the vast majority of U.N. member states. The United States has ratified the Genocide Convention, CERD, and the Torture Convention.

§ 6–6. Specialized agencies and regional organizations. The specialized agencies of the United Nations, particularly the International Labor Organization and UNESCO, have coordinated their codification efforts in the human rights area with those of the United Nations and adopted many treaties and other instruments on the subject. *See* K. Samson, *Human Rights Co-ordination within the UN System*, in *The United Nations and Human Rights* 620 (P. Alston ed., 1992). Three regional international organizations—the Council of Europe, the Organization of American States, and the Organization of African Unity—have established treaty-based regional systems for the protection of human rights, which were inspired in large measure by the Universal Declaration and other U.N. human rights efforts. *See infra* §§ 6–8 to 6–18.

§ 6–7. International human rights code and its legal effect. The treaties described in the preceding sections, and numerous other international agreements that were not mentioned for lack of space, have created a vast body of international human rights law. *See* United Nations, *Human Rights–A Compilation of International Instruments*, vol. I, pts. 1 & 2 (1993) (covering universal instruments); vol. II (1997) (covering regional instruments). The parties to these treaties are legally bound, of course, to comply with the obligations they have assumed thereunder. A more difficult question concerns the obligation of the states that have ratified the U.N. Charter and only some or a few of the other agreements. To the extent that multilateral international agreements can be the source of general or customary international law, *see supra* ch. 2, U.N. human rights practice can create and has created international human rights law. The primary source of that law is the U.N. Charter and the Universal Declaration, reinforced by the large body of existing conventional law, by the resolutions and other acts of international organizations, and by the practice of states. The proposition that there has emerged a body of general international human rights law is today no longer seriously disputed with regard to some of the most fundamental rights, which outlaw genocide, torture and slavery, and other large-scale violations of human rights. *See Restatement (Third)* § 702; *see also Filartiga v. Pena–Irala*, 630 F.2d 876 (2d Cir.1980). There is greater uncertainty with regard to violations involving rights of lesser magnitude that are guaranteed in all or some of these treaties. Few areas of international law have experienced and continue to experience as much legislative activity as has the human rights field.

An equally important effect of the human rights provisions of the U.N. Charter and the legislative practice described above concerns the internationalization of human rights. Prior to the Second World War, human rights issues were, in general, not regulated by international law and, therefore, were deemed to be matters within the national jurisdiction of each state. The manner in which a state treated its own nationals was, with some exceptions, not a matter of international concern and, hence, an issue that other states had no right to address on the international plane. Today, the manner in which a state treats its nationals is no longer *ipso facto* a matter within its national jurisdiction because such a large body of international law regulates the subject of human rights. Thus, for example, it would not be intervention in the national affairs of a state for another state to express concern about or to ask the former to explain alleged violations of internationally recognized human rights. *See* L. Henkin, *Human Rights and "Domestic Jurisdiction"*, in *Human Rights, International Law and the Helsinki Accord* 21 (T. Buergenthal ed., 1977); T. Meron, *Human Rights and Humanitarian Norms as Customary Law* 103 (1989).

B. Regional human rights law and institutions

1. European system

§ 6–8. European Convention on Human Rights. Drafted within the framework of the Council of Europe, the European Convention for the Protection of Human Rights and Fundamental Freedoms, Nov. 4, 1950, 312 U.N.T.S. 221 (European Convention), entered into force in 1953. Forty-one European states have ratified the Convention. The European Convention, as originally adopted, protected only a dozen fundamental civil and political rights. This catalog of rights has been substantially expanded with the entry into force of various additional protocols to the European Convention, which are used by the states parties to add new rights to the protected categories. The right to property, for example, became a right guaranteed in the European Convention with the entry into force of Protocol No. 1 in 1954. *See generally* P. van Dijk & G. van Hoof, *Theory and Practice of the European Convention on Human Rights* (3d ed. 1995); D. Harns, M. O'Boyle & C. Warbrick, *Law of the European Convention on Human Rights* (1995).

§ 6–9. Convention institutions. It is now generally agreed that the international enforcement machinery for the protection of human rights established by the European Convention is the most advanced system in existence today. It has become, in fact, the constitutional court of Europe for matters relating to political rights and civil liberties.

Prior to the entry into force of Protocol No. 11 to the European Convention, the Convention's enforcement system consisted of the European Commission of Human Rights and the European Court of Human Rights. The Protocol abolished the Commission, whose principal functions consisted of passing on the admissibility of applications charging violations of human rights, making findings on the facts alleged, attempting to negotiate a friendly settlement, and deciding whether to refer the cases to the Court for adjudication or to the Committee of Ministers, a political body of the Council of Europe. The jurisdiction of the Court was optional in the sense that a case could only be referred to the Court by and against states that had accepted its jurisdiction. Moreover, individuals lacked standing to submit their cases to the Court even if the respondent state had accepted its jurisdiction. Such cases could only come to the Court if referred to it by the Commission or another state. Under the system currently in effect, the Commission's functions are now performed by the Court, which has become a permanent body. Moreover, with the entry into force of Protocol No. 11, the Court's jurisdiction is no longer optional. A state that now ratifies the European Convention accepts the Court's jurisdiction to hear cases referred to it directly by individuals and other states parties to the Convention.

The Court is composed of judges whose number equals that of the states parties to the Convention—currently 43 judges. They are elected to six-year terms by the Parliamentary Assembly of the Council of Europe. The Court works in committees of three judges, chambers of seven judges and a Grand Chamber of 17 judges. The committees of three pass on the admissibility of individual cases. (Inter-state cases go directly to the chambers.) Individual cases deemed admissible are also decided on the merits by chambers. The Grand Chamber has a limited appellate jurisdiction as well as general jurisdiction. Within a period of three months from the date of a judgment rendered by a chamber, "any party to the case may, in exceptional cases, request that the case be referred to the Grand Chamber." European Convention, art. 43. If the Grand Chamber accepts the case, its judgment will supersede the judgment in the case. The Grand Chamber also has jurisdiction to deal with cases deemed by a chamber to raise serious questions of interpretation of the Convention or its Protocols, or where there is a risk of inconsistent judgments. *See* European Convention, art. 30. *See generally* A. Drzemczewski, *The European Human Rights Convention: Protocol No.*

11—Entry into Force and First Year of Application,
21 Hum. Rights L.J. 1 (2000). As in the past, the
Committee of Ministers of the Council of Europe
supervises compliance by the states parties with the
judgments rendered against them. Historically, the
European Convention institutions can claim a very
good compliance record.

§ **6–10. Admissibility requirements**. The
principal admissibility obstacle confronting states
and individuals is the requirement spelled out in
Article 35(1) of the European Convention. It provides that "the Court may only deal with the matter after all domestic remedies have been exhausted, according to the generally recognised rules of
international law, and within a period of six months
from the date on which the final decision was
taken." As applied to states, this provision is not to
be understood as requiring the applicant state itself
to exhaust these remedies in the courts of the
respondent state; it means only that the alleged
victims of the violation of the Convention whose
case the state is referring to the Court have done
so. The remaining admissibility requirements apply
only to individuals. They have to show, *inter alia*,
that the claim is not "incompatible with the provisions of the Convention or the protocols thereto,
manifestly ill-founded, or an abuse of the right of
application." European Convention, art. 35(3). An
application is incompatible with the Convention if it
seeks to vindicate rights not guaranteed in it or its
protocols. The manifestly ill-founded requirement
calls for a showing of a *prima facie* case. Over the
years, the Court and the Commission before it
developed a vast body of law on these requirements.

For the case law of the Court, see <www.echr.coe.int/Eng/Judgments.htm>.

2. *Inter–American System*

§ **6–11. Two sources of the system**. The inter-American system for the protection of human rights has two distinct legal sources. One is the Charter of the Organization of American States, Apr. 30, 1948, 2 U.S.T. 2394 (OAS Charter); the other is the American Convention on Human Rights, Nov. 22, 1969, 9 I.L.M. 673 (American Convention). The institutions of this system have a different history and different powers depending upon whether they were established pursuant to the OAS Charter or the American Convention. *See generally* T. Buergenthal, D. Shelton & D. Stewart, *International Human Rights in a Nutshell* ch. 4 (2002). It is useful, therefore, to treat them separately.

§ **6–12. OAS Charter system**. In 1960, based on some very general references to human rights in the OAS Charter, the OAS established the Inter–American Commission on Human Rights. (For a description of the OAS, *see supra* §§ 3.22–3.25.) The Commission, created as an ''autonomous entity'' of the OAS under a Statute adopted by the OAS Council, was charged with the task of promoting the human rights proclaimed by the American Declaration of the Rights and Duties of Man, which the OAS adopted in May 2, 1948 in the form of a non-binding resolution. When the OAS Charter was amended in 1970, the Commission became an OAS Charter organ. *See* OAS Charter, as amended, art. 51(e) (now art. 53(e)). The amendment strengthened the constitutional authority and legal powers of the Commission and, by necessary implication, the normative status of the American Declaration. OAS Charter, as amended, arts. 112 (now art. 106) & 150; T. Buergenthal, *The Revised OAS Charter and the Protection of Human Rights*, 69 Am. J. Int'l L. 828 (1975).

These and related developments establish that a member state of the OAS that has not ratified the American Convention is nevertheless deemed to have an OAS Charter obligation to promote the human rights that the American Declaration proclaims. *See* Statute of the Inter–American Commission on Human Rights, art. 1(2)(b). The power to ensure compliance with that obligation rests with the Inter–American Commission on Human Rights and, ultimately, the OAS General Assembly. In discharging this mandate, the Commission receives individual communications, prepares country studies, and undertakes on-site investigations. The publication of these reports and their review by the political organs of the OAS have on a number of occasions had a significant impact and resulted in an improvement of conditions in some of these states. *See generally* C. Medina, *The Battle of Human Rights: Gross, Systematic Violations and the Inter–American System* (1988).

§ **6–13. Convention system**. The American Convention entered into force in 1978 and has been ratified by 25 out of the 35 OAS member states. Only the United States, Canada and a number of Commonwealth Caribbean states to date have not ratified it. All Latin American states have done so except for Cuba, a member state whose government is excluded from the OAS. The American Convention was modelled on the European Convention and resembles the latter in its institutional structure as it existed prior to the entry into force of Protocol No. 11. The American Convention guarantees some 22 basic civil and political rights. Unlike its European counterpart, the American Convention contains a federal-state clause, which enables some federal states to assume more limited territorial obligations than those incumbent on unitary states.

The American Convention establishes an Inter–American Commission on Human Rights and an Inter–American Court of Human Rights. Both bodies consist of seven members, the former elected by the OAS General Assembly, the latter by the states parties to the Convention. This difference in the selection process of the judges of the Court and the members of the Commission is explained by the fact that the same Commission acts both as the OAS Charter organ referred to in the preceding section and as a Convention organ. Thus, all OAS member states have an interest in the Commission's composition. The Court does not perform a comparable function.

The principal function of the Inter–American Commission under the American Convention is to deal with communications charging violations of the rights the treaty guarantees. The American Convention is unique among international human rights instruments in making the right of individual petition mandatory and that of inter-state communications optional. That is to say, as soon as a state has ratified the American Convention, the Inter–American Commission has jurisdiction to deal with an individual petition directed against that state. A state may file a complaint against another state only if both of them, in addition to ratifying the American Convention, have accepted the Inter–American Commission's jurisdiction to receive inter-state applications.

The Inter–American Court has contentious and advisory jurisdiction. Under its contentious jurisdiction, the Court has the power to decide cases involving charges that a state party has violated the rights guaranteed in the American Convention. This jurisdiction is optional and must be accepted by the states parties before cases may be filed by or against them. Only the Inter–American Commission and the states may bring cases to the Court; individuals lack standing to do so. However, an amendment to the Court's Rules of Procedure, which entered into force in 2001, gives individuals the right to argue their cases in the Court once the case has been referred to it. Individuals are thus no longer dependent on the Inter–American Commission or another state to represent them in the Court.

The Inter–American Court's advisory jurisdiction authorizes it to render opinions interpreting the American Convention and other treaties dealing with the protection of human rights in the inter-American system. That jurisdiction, which may be invoked by all OAS member states, whether or not they have ratified the American Convention, and by all OAS organs, is more extensive than the advisory jurisdiction of any international tribunal in existence today. *See Advisory Opinion on "Other Treaties,"* Inter–Am. Court H.R., Sept. 24, 1982, 22 I.L.M. 51 (1983); *Advisory Opinion on the Right to Information on Consular Assistance,* Inter–Am. Court H.R. (ser. A) No. 16 (2000).

§ 6–14. Applying the Convention. The American Convention, unlike its European counterpart, confers standing on individuals and organizations generally, even if they are not the victims of the violation complained of, to bring the violation to the attention of the Commission. To be admissible, all available national remedies must have been exhausted in the case. It must also meet various other admissibility criteria, including the requirement that the complaint state a *prima facie* case.

Once a case has been admitted, the Commission investigates the facts and attempts to negotiate a friendly settlement. If a friendly settlement has not been achieved, the Commission prepares a report which is transmitted to the parties to the dispute, containing findings of fact and recommendations. If within a three-months period following the transmission of the report the Commission's recommendations are not accepted or the case has not been referred to the Court, the Commission has the power to make a final determination in the matter and to set deadlines within which the defendant state must adopt the measures indicated by the Commission. *See Godinez Cruz Case,* Inter–Am. Court H.R. (ser. C) No. 3 (1987).

The case may be referred to the Court by the Commission and by the states parties to the Convention, provided the states concerned have accepted the Court's jurisdiction. A case may only be dealt with by the Court under its contentious jurisdiction if the Commission proceedings in the matter have run their normal course. *See In re Viviana Gallardo (Costa Rica)*, Inter–Am. Court H.R. (ser. A) No. 11, 20 I.L.M. 1424 (1981). The judgments of the Court are final and binding on the parties. Besides having the power to award damages and render declaratory decrees, the Court may in certain special circumstances also enter preliminary injunctions. *See* T. Buergenthal, *Interim Measures in the Inter–American Court of Human Rights*, in *Interim Measures Indicated by International Courts* 69 (R. Bernhardt ed., 1994).

§ **6–15. Interplay with U.S. law**. A recent death penalty case in the United States demonstrates the current interplay of this system with U.S. law. A U.S. national on death row in Texas filed a petition with the Commission seeking a decision that the introduction of certain evidence during his sentencing violated his rights to life, equal protection, and due process. Both the defendant and the U.S. government filed pleadings with the Commission. In its report, the Commission found that the American Declaration did not prohibit capital punishment altogether, but did prohibit its application in an arbitrary manner, and that the introduction of the evidence was arbitrary, as well as a denial of the defendant's rights to a fair trial and due process of law. *See Case 12.243*, Inter–

Am. Comm. H.R., paras. 92–111 (Apr. 4, 2001).
Despite the Commission's report, the Seventh Circuit Court of Appeals declined to stay the defendant's execution. The court characterized the American Declaration as an "aspirational document" that "did not on its own create any enforceable obligations on the part of any of the OAS member states." *Garza v. Lappin*, 253 F.3d 918, 924–25 (7th Cir.2001). The court further noted that while the Inter–American Court's decisions are potentially binding on member states, the United States has not yet joined the American Convention, and therefore is not bound by the Court's decisions. *But see Advisory Opinion on Interpretation of the American Declaration of the Rights and Duties of Man*, Inter–Am. Court H.R. (ser. A) No. 10, para. 45 (1990) (declaring that for member states of the OAS the American Declaration is "a source of international obligations related to the Charter of the Organization").

3. African System

§ 6–16. African Charter on Human and Peoples' Rights. The African Charter, June 26, 1981, 21 I.L.M. 59, was adopted in 1981 by the Organization of African Unity (now the African Union) and entered into force in 1986. Africa thus becomes the third region in the world with its own human rights system. All 53 African Union member states have ratified the African Charter. *See generally* V. Nmehielle, *The African Human Rights System* (2001).

§ 6–17. Charter institutions. The African human rights system differs in a number of respects from the two other regional systems described in the preceding sections. The African Charter does not establish a human rights court. Moreover, a Protocol to the Charter, adopted in 1998, provides for an African Court of Human and Peoples' Rights. The Protocol as yet (mid-2002) has not entered into force. The Charter creates an African Commission on Human and Peoples' Rights with power to deal with inter-state and individual petitions. The Charter places much greater emphasis on friendly settlement and negotiations to resolve charges of violations of human rights than the instruments in force in Europe and in the Americas. *See* C. Flinterman & E. Ankumah, *The African Charter on Human Rights and Peoples' Rights*, in *Guide to International Human Rights Practice* 163 (Hannum ed., 3d ed. 1999).

§ **6–18. Rights guaranteed**. As for the rights it guarantees, the African Charter draws heavily on the two U.N. Covenants on human rights, although it weakens these rights with provisions that permit the imposition of far-reaching restrictions and limitations. The Commission has been given broad interpretative power, however, which might enable it over time to narrow the scope of these restrictions and limitations. This power is amplified by Article 60 of the Charter, which authorizes the Commission, in interpreting the Charter, to "draw inspiration from international law on human and peoples' rights." That law is described in Article 60 by reference to "the provisions of various African instruments on human and peoples' rights, the Charter of the United Nations, the Charter of the Organization of African Unity, the Universal Declaration of Human Rights ..." as well as other

OAU and U.N. instruments. It is still too early to say how this provision will be applied.

C. International humanitarian law

§ 6–19. Definition and sources. International humanitarian law can be said to be a branch of the international law of human rights that applies to situations of international armed conflict and, to a more limited extent, to internal armed conflict. Some humanitarian law has its source in customary international law and in various treaties relating to the law of war adopted at the Hague Peace Conferences of 1899 and 1907. The principal sources of this law, however, are the four Geneva Conventions of 1949, which entered into force in 1950, and the two Protocols Additional to these Conventions, which entered into force in 1978. *See generally* F. Kalshoven & L. Zegveld, *Constraints on the Waging of War: An Introduction to International Humanitarian Law* (2001); T. Meron, *Humanization of Humanitarian Law*, 94 Am. J. Int'l L. 239 (2000); L. Green, *The Contemporary Law of Armed Conflict* (2d ed. 2000). The United States has ratified the Geneva Conventions, but it is not a party to the Protocols.

§ 6–20. 1949 Geneva Conventions. These four treaties consist of Geneva Convention I for the Amelioration of the Condition of the Wounded and Sick in Armed Forces in the Field, Aug. 12, 1949, 75 U.N.T.S. 31; Geneva Convention II for the Amelioration of the Condition of the Wounded, Sick, and Shipwrecked Members of Armed Forces at Sea, Aug. 12, 1949, 75 U.N.T.S. 85; Geneva Convention III Relative to the Treatment of Prisoners of War, Aug. 12, 1949, 75 U.N.T.S. 135; and Geneva Convention

IV Relative to the Protection of Civilian Persons in Time of War, Aug. 12, 1949, 75 U.N.T.S. 287. More than 150 states are parties to these treaties, making them, together with the U.N. Charter, the most widely ratified international agreements dealing with human rights issues. These four conventions set forth in considerable detail protections that must be accorded to these victims of war, such as the medical treatment they should receive, the conditions of their captivity if they are detained, and their right to repatriation after the conflict ends.

The 1949 Geneva Conventions apply principally to armed conflicts between two or more of the states parties to these treaties. *See* Geneva Conventions, art. 2 ("common Article 2"). That is, they apply to *international* armed conflicts. Only one provision—the so-called "common Article 3"—lays down rules applicable to conflicts "not of an international character occurring in the territory" of one of the states parties. The distinction between an international and non-international armed conflict is not always easy to make, particularly in civil war situations involving contested claims of foreign intervention. *See* H. Gasser, *Internationalized Non–International Armed Conflicts: Case Studies of Afghanistan, Kampuchea, and Lebanon*, 33 Am. U.L. Rev. 145 (1983). Equally difficult to ascertain in practice is the threshold for the application of common Article 3. The dispute here usually involves the question of when may a situation be validly characterized as a conflict "not of an international character," which would make common Article 3 applicable, rather than a minor internal disturbance to which the Geneva Conventions would not apply. *See, e.g.*, R. Goldman, *International Humanitarian Law and the Armed Conflicts in El Salvador and Nicaragua*, 2 Am. U.J. Int'l L. & Pol'y 539 (1987).

Many contemporary conflicts involve large-scale internal armed insurgencies that may not qualify as international armed conflicts. Here common Article 3 of the Geneva Conventions is often the only applicable humanitarian law provision. Article 3 requires the parties to the conflict—the government and the insurgents—to treat "humanely" all "persons taking no active part in the hostilities, including members of armed forces who have laid down their arms and those placed *hors de combat* by sickness, wounds, detention, or any other cause…." Adverse distinctions in treatment based "on race, colour, religion or faith, sex, birth or wealth, or any other similar criteria" are prohibited. Also prohibited are the following acts:

(a) violence to life and person, in particular murder of all kinds, mutilation, cruel treatment and torture;

(b) taking of hostages;

(c) outrages upon personal dignity, in particular, humiliating and degrading treatment;

(d) the passing of sentences and the carrying out of executions without previous judgment pronounced by a regularly constituted court, affording all judicial guarantees which are recognized as indispensable by civilized peoples.

Common Article 3 requires, furthermore, that "the wounded and sick . . . be collected and cared for." It also permits the International Committee of the Red Cross to offer its humanitarian services to the parties to the conflict. Although the guarantees spelled out in common Article 3 are not very extensive, they provide some protection in circumstances where any humane treatment, however elementary, amounts to progress. *See generally* T. Meron, *Human Rights in Internal Strife: Their International Protection* 36 et seq. (1987).

§ 6–21. Protocols additional to the Geneva Conventions. In 1977, an intergovernmental conference adopted two protocols to supplement the 1949 Conventions, known as Protocol Relating to the Protection of Victims of International Armed Conflicts, June 8, 1977, 1125 U.N.T.S. 3 (Protocol I); and Protocol Relating to the Protection of Victims of Non–International Armed Conflicts, June 8, 1977, 1125 U.N.T.S. 609 (Protocol II). *See generally* M. Bothe, K Partsch & W. Solf, *New Rules for Victims of Armed Conflicts* (1982); *Commentary on the Additional Protocols of 8 June 1977 to the Geneva Conventions of 12 August 1949* (Y. Sandoz, C. Swinarski & B. Zimmermann eds., 1987).

Each protocol is designed to serve a different function. Protocol I applies, in general, to international armed conflicts, while Protocol II applies to internal conflicts. Protocol II amplifies and clarifies the protections provided in common Article 3 of the Geneva Conventions. Protocol I does that in part as well because it applies not only to international conflicts within the meaning of common Article 2 of the Geneva Conventions, but also to "armed conflicts in which peoples are fighting against colonial domination and alien occupation and against racist régimes...." Protocol I, art. 1(4). Thus, to the extent that an internal armed conflict comes within this latter definition, the parties to the conflict are required to accord the individuals concerned the additional rights and protection they would otherwise enjoy only if the conflict were international in character. *See, e.g.*, Protocol I, art. 75.

§ 6–22. **Human rights conventions, derogation, and humanitarian law**. The major international human rights instruments in force today contain so-called derogation clauses, which permit the states parties to suspend, in time of war or other national emergency, certain of the rights guaranteed by these treaties. *See* ICCPR, art. 4; European Convention, art. 15; American Convention, art. 27. The right of derogation is limited, however, in two very important respects. First, all derogation clauses list certain fundamental rights that may not be suspended under any circumstances. Second, they provide that, even with regard to the rights that are suspendable, the measures which the states parties may take in emergency situations must not be "inconsistent with [their] ... other obligations under international law." *See, e.g.*, American Convention, art. 27(1).

The reference to other international obligations has important consequences. For a state party to one of the aforementioned human rights treaties, which has also ratified the Geneva Conventions and the two Protocols, the derogation clause bars any derogation inconsistent with the humanitarian law conventions. Moreover, certain measures not prohibited by the Geneva Conventions or the Protocols in time of war or national emergency could not be lawfully adopted by a state party to the human rights treaty, if such measures violated a human right that was non-derogable under the treaty.

§ 6–23. **War crimes and crimes against humanity**. The Statutes of the international criminal tribunals for the former Yugoslavia and for Rwanda, as well as the Statute of the permanent International Criminal Court, draw heavily on the Geneva Conventions and the decisions of Nuremberg War Crimes Tribunal in defining the crimes that fall within the jurisdiction of these tribunals, i.e., grave breaches of these conventions and other serious violations of international humanitarian law. *See supra* § 4–29 & –33; *see also* Draft Code of Crimes Against the Peace and Security of Mankind, arts. 18 & 20, Report of the International Law Commission, 48th Sess., U.N. G.A.O.R., 51st Sess., Supp. No.10, at 125, U.N. Doc. A/51/10 (1996).

III. STATE RESPONSIBILITY FOR INJURIES TO ALIENS

§ 6–24. **Historical development**. Whereas the international law of human rights has a very recent history, the basic principles of the law of state responsibility for injuries to aliens can be traced to the early days of modern international law. These principles were amplified and refined by international arbitral tribunals in the 19th and early 20th centuries and to a lesser extent by the Permanent Court of International Justice.

The relevant law can be divided into two parts: the procedural law of state responsibility and its substantive counterpart. The latter relates to the content of the law, that is, to the legal rights and obligations that it creates. The procedural law deals with the manner in which these rights and obligations are enforced. Although the relevant procedural law is today quite clear, considerable uncertainty exists about the content of some substantive norms.

The international law of state responsibility for injuries to aliens is closely related to the broader topic of state responsibility for internationally wrongful acts. This more general topic was extensively studied over a period of many years by the International Law Commission (I.L.C.). The I.L.C. concluded that work in 2001 with the adoption of the Draft Articles on the Responsibility of States for Internationally Wrongful Acts, Report of the International Law Commission, 53d Sess., U.N. G.A.O.R., 56th Sess., Supp. No. 10, U.N. Doc. A/56/10 (2000) (I.L.C. Draft Articles). The I.L.C. Draft Articles do not define the content of international obligations as such. Instead, they address the circumstances in which states may be held responsible for wrongful acts—a topic relevant to the subject here under consideration. Moreover, many of its provisions no doubt also reflect customary international law. *See generally* J. Crawford, *The International Law Commission's Articles on State Responsibility: Introduction, Text and Commentaries* (2002).

A. Procedural issues

§ 6–25. Nationality requirement. The law of state responsibility for injuries to aliens can only be invoked on the international plane by a state whose national is alleged to be a victim of a violation of that law. On nationality, see *infra* § 8–7. For the purpose of asserting a claim, the injury, if there be any, is deemed to be an injury to the state of the alien's nationality. *See Mavrommatis Palestine Concessions*, 1924 P.C.I.J. (ser. A) No. 2 (Aug. 30); *see also* I.L.C. Draft Articles, art. 44(a) & cmts. para. 2. Hence, if the alien is a stateless person, has the nationality of the state alleged to have acted wrongfully or, although formally a national of the espousing state, his/her nationality is not entitled to recognition on the international plane, the claim will have to be dismissed. *See Nottebohm Case* (Liech. v. Guat.), 1955 I.C.J. 4 (Apr. 6). If an individual has dual nationality, either state of his/her nationality may file a claim against a third state. The former may not, however, sue each other because either state is free to treat the individual as its national, *Mergé v. Italian Republic*, 14 R.I.A.A. 238 (1955), unless it can be shown that the individual has much stronger ties (dominant nationality) to the claimant state. *See Restatement (Third)* § 713, cmt. c; *see also* G. Aldrich, *The Jurisprudence of the Iran–United States Claims Tribunal* 54–79 (1996).

Claims under the law of state responsibility may be asserted also on behalf of legal persons such as corporations. A state espousing the claim of a corporation will have to show that the corporation has its nationality. That question is usually determined by reference to the entity's place of incorporation and/or its principal place of business (*siège social*). *See* Barcelona Traction, Light & Power Co. (Belg. v. Spain), 1970 I.C.J. 3 (Feb. 5).

§ 6–26. Exhaustion of local remedies. Before a state may espouse a claim on behalf of its national, it must be shown that the latter has exhausted all available legal remedies in the courts and before the administrative agencies of the state against which the claim is brought. *See Elettronica Sicula S.p.A. (ELSI)* (U.S. v. Italy), 1989 I.C.J. 15 (July 20); *Interhandel Case* (Switz. v. U.S.), 1959 I.C.J. 6 (Mar. 21). This requirement is designed to permit a state to remedy a wrong at the national level before it is transformed into a dispute on the international plane, where it might disrupt unnecessarily relations between states. It should be noted, in this connection, that the exhaustion of local remedies is also a requirement found in various international human rights instruments. Today there exists a vast body of law and practice on this subject, most of it developed in the context of human rights complaints but equally applicable to state responsibility cases. *See* A. Trindade, *The Application of the Rule of Exhaustion of Local Remedies in International Law* (1983); C. F. Amerasinghe, *Local Remedies in International Law* (1990).

The exhaustion of local remedies requirement may be waived by the state against which the claim is lodged. *See De Wilde, Ooms & Versyp v. Belgium*, Eur. Ct. H.R. (ser. A) No. 12 at 34–35 (1971). It is also excused if it can be established that it would be futile to resort to local remedies or because none are in fact available. *See Velasquez Rodriguez Case*,

Inter–Am. Court H.R. (ser. C) No. 1 (1987); *see also* I.L.C. Draft Articles, art. 44(b) & cmts. para 2.

§ 6–27. Presentation and settlement of claims. After a claimant has failed to obtain satisfaction in the state alleged to have violated his/her rights, the claim may be espoused by the state of the claimant's nationality. The decision whether to espouse the claim is a political question within the discretion of each individual state. On the U.S. Secretary of State's discretion, see, e.g., *Chytil v. Powell*, 15 Fed.Appx. 515 (9th Cir.2001).

Once the claim has been espoused, it takes on an international character in the sense that it becomes the subject of international negotiations between the state of the claimant's nationality and the state against which the claim is asserted. Sometimes the claim is settled at this stage. If this does not happen, the states concerned might decide to litigate it either in an international arbitral tribunal or in the International Court of Justice. *See, e.g.,* S. Murphy, *The ELSI Case: An Investment Dispute at the International Court of Justice*, 16 Yale J. Int'l L. 391 (1991). In some instances, a case may be discontinued because negotiations bear fruit following the filing of a claim. *See, e.g., Aerial Incident of 3 July 1988* (Iran v. U.S.), 1996 I.C.J. 9 (Feb. 22) (ordering discontinuance of the case following a settlement). Sometimes, too, states will negotiate a lump sum settlement of all outstanding claims, *see. e.g.,* B. Weston, R. Lillich & D. Bederman, *International Claims: Their Settlement by Lump Sum Agreements, 1975–1995* (1999), or decide to submit the claims to a special arbitral tribunal. The Iran–U.S. Claims Tribunal is a recent example of the latter. *See* C. Brower & J. Brueschke, *The Iran–United States Claims Tribunal* (1998); *The Iran–United States Claims Tribunal: Its Contribution to the Law of State Responsibility* (R. Lillich & D. McGraw eds., 1998). Some claims, though, may never be satisfactorily resolved.

When a claim has been espoused by a state, it has the right under international law to waive the claim, to settle it, and, in all respects, to control the negotiations or litigation relating to it. Moreover, the funds a state receives in satisfaction of a claim are deemed under international law to belong to the state receiving them. National law may require a state to pay the money to the individual claimant, but international law does not impose that requirement. Some states, including the United States, have from time to time established national commissions to adjudicate the claims of their nationals to a share of the funds comprising the lump sum settlement. *See* R. Lillich, *International Claims: Their Adjudication by National Commissions* (1962); *Restatement (Third)* § 713, rptrs. note 9. For the remedies available under international law to a state espousing a claim, see I.L.C. Draft Articles, arts. 34–37.

In order to prevent international claims from being brought against them on behalf of foreign nationals, some states in the past have sought to force foreigners, as a condition of doing business within their territories, to waive the right to seek diplomatic protection from their home states. Provisions requiring such waivers were included in national legislation or concession contracts, particularly in Latin America. These "Calvo clauses," named after the Argentine diplomat and scholar who proposed them, have been held by international tribunals to be incapable of depriving the state of the alien's nationality of the right to espouse a national's claim if the individual's rights under international law were violated. *Cf. North Am. Dredging Co. v. United Mexican States*, 44 R.I.A.A. 26 (U.S.-Mex. Gen. Claims Comm'n 1927). The theory of these holdings is that the right of diplomatic protection belongs to the state and not to the claimant. Some of these problems are today being resolved by so-called Bilateral Investment Treaties (BITs). As a rule, these treaties provide for arbitration in an international forum of investment disputes arising between the nationals of the states parties and the state of their investment. These treaties frequently also provide for a waiver of the exhaustion of local remedies requirement. *See* R. Dolzer & M. Stevens, *Bilateral Investment Treaties* (1995). For a case involving some of these and related issues, see *Maffezini v. Spain*, 40 I.L.M. 1129 (Int'l Ctr. for Settlement of Inv. Disputes 2001). A state's failure, for example, to comply with the provision of the BIT calling for arbitration of a dispute between a state party and the investor would constitute a violation of the treaty obligation, which the state of the investor's nationality would be entitled to challenge on the international plane.

B.   Substantive aspects

§ 6–28.   Attributable liability. A state is liable under international law for an injury to a foreign national only if the wrongful act or omission is attributable to the state. Under this principle of attribution, a state is responsible for the conduct of its government organs, agencies or officials, acting within the scope of their authority or under color of such authority. It matters not whether the agencies or officials belong to the national government or to local governmental entities. *See Restatement (Third)* § 207; I.L.C. Draft Articles, arts. 4–7. In a recent decision, the International Court of Justice declared that it was "a well-established rule of international law" that "the conduct of any organ of a State must be regarded as an act of that State". *Advisory Opinion on Difference Relating to Immunity from Legal Process of a Special Rapporteur of the Commission on Human Rights*, 1999 I.C.J. 62, at para. 62 (Apr. 29).

As a general rule, the private acts of individuals will not be treated as state action unless the state has encouraged such action or fails to take reasonable measures to protect the aliens. Failure to punish persons who have injured an alien or refusal to permit redress in national courts may implicate the state. A state may also become responsible for private acts by ratifying them. *See United States Diplomatic and Consular Staff in Tehran* (U.S. v. Iran), 1980 I.C.J. 3 (May 24); *Laura Janes Claim*, 4 R.I.A.A. 82 (U.S.-Mex. Gen. Claims Comm'n 1926); *Garcia & Garza Claim*, *id.* at 119; *see also* I.L.C. Draft Articles, art. 11.

§ **6–29. Scope of liability**. Under traditional international law, states were deemed to be liable for official acts or omissions involving a "denial of justice" falling below the "international minimum standard." The phrase "denial of justice" was sometimes applied only to violations committed by the judicial authorities of the states. At other times it was used to describe all wrongful acts attributable to a state. The test for determining whether an act or omission was wrongful was the so-called "international minimum standard." Some states, notably those of Latin America, contended that aliens were entitled to no more and no less than "national treatment," which meant that an alien had no right to receive better treatment than the state's own nationals. Most states, however, viewed the international minimum standard as being different than national treatment, but its precise substantive content remained an issue of considerable controversy. *See e.g.*, the separate opinions in *Chattin Claim*, 4 R.I.A.A. 282 (U.S.-Mex. Gen. Claims Comm'n, 1927). The arbitral tribunals could point to few principles of customary international law on the subject and, therefore, relied mainly on general principles of law derived from national legislation and court decisions when deciding what constituted a denial of justice. Some states viewed these principles as European standards of justice that were imposed on them without regard for national legal and political realities. With the adoption of the Universal Declaration of Human Rights and other instruments dealt with in part II of this Chapter, the debate has lost much of its significance. These instruments supply an international standard that has been developed and accepted by the international community for the treatment of all human beings, regardless of the nationality they might have. The *Restatement (Third)* § 711 declares that a state is responsible for injuries incurred by foreign nationals that were caused by official acts or omissions violating internationally recognized human rights. *See also Restatement (Third)* § 701. Of course, a state is also liable for violations of treaties for the protection of the rights of foreign nationals residing in its territory. Many treaties exist today which guarantee a variety of civil, economic and other rights to certain aliens. *See, e.g., Swendig v. Washington Water Power Co.*, 265 U.S. 322 (1924); *Avigliano v. Sumitomo Shoji Am., Inc.*, 638 F.2d 552 (2d Cir.1981).

§ **6–30. Economic rights**. Claims under the law of state responsibility for the infringement of economic rights usually involve either measures infringing upon property rights or government cancellation of or interference with an alien's contract or concession agreement. While it is clear that a state may take alien-owned property located within its borders as an incident of its sovereignty, controversy exists about how much compensation is required when such a taking occurs. The capital exporting states have adopted the position that expropriation is lawful only if the taking is for a public purpose, is not discriminatory, and is accompanied by "full compensation". In the past, Communist states contended that a state may expropriate the means of production at any time for any purpose with whatever compensation it decides is appropriate. Treaties between these states did provide, however, for payment of compensation for the taking of property belonging to their respective nationals. The developing states took a middle course, acknowledging the right of a state to expropriate foreign-owned property, but recognizing a requirement of "just" or "appropriate" compensation, defined in the light of all the circumstances surrounding the taking, including the purpose of the taking and the expropriating state's ability to pay. A somewhat more restrictive attitude is reflected in the Charter of Economic Rights and Duties of States, G.A. Res. 3281 (May 1, 1974), 14 I.L.M. 251 (1975) (adopted by a vote of 120 to 6 with 10 abstentions). That Charter declares a right in each state

to nationalize, expropriate or to transfer ownership of foreign property, in which case appropriate compensation should be paid by the State adopting such measures, taking into account its relevant laws and regulations and all circumstances that the State considers pertinent. In any case where the question of compensation gives rise to controversy, it shall be settled under the domestic law of the nationalizing State and by its tribunals . . . [unless otherwise agreed].

This provision would deny the relevance of international law as a source for defining standards for compensation. *But see Texaco Overseas Petroleum v. Libya*, 17 I.L.M. 1 (1978).

There is a dispute also over whether contractual rights and concession agreements should be accorded the same treatment as rights in tangible property when the value of those rights is impaired or nullified by state action. The mere breach of a contract by a state does not raise international legal liability unless the breach is accompanied by an abuse of governmental power, such as a failure to permit access to local courts to try the issue of breach. On the other hand, the arbitrary nullification of a contract or concession agreement is deemed to be a violation of international law. Most of these issues are today regulated by bilateral and multilateral investment treaties that spell out the obligations assumed by states in relation to foreign investment and provide for third-party dispute resolution mechanisms. *See, e.g., Companía de Aguas v. Argentina*, 40 I.L.M. 426 (Int'l Ctr. for Settlement of Inv. Disputes 2001).

The United States maintains the position that the taking of property is unlawful under international law if it is not for a public purpose, if it is discriminatory or if "just compensation" is not paid. *Restatement (Third)* § 712. The *Restatement (Third)* defines "just compensation" as "fair market value" except in very exceptional circumstances. As a practical matter, in the majority of international dispute settlements, the traditional measure of compensation as set forth in the *Restatement (Third)* has been applied, i.e., that compensation must be an amount equivalent to the value of the property taken and must be paid at the time of the taking, or with interest from that date, and in a form economically usable by the foreign national. This conclusion is reflected in provisions of recent bilateral investment treaties and in friendship, commerce and navigation treaties, as well as in decisions of the Iran–U.S. Claims Tribunal. *See, e.g., Starret*

Housing Corp. v. Iran, 23 I.L.M. 1090 (Iran–U.S. Claims Trib. 1984); *America Int'l Group v. Iran*, 23 I.L.M. 1 (Iran–U.S. Claims Trib. 1983); *Kuwait v. America Indep. Oil Co.*, 21 I.L.M. 976 (1982); *Sedco v. National Iranian Oil Co.*, 25 I.L.M. 629 (Iran–U.S. Claims Trib. 1986); *see also* P. Norton, *A Law of the Future or a Law of the Past? Modern Tribunals and the International Law of Expropriation*, 85 Am. J. Int'l L. 474 (1991).

The end of the Cold War and the gradual recognition by many governments that state ownership of the means of production has on the whole proved to be an obstacle to economic development have tended increasingly to reduce the significance and relevance of this debate. This process has been further accelerated by the desire of many states to attract foreign investment, which is unlikely to be drawn to states where the risk of expropriation is great.

CHAPTER 7

FOREIGN RELATIONS LAW IN THE UNITED STATES

I. INTRODUCTION

Foreign relations law in the United States falls principally into two areas. One area concerns the division of power among the three branches of the federal government, and between the federal government and the several states, in matters touching upon foreign affairs. The other area deals with the manner in which international law is regarded as a part of U.S. law, such as the circumstances under which an individual can invoke a treaty provision before a U.S. court. This chapter provides an overview of these two areas of U.S. foreign relations law.

II. SEPARATION OF POWERS IN FOREIGN AFFAIRS

§ 7–1. Congressional power. Under the U.S. Constitution, Congress has several powers touching upon foreign affairs, such as the powers to lay and collect duties, to provide for the common defense, to regulate commerce with foreign nations, to regulate naturalization, to define and punish piracies and felonies committed on the high seas (as

171

well as offenses against the law of nations), and to declare war. *U.S. Const.* art. I, § 8. Moreover, two-thirds of the U.S. Senate must provide advice and consent before the President may ratify a treaty. *U.S. Const.* art. II, § 2(2). Congress also, of course, has the power of appropriating funds for the U.S. government. *U.S. Const.* art. I, § 7. As in other areas of the law, U.S. courts have interpreted these Congressional powers broadly in the field of foreign affairs when Congress chooses to act, absent some limitation found in the Constitution, such as in the Bill of Rights. *See* L. Henkin, *Foreign Affairs and the United States Constitution* 64, 80 (2d ed. 1996).

§ 7–2. **Executive power**. By contrast, the Constitution expressly allocates only a few foreign affairs powers to the President: he serves as the commander in chief of the armed forces, and has the powers to receive and appoint ambassadors and to make treaties (with the consent of two thirds of the Senate). *U.S. Const.* art. II, §§ 2 & 3. Nevertheless, as a practical matter, an extraordinary amount of U.S. government authority in the field of foreign affairs is exercised by the executive branch, which alone represents the United States in diplomatic relations with other governments and in U.S. courts. Such power is derived from the few express powers noted above and from the express grant of the "executive power" in the first sentence of Article II. Much of the content of this general executive power is derived from customary practice, often as the result of struggles between the executive and legislative branches for the right to exercise a given element of foreign affairs authority.

A key dynamic of this executive-legislative struggle is described in *Youngstown Sheet & Tube Co. v. Sawyer*, 343 U.S. 579 (1952) (the "Steel Seizure" case). During the Korean war, the U.S. steel industry was on the verge of a strike. President Truman issued an executive order, without express statutory authority, directing the Secretary of Commerce to seize and operate the steel mills. The President explicitly tied this action to the need for steel in the war effort. The U.S. Supreme Court found the President's order unconstitutional because it was not authorized by Congress and, perhaps, was implicitly prohibited by the Taft–Hartley Act. Justice Jackson, concurring, wrote (*id.* at 635–638):

1. When the President acts pursuant to an express or implied authorization of Congress, his authority is at its maximum, for it includes all that he possesses in his own right plus all that Congress can delegate. . . . If his act is held unconstitutional under these circumstances, it usually means that the Federal Government as an undivided whole lacks power. . . .

2. When the President acts in absence of either a congressional grant or denial of authority, he can only rely upon his own independent powers, but there is a zone of twilight in which he and Congress may have concurrent authority, or in which its distribution is uncertain. . . . In this area, any actual test of power is likely to depend on the imperatives of events and contemporary imponderables rather than on abstract theories of law.

3. When the President takes measures incompatible with the expressed or implied will of Congress, his power is at its lowest ebb, for then he can rely only upon his own constitutional powers minus any constitutional powers of Congress over the matter. Courts can sustain exclusive Presidential control in such a case only by disabling the Congress from acting upon the subject.

An example of this dynamic arose when the President agreed in the 1981 Algiers Accords to terminate claims that had been filed by U.S. nationals in U.S. courts against the government of Iran, in exchange for the release by Iran of U.S. nationals being held hostage. The Algiers Accords also provided for the establishment of a claims tribunal in The Hague to resolve, *inter alia*, claims by U.S. nationals against the government of Iran. In *Dames & Moore v. Regan*, 453 U.S. 654 (1981), claimants against the Iranian government sought a declaration that the executive action, which nullified their claims in U.S. courts, was unconstitutional. Relying heavily on the *Steel Seizure Case,* the Court concluded that the President's action was valid. While there was no statutory authority expressly supporting such termination of claims, the Court found significant certain statutes that provided the President with broad authority in times of national emergency. Further, the Court noted Congress' longstanding acquiescence to presidential settlement of international claims by executive agreement. From cases such as *Dames & Moore*, it is clear that guides to the scope of executive power in foreign affairs are not found primarily in judicial definitions or even in the synthesis of results in decided cases. Rather that authority is defined in an inter-branch demand/response/accommodation process that characterizes much of U.S. constitutional law as between the political branches.

§ **7–3. Treaty power**. As noted above, the President may only ratify treaties after receiving the advice and consent of the Senate. By some estimates, however, only about five percent of all the international agreements concluded by the United States have gone through the process set forth in the U.S. Constitution for approval of treaties. Indeed, the vast majority of international agreements entered into by the United States are never submitted to the Senate for advice and consent. Rather, they are based on one of three other forms of authority and are referred to as "executive agreements."

First, if there exists a prior treaty that contemplates explicitly or implicitly follow-on international agreements, the President may conclude those agreements without obtaining further approval by the Senate (sometimes referred to as a "treaty-based executive agreement"). For instance, while the Senate provided advice and consent to the NATO Status of Forces Agreement, June 19, 1951, 4 U.S.T. 1792, 199 U.N.T.S. 67, concerning the status of U.S. troops in NATO states, the President thereafter concluded, without further congressional approval, a series of bilateral agreements with individual states in order to implement that treaty.

Second, the President may conclude an executive agreement when it is based on one of his constitutional powers (sometimes referred to as a "sole-executive agreement"). Thus, based solely on his constitutional power to appoint and receive ambassadors (*see supra* §§ 3–5, 7–2), the President might conclude an executive agreement with another state to establish diplomatic relations, which might even involve the settlement of outstanding claims between the two nations. For example, when President Roosevelt recognized the Soviet Government in 1933, he also concluded an agreement by which there was an assignment (the "Litvinov Assignment") from the Soviet Government of all its rights in properties located in the United States, rights which the Soviets had previously claimed pursuant to expropriation decrees issued after the Russian Revolution. The assignment was part of a larger process for settling claims between the two governments. When the U.S. Government appeared in U.S. state courts to exercise its newly acquired rights in the properties in the United States, state courts refused to accept that the Soviets had ever acquired rights in such properties (and thus could not assign rights in them), because state law denied extraterritorial effect to the Soviet expropriation decrees. The U.S. Supreme Court, however, held that accepting the Assignment was an essential component of the normalization of relations between the United States and the Soviet Union, and that the agreement was properly concluded based solely on the President's constitutional powers.

Therefore, U.S. property rights under the Assignment could not be questioned under state law. *See United States v. Belmont*, 301 U.S. 324, 330 (1937); *United States v. Pink*, 315 U.S. 203, 230 (1942).

Third, the President may conclude an executive agreement if he has obtained a *majority* approval (not two-thirds approval) from *both* houses of Congress. This third form of executive agreement (sometimes referred to as a "congressional-executive agreement") may be based on prior congressional approval, such as might be embodied in a long-standing statute. Thus, Congress has authorized the President by statute to conclude stratospheric ozone protection agreements with other states, 42 U.S.C. § 7671p (1994); project agreements with NATO states, 22 U.S.C. § 2767 (1994); and numerous other kinds of agreements, typically subject to certain conditions. Yet this type of executive agreement may also be based on *ad hoc* congressional approval of a particular agreement after its negotiation. For instance, after the President completed negotiation of the North American Free Trade Agreement, Dec. 12, 1992, Can.-Mex.-U.S., 32 I.L.M. 289 (1993) (NAFTA), he submitted the agreement to both houses of the Congress. After majority approval in both houses (the vote in the Senate was less than a two-thirds majority), the President proceeded to ratify the treaty.

It may seem startling that U.S. practice in concluding international agreements deviates so starkly from the means contemplated in Article II of the Constitution. However, there is an indirect recognition in the U.S. Constitution of the ability to conclude other types of international agreements, such as agreements by "alliance," "confederation," and "compact". *U.S. Const.* art. I, § 10; *see also* L. Tribe, *American Constitutional Law* § 4–5 (3d ed. 2000). Further, this practice is long-standing in U.S. history and reflects a practical accommodation of the President's need to conclude numerous agreements, many of marginal significance, without adhering to the formal treaty process. Nevertheless, on occasion, this practice has been challenged in U.S. courts. *See infra* § 7–5.

Congressional concern over the use of the treaty power led to the enactment of the Case Act, 1 U.S.C. § 112b (1994), which requires the Secretary of State to transmit to Congress the text of any international agreement, other than a treaty, concluded by the President. By this means, Congress can monitor the President's practice of concluding executive agreements. Further, the Department of State adopted Circular 175, an administrative instruction laying out the procedures to be followed, including consultative procedures with Congress, when considering whether an intended agreement should be concluded as a treaty or an executive agreement. Circular 175 calls upon the State Department to consider the extent to which the agreement involves the nation as a whole, whether the agreement will affect state laws, whether the agreement can be self-executing (*see infra* § 7–9), the relevant past practice concerning similar agreements, the preferences of Congress, the degree of formality of the agreement, the agreement's expected duration, and general international practice in connection with the type of agreement in question.

Whether by treaty or executive agreement, the authority of the United States to enter into international agreements is coextensive with the foreign affairs interests of the United States.

The treaty power, as expressed in the Constitution, is in terms unlimited except by those restraints which are found in that instrument against the action of the government or of its departments, and those arising from the nature of government itself and of that of the States. It would not be contended that it extends so far as to authorize what the Constitution forbids, or a change in the character of the government or in that of one of the States, or a cession of any portion of the territory of the latter without its consent. ...But with these exceptions, it is not perceived that there is any limit to the questions which can be adjusted touching any matter which is properly the subject of negotiation with a foreign country.

Geofroy v. Riggs, 133 U.S. 258, 267 (1890); *see Santovincenzo v. Egan*, 284 U.S. 30, 40 (1931).

Indeed, there is support for the proposition that the federal government may do by treaty what it cannot do by statute. In *Missouri v. Holland*, 252 U.S. 416, 433–35 (1920), the Supreme Court found that the federal government could regulate migratory birds pursuant to a treaty, even though a statute to the same effect had been struck down previously by lower courts as unconstitutional. The state of Missouri asserted that regulation of birds was a matter "reserved" to the states under the Tenth Amendment of the U.S. Constitution. Justice Oliver Wendell Holmes, in upholding the treaty, found that the scope of the legislative powers granted to Congress did not govern the scope of the treaty power. *See* D. Golove, *Treaty-Making and the Nation: The Historical Foundations of the Nationalist Conception of the Treaty Power*, 98 Mich. L. Rev. 1075 (2000).

At the same time, treaties are subject to constitutional limitations on governmental power and may not contravene specific constitutional prohibitions. In *Reid v. Covert*, 354 U.S. 1 (1957), the Supreme Court found that U.S. civilian defendants could not be tried by a court-martial, where they were denied a jury trial and other constitutional rights, even if that process was the only means of carrying out an exercise of U.S. criminal jurisdiction as set forth in an international agreement. *See* American Law Institute, *Restatement of the Foreign Relations Law of the United States (Third)* § 302 (1987) (*Restatement (Third)*).

§ 7–4. War power. As noted above, Congress has the power to declare war, to raise and support an army and navy, and to control the federal "purse," while the President serves as commander-in-chief of the armed forces and is the chief executive. These concurrent powers of the President and Congress on matters relating to war sometimes are

in great tension, such as when the President continued to prosecute the Vietnam War in the face of
significant congressional opposition (Congress was
unable to muster a majority to cut off funds for the
war).

Concerned that the President might commit
troops without congressional approval in situations
short of war, which could then evolve into full-scale
armed conflicts, Congress passed during the Vietnam War the 1973 War Powers Resolution, 50
U.S.C. §§ 1541–48 (1994). The Resolution requires
consultation between the President and Congress
''in every possible instance'' before introducing U.S.
forces into hostilities or into eminent danger of
hostilities. After troops are introduced into such
hostilities or into a foreign territory ''equipped for
combat,'' the President is required to report to
Congress concerning the circumstances. If the President reports that troops have been introduced into
hostilities or eminent danger of hostilities, the
troops must be withdrawn within sixty days (ex-
tendable to ninety days), unless Congress has authorized a continuation of the action.

The War Powers Resolution represented the first
overt recognition by the Congress of the inherent
power of the President to send troops abroad for at
least a period of time without prior Congressional
approval. The Resolution, however, has not proven
particularly effective. Politically, it is difficult for
Congress not to support the President once U.S.
troops are placed in harm's way. Further, the sixty-
day withdrawal provision is not triggered when the

President simply reports that he has introduced troops into a foreign state "equipped for combat"; by not mentioning "hostilities," the President avoids the withdrawal provision while at the same time maintaining an appearance of cooperation with Congress. Finally, the Executive Branch has consistently maintained that the withdrawal provision of the War Powers Resolution represents an unconstitutional congressional attempt to interfere with the powers of the President as Chief Executive and Commander in Chief. The courts are likely to treat disputes over such matters as a political question unless a majority of both houses of Congress forbid executive action. *See infra* § 7—5. Lacking judicial intervention, the effect of the Resolution on executive power is determined principally by whether U.S. public opinion supports or opposes the use of U.S. troops abroad under the circumstances. For the most recent large-scale deployments of U.S. military troops, Congress has passed joint resolutions supporting the President. *See, e.g.*, Pub. L. No. 107–40, 115 Stat. 224 (2001) (authorizing the use of military force in response to the terrorist attacks of September 2001 on the World Trade Center and the Pentagon).

§ 7–5. Judicial power. The Constitution provides that the federal judicial power extends to all cases concerning treaties, ambassadors, and admiralty and maritime jurisdiction, and cases between a state (or its nationals) and foreign states (or their nationals). *U.S. Const.*, art. III, § 2. On a regular basis, U.S. courts are called upon to decide matters touching on foreign affairs, as may be seen in the numerous U.S. cases cited throughout this volume.

Yet U.S. courts are generally hesitant to second-guess actions of the Congress or the President in the field of foreign affairs. The Supreme Court has stated that "the conduct of foreign relations is committed by the Constitution to the political departments of the Federal Government; that the propriety of the exercise of that power is not open to judicial inquiry." *United States v. Pink*, 315 U.S. 203, 222–23 (1942); *see Haig v. Agee*, 453 U.S. 280, 292 (1981). Further, U.S. courts are reluctant to resolve controversies between the President and the Congress over the exercise of the foreign affairs powers, typically choosing to invoke the "political question doctrine." That hesitancy grows in large part from a desire not to crystallize erroneous judicial perceptions of appropriate power allocations.

The modern statement of the political question doctrine is found in *Baker v. Carr*, 369 U.S. 186 (1962). In that case (which involved the apportionment of state legislative districts), the Supreme Court identified six factors that would weigh against judicial review, including in cases touching on foreign relations. Those factors were:

a textually demonstrable constitutional commitment of the issue to a coordinate political department; or a lack of judicially discoverable and manageable standards for resolving it; or the impossibility of deciding without an initial policy determination of a kind clearly for nonjudicial discretion; or the impossibility of a court's undertaking independent resolution without expressing lack of the respect due coordinate branches of the government; or an unusual need for unquestioning adherence to a political decision already made; or the potentiality of embarrassment from multifarious pronouncements by various departments on one question.

Id. at 217. Application of these principles may be seen in various cases. For example, in *Ramirez v. Weinberger*, 745 F.2d 1500 (D.C.Cir.1984), *remanded for reconsideration on other grounds*, 471 U.S. 1113 (1985), a U.S. national challenged the authority of the executive branch to confiscate in effect his plantation in Honduras by permitting its use for military exercises to train soldiers for El Salvador. The court concluded that the claims were not "exclusively committed for resolution to the political branches" for three reasons: federal courts historically have resolved disputes over land; adjudication of this claim was not beyond judicial expertise; and none of the circumstances of the case gave rise to prudential concerns. 745 F.2d at 1512–13; *see also Lamont v. Woods*, 948 F.2d 825 (2d Cir.1991) (declining to invoke the political question doctrine in a case challenging U.S. foreign aid to religious institutions).

By contrast, in *Made in the USA Found. v. United States*, 242 F.3d 1300 (11th Cir.2001), the plaintiffs ultimately were not successful in obtaining judicial review. In that case, the plaintiffs sought a judicial declaration that NAFTA (discussed *supra* § 7–3) was unconstitutional, since it received a majority approval in both houses of Congress but not did not obtain the consent of two-thirds of the Senate. The Eleventh Circuit found that with respect to international commercial agreements such as NAFTA, the question of what constitutes a "treaty" requiring Senate ratification presents a nonjusticiable political question. Relying on *Goldwater v. Carter*, 444 U.S. 996 (1979) (a challenge to the President's power to terminate a treaty without congressional consent), the court in *Made in the USA Foundation* stated that "just as the Treaty Clause fails to outline the Senate's role in the abrogation of treaties, we find that the Treaty Clause also fails to outline the circumstances, if any, under which its procedures must be adhered to when approving international commercial agreements." 242 F.3d at 1315; *see also Weinberger v. Rossi*, 456 U.S. 25 (1982).

Resort to the courts to challenge the President's power to deploy armed forces in the absence of a congressional declaration of war has also fallen victim to the political question doctrine. For example, in April 1999, seventeen members of the House of Representatives filed a lawsuit in federal court challenging President Clinton's ability to maintain a bombing campaign against Yugoslavia (in response to its treatment of Kosovar Albanians) without authorization from Congress. The complaint requested the court to issue declaratory relief that the President "is unconstitutionally conducting an offensive military attack," and that "no later than May 25, 1999, the President must terminate" such action.

The district court, however, dismissed the case, noting that Congress had not expressly opposed the President's actions and that courts traditionally have been reluctant to intervene in political disputes concerning matters of war. *See Campbell v. Clinton*, 52 F. Supp.2d 34 (D.D.C.1999), *aff'd*, 203 F.3d 19 (D.C.Cir.2000); *see also Dellums v. Bush*, 752 F.Supp. 1141 (D.D.C.1990) (dismissing a challenge by members of Congress to President George Bush's deployment of forces to assist Kuwait against Iraq's invasion).

III.   ROLE OF THE STATES

§ 7–6.   Federal supremacy under the Constitution. There are several reasons why the foreign affairs power resides in the federal government, rather than in the governments of the several states. First, there is some authority for the proposition that the foreign affairs power is a necessary attribute of sovereignty itself and, therefore, needs no constitutional source other than the intent to create a nation. *See United States v. Curtiss–Wright Export Corp.*, 299 U.S. 304 (1936).

Second, U.S. constitutional history makes clear that matters touching upon foreign affairs were intended to be dealt with under federal law. The founders meeting in Philadelphia were dissatisfied with the lack of centralized control over matters of foreign affairs under the Articles of Confederation and ultimately urged ratification of the new constitution as a means of correcting that deficiency. *See, e.g., The Federalist*, Nos. 1, 6, 8–9, 11, 21 (A. Hamilton), Nos. 2–5 (J. Jay), No. 49 (J. Madison).

Third, in the Constitution itself, all the important foreign affairs powers are explicitly denied to the states. The states are absolutely prohibited from entering into treaties or alliances with other nations, *U.S. Const.* art. I, § 10(1), and may not, without the consent of Congress, impose duties on imports or exports or keep military forces in times of peace. *Id.* § 10(2) & (3). At the same time, as noted *supra* §§ 7–1, 7–2 & 7–5, the U.S. Constitution explicitly assigns considerable law-making power to the national government in the field of foreign affairs, such as the power to regulate foreign commerce. Moreover, the Constitution's supremacy clause, *U.S. Const.*, art. VI(2), expressly makes federal legislation passed pursuant to these federal constitutional powers—as well as all treaties—binding upon the several states as "the supreme Law of the Land."

§ 7–7. Case law on federal supremacy. U.S. courts have readily recognized federal authority over the several states on matters concerning foreign affairs. For example, to protest human rights violations, Massachusetts enacted in 1996 a law prohibiting its government from purchasing goods or services from individuals or companies that engaged in business with or in Myanmar (Burma), except in certain limited situations. The First Circuit Court of Appeals found the law unconstitutional on three grounds. *National Foreign Trade Council v. Natsios*, 181 F.3d 38 (1st Cir.1999). First, the law infringed on the general foreign affairs power of the federal government, because it had more than an "incidental or indirect effect in foreign countries" (as evidenced by the intent of the law, by Massachusetts' purchasing power, and by protests from foreign states). In reaching this conclusion, the court relied heavily on *Zschernig v. Miller*, 389 U.S. 429 (1968). Second, the Massachusetts law violated the foreign commerce clause because it facially discriminated against foreign commerce without a legitimate local justification and because it attempted to regulate conduct beyond its borders. Third, the law was unconstitutional under the supremacy clause, because there already existed federal sanctions against Myanmar, which the President could increase or decrease in response to actions by the Myanmar government. The U.S. Supreme Court also found the law unconstitutional, but limited its decision to the third ground. *Crosby v. National Foreign Trade Council*, 530 U.S. 363 (2000).

As the lower court decision in *Crosby* makes clear, state interference with federal policies may be prohibited even when those policies are not reduced to legislative form. *See also United States v. Belmont*, 301 U.S. 324 (1937). States may not act to exacerbate relations with foreign nations, *Banco Nacional de Cuba v. Sabbatino*, 376 U.S. 398, 423 (1964), nor may they contravene the policies advanced in a U.S. international agreement even if no direct conflict with the agreement exists. *Kolovrat v. Oregon*, 366 U.S. 187 (1961).

State courts themselves have balanced the importance of exercising state authority against the need for national control. *Compare Springfield Rare Coin*

Galleries v. Johnson, 503 N.E.2d 300 (Ill.1986) (finding that the exclusion of South African coinage from state tax exempt status "is an impermissible encroachment upon a national prerogative—the authority of the Federal government to conduct foreign affairs"); *with Board of Trustees of Employees' Retirement System of City of Baltimore v. Mayor and City Council of Baltimore City,* 562 A.2d 720 (Md.1989) (upholding state and local measures directed against investment in South Africa).

IV. INTERNATIONAL LAW AS A PART OF U.S. LAW

§ 7–8. Introduction. In Chapter I, we emphasized the importance of keeping the difference between the national and international applications of international law constantly in mind. We pointed out that in the United States, parties before national courts invoke international law whenever it appears relevant. In a very real sense, then, it is not the international legal *system* that operates in United States courts but, rather, those rules and principles of international law that a U.S. court considers to be applicable because they are deemed to be a part of U.S. law that is appropriate to the particular case.

In fact, international law has been a part of U.S. law since the founding of the nation. *See* L. Henkin, *International Law as Law in the United States,* 82 Mich. L. Rev. 1555 (1984). Although there are important issues about how international law operates within the U.S. legal system—and the relative hierarchy between it and other sources of U.S. law—U.S. courts at both the state and federal level have drawn upon international law since 1776, just as the courts of England did prior to U.S. independence. In the first great treatise on U.S. law, Chancellor James Kent stated that the "faithful observance" of the law of nations "is essential to national character, and to the happiness of mankind." J. Kent, *Commentaries on American Law*, pt. 1, lect. 1, at 1 (1826). This section considers the manner in which international law is regarded as a part of U.S. law.

§ 7–9. **Treaties in U.S. law**. The Supremacy Clause of the U.S. Constitution provides:

This Constitution, and the Laws of the United States which shall be made in Pursuance thereof; *and all Treaties made*, or which shall be made under the Authority of the United States, *shall be the supreme Law of the Land*; and the Judges in every State shall be bound thereby, any Thing in the Constitution or Laws of any State to the Contrary notwithstanding.

(emphasis added). On the text of this clause, it would appear that treaties should be regarded just like statutes passed by Congress and signed by the President. Certainly, in terms of their supremacy over state law, treaties are like statutes. *See Asakura v. Seattle*, 265 U.S. 332 (1924) (striking down a Seattle ordinance that discriminated against Japanese as inconsistent with a U.S.–Japan commercial treaty). Moreover, to the extent that there is a conflict between a treaty and a statute, the later-in-time rule prevails, just as it would between two statutes. *See United States v. Palestine Liberation Org.*, 695 F.Supp. 1456 (S.D.N.Y.1988) (considering the normative hierarchy between a U.S. treaty commitment to the United Nations as against a later-in-time statute affecting the PLO mission in New York). Whenever possible, courts will seek to interpret a later-in-time statute as consistent with an earlier treaty, unless Congress evinces a contrary intent, on an assumption that Congress normally does not seek to violate U.S. obligations under international law. *See id.*; *Murray v. The Schooner Charming Betsy*, 6 U.S. (2 Cranch) 64, 118 (1804); *Restatement (Third)* §§ 114–15; R. Steinhardt, *The Role of International Law as a Canon of Domestic Statutory Construction*, 43 Vand. L. Rev. 1103 (1990).

However, there is an important way in which treaties are not like U.S. statutes. Beginning with Chief Justice Marshall's decision in *Foster v. Neilson*, 27 U.S. (2 Pet.) 253, 314 (1829), U.S. courts have developed a doctrine that treaties may be either "self-executing" or "non-self-executing." *See* T. Buergenthal, *Self-Executing and Non Self–Executing Treaties in National and International Law*, 235 R.C.A.D.I. 303, 370 (1992). A self-executing treaty becomes internal law in the United States immediately upon entry into force of the agreement. This means that courts will look to it for the rule of decision in cases affected by its terms. Non-self-executing treaties, however, require legislation to implement them in the United States. For such agreements, it is the implementing legislation, not the agreement itself, that becomes the rule of decision in U.S. courts.

When will a court determine that a treaty is self-executing? Courts in the United States answer that question by focusing on different kinds of factors. For instance, many courts say that whether an agreement is self-executing is determined by the intent of the states parties. For example, in *Cheung v. United States*, 213 F.3d 82, 95 (2000), the Second Circuit found an agreement between the United States and Hong Kong to be self-executing by reference to statements made by the executive when transmitting the agreement to Congress, to the effect that "this Agreement will not require implementing legislation."

Yet some courts focus more on whether the language of the treaty is susceptible to enforcement; thus, a treaty containing hortatory or indeterminate language may be found non-self-executing. Still other courts consider whether the treaty seeks to regulate a matter over which Congress has the sole competence to legislate (e.g., the appropriation of funds). If so, then it is not self-executing. Finally, some courts are interested in whether the treaty purports to create a private right of action; if not, then the treaty might not be found self-executing. Whether these are sensible distinctions to draw is subject to debate. *See, e.g.*, Carlos Manuel Vázquez, *The Four Doctrines of Self–Executing Treaties*, 89 Am. J. Int'l L. 695 (1995); Jordan Paust, *Self-Executing Treaties*, 82 Am. J. Int'l L. 760 (1988).

For a spirited discussion of whether *any* treaties should be self-executing, see 99 Colum. L. Rev. 1955–2258 (1999).

Although it is clear today that both treaties and executive agreements are constitutionally acceptable instruments for conducting U.S. foreign policy, there are some differences between the two types of agreements in terms of their internal legal effect. Executive agreements authorized by a federal statute or treaty have the same normative rank as the statute or treaty on which they are based, with the later in time having precedence. Sole-executive agreements (agreements made by the President based solely on his own constitutional power) will supersede inconsistent state laws, but may not prevail against a conflicting prior federal statute. *See Restatement (Third)* § 115, rptrs. note 5.

§ 7–10. Customary international law in U.S. law. The role of customary international law in U.S. law is most famously addressed in *The Paquete Habana*, 175 U.S. 677 (1900). In that case, the President of the United States ordered a naval blockade of the Cuban coast "in pursuance of the laws of the United States, and the law of nations applicable to such cases." *Id.* at 712. The blockade commander captured two small fishing vessels that were sold in the United States as prize vessels. In a suit by the original owners to recover those proceeds, the U.S. Supreme Court, sitting as a prize court, held that international law prohibited seizing coastal fishing vessels during time of war. The Court wrote:

International law is part of our law, and must be ascertained and administered by the courts of justice of appropriate jurisdiction, as often as questions of right depending upon it are duly presented for their determination. For this purpose, where there is no treaty, and no controlling executive or legislative act or judicial decision, resort must be had to the customs and usages of civilized nations. . . .

Id. at 700. The meaning of this broad language has been the subject of considerable controversy. Some writers emphasize the first sentence in the quotation, arguing that customary international law is automatically and directly applicable in U.S. courts whenever issues to which it is relevant are up for decision. Under this analysis, customary international law is one of the "Laws of the United States" that are the "supreme Law of the Land" under the Supremacy Clause (preempting state law), which the President must faithfully execute under Article II, § 3 of the Constitution. *See, e.g.*, L. Henkin, *International Law as Law in the United States*, 82 Mich. L. Rev. 1555, 1566 (1984).

Other writers, however, emphasize the second sentence in the quotation, pointing out that international legal rules were relevant in *The Paquete Habana* because the President had incorporated the limitations of customary international law into his orders to the commander. Acts in violation of those rules were therefore *ultra vires* under the President's own orders and, consequently, void; they were not void simply because they transgressed customary international law. A more recent example of this thinking may be seen in *Garcia-Mir v. Meese*, 788 F.2d 1446 (11th Cir.1986). In that case, many Cubans came to the United States who the United States did not want to admit and who could not be deported elsewhere. Consequently, the U.S. Attorney General ordered that they be held in detention for many months. The Cubans filed suit charging that their prolonged detention was arbitrary and thus a violation of customary international law. The Eleventh Circuit agreed that the detention violated international law, but saw the Attorney General's decision as a "controlling executive act" (see the *Paquete Habana* excerpt above) that trumped international law.

A few scholars writing about customary international law have questioned whether locating lawmaking authority outside U.S. institutions (i.e., in the practice of states globally) fits within the U.S. political tradition. *See* P. Trimble, *A Revisionist View of Customary International Law*, 33 UCLA L. Rev. 665 (1986). Further, some scholars view customary international law as part of the common law of the several states, to be incorporated as U.S. federal law only after express authorization by the federal political branches. *See* C. Bradley & J. Goldsmith, *Customary International Law: A Critique of the Modern Position*, 110 Harv. L. Rev. 815 (1997); *but see* H. Koh, *Is International Law Really State Law?*, 111 Harv. L. Rev. 1824 (1998). The U.S. Supreme Court has also evinced caution. *See, e.g., Stanford v. Kentucky*, 492 U.S. 361, 369 n. 1 (1989) (emphasizing "that it is *American* conceptions of decency that are dispositive" in interpreting the Eighth Amendment, not the sentencing practices of foreign states); *see also United States v. Yunis*, 924 F.2d 1086, 1091 (D.C.Cir.1991) ("Our duty is to enforce the Constitution, laws and treaties of the United States, not conform the law of the land to norms of customary international law.")

Whether customary international law supersedes a pre-existing treaty or a pre-existing statute under U.S. law is also unclear. *Compare* L. Henkin, *The Constitution and United States Sovereignty: A Century of Chinese Exclusion and Its Progeny*, 100 Harv. L. Rev. 853, 867–78 (1987) (asserting that customary international law is not inferior to treaties or statutes), *with* J. Goldklang, *Back on Board the Paquete Habana: Resolving the Conflict Between Statutes and Customary International Law*, 25 Va. J. Int'l L. 143 (1984) (finding that customary international law is inferior). What is clear is that when the existence of a specific norm of customary international law is denied by the political branches, U.S. courts normally will not give effect to the norm. Further, U.S. courts will give special weight to views of the executive branch in interpreting customary international law. *See Restatement (Third)* § 112, cmt. c.

§ 7–11. Alien Tort Claims Act. A modern and important development in the role of international law in U.S. courts is found in recent cases decided under the Alien Tort Statute, 28 U.S.C. § 1350 (1994) (also referred to as the Alien Tort

Claims Act or ATCA). The ATCA confers original jurisdiction on federal district courts over "any civil action by an alien for a tort only, committed in violation of the law of nations or a treaty of the United States." The original purpose of the statute may have been to avoid international conflict by opening U.S. federal courts (which would be less political than state courts) to foreign diplomats for redress of injuries suffered at the hands of U.S. nationals, either in the United States or abroad. However, the intent of Congress when enacting the statute is not entirely clear and, because the statute lay dormant for some 200 years, its scope was never clarified by U.S. courts. *See* A. Burley, *The Alien Tort Statute and the Judiciary Act of 1789: A Badge of Honor*, 83 Am. J. Int'l L. 461 (1989).

The ATCA was dramatically resurrected in *Filartiga v. Pena–Irala*, 630 F.2d 876 (2d Cir.1980). In that case, a federal court used the statute to find jurisdiction over a claim by Paraguayan plaintiffs against an official of their own government for the torture-slaying of a family member in Paraguay. The Court found that torture conducted under "color of law" was a violation of the law of nations, even when conducted by a government against its own nationals. Such a case—involving a tort that occurred abroad by an alien against another alien— highlights the extraordinary nature of the ATCA. However, not all courts have been receptive to a robust use of the statute. *See e.g.*, *Tel-Oren v. Libya*, 726 F.2d 774, 798 (D.C.Cir.1984) (Bork, J., concurring) (seeking to limit the ATCA to 18th century torts, specifically violation of safe-conducts or passports, infringement of the rights of ambassadors, and piracy); *Beanal v. Freeport–McMoran, Inc.*, 197 F.3d 161 (5th Cir.1999) (finding that the environmental agreements upon which the claim was pled did not provide discernable standards for identifying international environmental torts).

To succeed on an ACTA claim, three key elements must exist: (1) the claim must be filed by an alien (i.e., not a national of the United States); (2) the claim must be for a tort; and (3) the action in controversy must have violated international law. Further, ACTA claims generally have been limited to suits against individuals, since suits against governments must be brought under the Foreign Sovereign Immunities Act. *See Argentine Republic v. Amerada Hess Shipping Corp.*, 488 U.S. 428 (1989) (finding that the ATCA does not grant jurisdiction for a suit against a foreign government); *see also infra* ch. 9, pt. III. The individual sued, however, must be acting under "color of law," since it generally is assumed that only states can violate international law. Yet, recent case law also permits claims against individuals that are based on a handful of egregious offenses (such as piracy, slave trading, and certain war crimes), since those offenses can lead to individual liability under international law. *See, e.g., Kadic v. Karadzic*, 70 F.3d 232 (2d Cir. 1995).

A notable use of the ATCA is against U.S. corporations which enter into business relationships with foreign governments, which in turn engage in human rights violations. For example, in 1996, villagers from Myanmar (Burma) filed a class action lawsuit in a U.S. federal court against, *inter alia*, a U.S. corporation called Unocal that was involved in a joint venture to extract natural gas. The plaintiffs alleged that the defendant was responsible under the ACTA for international human rights violations, including forced labor, perpetrated by the Burmese military in furtherance of the pipeline portion of the project. The district court found that corporations are within the ambit of the ATCA when they engage in cooperative behavior with governments engaged in human rights violations. *Doe v. Unocal Corp.*, 963 F.Supp. 880 (C.D.Cal.1997). While this decision was heralded as a new step in promoting transnational corporate responsibility, the court eventually granted Unocal's motion for summary judgment because—as a factual matter— the corporation was not sufficiently connected to the construction and operation of the gas pipeline to sustain a claim that it engaged in a tort "in violation of the law of nations or a treaty of the United States." *Doe v. Unocal Corp.*, 110 F. Supp.2d 1294 (C.D.Cal.2000); *see Bigio v. Coca–Cola Co.*, 239 F.3d 440 (2d Cir.2000).

CHAPTER 8

JURISDICTION

I. INTRODUCTION

This chapter deals with the right of a state under international law to exercise jurisdiction over persons or things outside its territory. Its principal focus is the relevant practice of the United States. First, this chapter considers presumptions that exist under U.S. law regarding whether U.S. statutes apply extraterritorially. Second, if a U.S. statute does apply extraterritorially, this chapter considers whether such application of U.S. law is viewed as permissible under international law. Third, this chapter discusses how jurisdiction can be applied extraterritorially, not just through legislation but also through adjudication and enforcement.

II. PRESUMPTIONS UNDER U.S. LAW

§ 8–1. Statutes normally govern conduct only within U.S. territory. It is well-established that the Congress has the *power* to regulate conduct performed outside U.S. territory. As the Supreme Court has stated, "Congress has the authority to enforce its laws beyond the territorial boundaries of the United States." *EEOC v. Arabian Am. Oil Co.*, 499 U.S. 244, 248 (1991). However, it is equally well-established that U.S. courts are to presume that Congress has *not* exercised this power, unless Congress manifests an intent to reach acts performed outside U.S. territory. Thus, the normal presumption by U.S. courts is that U.S. statutes apply only to acts performed within U.S. territory. *See Sale v. Haitian Ctrs. Council, Inc.*, 509 U.S. 155, 188 (1993) (holding that a U.S. immigration statute does not apply extraterritorially); *Smith v. United States*, 507 U.S. 197, 209 (1993) (holding that the Federal Tort Claims Act does not apply extraterritorially).

For instance, U.S. law criminalizes the sale of cocaine. However, if a U.S. national traveled to The Netherlands, bought and sold a small amount of cocaine, and then returned to the United States, a U.S. court would not apply the U.S. law to such an act occurring outside the United States. Reasons for this presumption against extraterritoriality include that Congress legislates with national (not international) concerns in mind and that the presumption serves to protect against unintended clashes between our laws and those of other nations. *See EEOC*, 499 U.S. at 248; *Smith*, 507 U.S. at 204.

§ 8–2. Congressional intent to apply statute extraterritorially. As noted in the prior section, U.S. courts will apply a statute to regulate conduct outside the United States if Congress manifests an intent that the statute have such effect. Intent can be discerned by looking to "see whether 'language in the [relevant Act] gives any indication of a congressional purpose to extend its coverage beyond places over which the United States has sovereignty or has some measure of legislative control.' " *EEOC*, 499 U.S. at 248 (quoting *Foley Bros. v. Filardo*, 336 U.S. 281, 285 (1949)). For example, the Foreign Corrupt Practices Act, Pub. L. No. 95–213, 91 Stat. 1494 (1977), as amended, expressly focuses on bribery occurring outside the United States. However, this "clear manifestation" test does not require that the statute itself expressly provide for extraterritorial application. Rather, courts consider "all available evidence about the meaning" of the statute. *Sale*, 509 U.S. at 177; *see Smith*, 507 U.S. at 201–03 (examining text, structure, and legislative history of the statute).

§ 8–3. Example: East Africa Embassy Bombings. The presumption against extraterritoriality may be seen in a recent U.S. criminal law case. In 1998, two U.S. embassies in East Africa were bombed by terrorists. The United States succeeded in taking into custody several persons who had allegedly conspired in the bombings. In pre-trial proceedings, some of the defendants challenged the extraterritorial application of some of the U.S. statutes under which they were charged. Those statutes prohibited the malicious destruction by means of fire or an explosive of property owned or possessed by the United States, but the statutes were silent about whether the actions regulated were only those that occurred within U.S. territory. The court acknowledged the general presumption that U.S. laws are not applied extraterritorially, but stated that, in this instance, the presumption could be overcome. Quoting from *United States v. Bowman*, 260 U.S. 94, 98 (1922), the court said that the presumption did not apply to "criminal statutes which are, as a class, not logically dependent on their locality for the Government's jurisdiction, but are enacted because of the right of the Government to defend itself against obstruction, or fraud wherever perpetrated, especially if committed by its own nationals, officers or agents." *United States v. Bin Laden*, 92 F.Supp.2d 189, 193 (S.D.N.Y.2000). For such statutes, courts may infer the intent of Congress that the statutes are to be applied extraterritorially, because otherwise it would greatly curtail the scope and usefulness of the statute. In this case, federal criminal statutes protecting U.S. government property would be undermined if they did not apply to the extensive U.S. properties located abroad. *Cf. United States v. Mitchell*, 553 F.2d 996 (5th Cir.1977) (finding that the Marine Mammal Protection Act, 16 U.S.C. § 1372 (1994) does not criminalize a U.S. national's capture, without a U.S. permit, of a dolphin in Bahamian waters for transport to the United Kingdom).

§ 8–4. **Presumption of consistency with international law**. There is a presumption in U.S. law that an act of Congress ought never to be construed to violate the "law of nations" if any other possible construction remains. *See Murray v. The Schooner Charming Betsy*, 6 U.S. (2 Cranch) 64, 118 (1804); R. Steinhardt, *The Role of International Law as a Canon of Domestic Statutory Construction*, 43 Vand. L. Rev. 1103 (1990). Consequently, when considering whether Congress intended a statute to be applied extraterritorially, U.S. courts typically are interested in whether the statute is compatible with the extraterritorial jurisdiction of states recognized as permissible under international law.

III. PERMISSIBLE BASES OF JURISDICTION UNDER INTERNATIONAL LAW

§ 8–5. General approach of international law. Over the centuries, states have developed through their practice (and in some instances, through treaties) rules on what kinds of national jurisdiction are acceptable as a matter of international law. Generally, these rules view the permissible scope of a state's jurisdiction over persons or conduct as a function of the state's linkages with those persons or conduct. The stronger the link, the more likely the exercise of jurisdiction will be regarded as permissible.

A case often referred to in this regard is the opinion of the Permanent Court of International Justice (P.C.I.J.) in the *S.S. "Lotus" Case*, 1927 P.C.I.J. (ser. A) No. 10 (Sept. 7). In that case, France objected to Turkey's attempt to try a French merchant ship officer for criminal negligence that caused a collision between his ship and a Turkish vessel on the high seas, killing several Turkish nationals. The P.C.I.J. concluded that Turkey was free to act unless a customary prohibition *against* the exercise of jurisdiction could be found. After stating that territorial jurisdiction was a fundamental element of the sovereignty principle in the international legal system, the Court wrote:

Far from laying down a general prohibition to the effect that States may not extend the application of their laws and the jurisdiction of their courts to persons, property and acts outside their territory, it leaves them in this respect a wide measure of discretion which is only limited in certain cases by prohibitive rules; as regards other cases, every State remains free to adopt the principles which it regards as best and most suitable.

Id. at 19. The Court concluded: "All that can be required of a State is that it should not overstep the limits which international law places upon its jurisdiction; within these limits, its title to exercise jurisdiction rests in its sovereignty." *Id.*

When considering the "limits which international law places" on the exercise of jurisdiction by a state, reference typically is made to "principles" of jurisdiction that international law has come to accept in one form or another. The five principles are known as: (1) the territorial principle; (2) the nationality principle; (3) the passive personality principle; (4) the protective principle; and (5) the universality principle. Each is discussed in turn.

§ 8–6. Territorial principle. A state has absolute, but not necessarily exclusive, power to regulate conduct that occurs within its own territory. It may also act to affect interests in a *res* or the status of persons located within its territory. *See* American Law Institute, *Restatement of the Foreign Relations Law of the United States (Third)* § 402(1) (1987) (*Restatement (Third)*). This "territorial principle" reflects the global community's recognition that without the power to control acts or things located in its territory, a state could not exist. Further, other states must be able to rely on that power so as to protect their own rights and interests within that state's territory. Thus, the territorial principle in part serves to distribute competence among the members of the international community. *See The Island of Palmas Case* (Neth. v. U.S.), 2 R.I.A.A. 829, 839 (1928).

In addition, a state has jurisdiction to regulate conduct that occurs outside its territory but which has, or is intended to have, substantial *effects* within its territory. This "objective territorial" principle recognizes that, without the authority to regulate foreign-based acts that have national effects, a state could not fully protect its nationals and residents. The most controversial application of the "objective territorial" principle is to support the assertion of jurisdiction to regulate foreign-based activities that have, or threaten to have, adverse economic effects within the regulating state. For instance, in *United States v. Aluminum Co. of Am.*, 148 F.2d 416 (2d Cir.1945), the Second Circuit ruled that the Sherman Antitrust Act applied to a foreign agreement that was intended to affect the U.S. market, even though that agreement was solely between foreign companies and was performed entirely on foreign soil.

§ 8–7. Nationality principle. States may exercise jurisdiction over their nationals and over the conduct of their nationals even when those nationals or conduct are physically outside the state's territory. Thus, the Foreign Corrupt Practices Act (referred to *supra* § 8–2) expressly criminalizes certain actions by U.S. nationals and corporations even if the acts occur abroad. The justifications for this principle are that: (1) the national owes allegiance to his or her state no matter where he or she is located; (2) each state has certain responsibilities to other states for the conduct of its nationals; and (3) each state has an interest in the welfare of its nationals while they are abroad. *See generally* G. Watson, *Offenders Abroad: The Case for Nationality–Based Criminal Jurisdiction*, 17 Yale J. Int'l L. 41 (1992).

Each state has the right to determine how a person may acquire its nationality. However, to be entitled to recognition on the international plane, that nationality must be based on a genuine link between the state asserting jurisdiction and the person or entity over whom jurisdiction is asserted. *See Nottebohm Case* (Liech. v. Guat.), 1955 I.C.J. 4 (Apr. 6). As a general proposition, nationality may be acquired as the result of birth, either by being born within a state's territory (*jus soli*) or through the nationality of one's parents (*jus sanguinis*), or both. It may also be acquired by "naturalization." Naturalization can occur by voluntary application and acceptance in a formal process or as the result of marriage, adoption or the reacquisition of an original nationality by operation of law. An individual may also become a national of a state that acquires the territory on which he or she lives, although the consent of an individual is normally required before a state can impose its nationality upon that person. Individuals may also have more than one nationality, that is, they may be dual nationals. For example, one and the same person may have the nationality of state X by operation of the *jus soli* principle and of state Y under the *jus sanguinis* principle.

A corporation is deemed to have the nationality of the state where it is incorporated. *See Barcelona Traction Light & Power Co.* (Belg. v. Spain), 1970 I.C.J. 3, 168 (Feb. 5). The connection provided by the act of creation is sufficient to permit a state to exercise jurisdiction over a corporation under the nationality principle. Whether a state may treat a corporation that is *not* incorporated under its laws as its national is unclear. A genuine link must exist between the state asserting nationality and the corporation subject to the claim. *See Restatement (Third)* § 211, cmt. c. Among such links are the nationality of owners of a substantial number of the corporation's shares, location of the corporate management office (called the *siège social* or corporate seat in some continental corporate codes), or the location of a principal place of business. *See Restatement (Third)* § 213, cmt. d. In certain circumstances—e.g. where the corporation is in fact only a corporate shell—it may be treated as having the nationality of its shareholders for limited purposes. In some circumstances, a state may exercise jurisdiction over foreign branches of nationally organized corporations by virtue of its jurisdiction over the parent or home office as long as that attempted exercise is reasonable; that is, it may lift the corporate veil for these limited purposes. *See Restatement (Third)* § 414(1) & cmt. c; § 403(2).

A vessel has the nationality of the state in which it is registered and whose flag it flies, regardless of the owner's nationality. Some states, such as Liberia and Panama, permit vessel registry with few requirements, except the payment of a fee. These "flags of convenience" have been challenged in modern times on the grounds that a "genuine link" must exist between the ship and the state whose flag it flies. *See* U.N. Convention on the Law of the Sea, art. 91, *S. Treaty Doc.* 103–39 (1994). U.S. courts have held that U.S. maritime regulatory legislation will apply to ships registered in foreign states when those ships have significant contacts with the United States. *See Hellenic Lines, Ltd. v. Rhoditis*, 398 U.S. 306 (1970). The same general rules that determine the nationality of ocean vessels apply to aircraft under the Convention on International Civil Aviation, Dec. 7, 1944, 61 Stat. 1180, 15 U.N.T.S. 295.

§ 8–8. Passive personality principle. In limited circumstances, states have asserted the authority to exercise jurisdiction over acts committed abroad on the ground that they injure a national of the claiming state. The Ninth Circuit Court of Appeals has stated:

> In general, this principle has not been accepted as a sufficient basis for extraterritorial jurisdiction for ordinary torts and crimes. . . . [T]he passive personality principle has become increasingly accepted as an appropriate basis for extraterritoriality when applied to terrorist activities and organized attacks on a state's nationals because of the victim's nationality.

United States v. Vasquez–Velasco, 15 F.3d 833, 841 n. 7 (9th Cir.1994); *see generally* G. Watson, *The Passive Personality Principle*, 28 Tex. Int'l L.J. 1 (1993).

For the United States, one interesting application of the passive personality principle concerns crimes against U.S. nationals aboard foreign vessels on the high seas. Federal criminal statutes typically apply not only within U.S. territory but also within the "special maritime and territorial jurisdiction" of the United States. The Violent Crime Control and Law Enforcement Act of 1994, Pub. L. No. 103–322, § 120002, 108 Stat. 2021 (1994), extended this "special maritime jurisdiction" to include, "to the extent permitted by international law, any foreign vessel during a voyage having a scheduled departure from or arrival in the United States with respect to an offense committed by or against a national of the United States." 18 U.S.C. § 7(8) (1994). In *United States v. Roberts*, 1 F. Supp.2d 601 (E.D.La.1998), a foreign national allegedly accosted a U.S. national on a Liberian-flagged cruise ship on the high seas. The ship began and ended its cruises in the United States. The court found that it had jurisdiction over the case on the ground that international law permitted a state to apply its law to an act committed outside its territory by an alien where the victim of the act was its national. It remains to be seen whether this expansive interpretation of the passive personality principle will be followed by other courts.

§ 8–9. Protective principle. A state may exercise jurisdiction over conduct outside its territory that threatens its security (such as counterfeiting the state's money or fabricating its visa documents), as long as that conduct is generally recognized as criminal by states in the international community. *See generally* I. Cameron, *The Protective Principle of International Criminal Jurisdiction* (1994).

The protective principle has had somewhat limited use in the United States, perhaps because of a common law preference for jurisdiction tied to territorial relationships. Nevertheless, U.S. courts have invoked the protective principle, for example, to punish perjury before a U.S. consular officer abroad, *see, e.g., United States v. Pizzarusso*, 388 F.2d 8 (2d Cir.1968), to punish falsification of official U.S. documents abroad, *see, e.g., United States v. Birch*, 470 F.2d 808 (4th Cir.1972), and to punish foreign conspiracies to smuggle drugs into the United States. *See, e.g., United States v. Cardales,* 168 F.3d 548 (1st Cir.1999); *United States v. Gonzalez*, 776 F.2d 931 (11th Cir.1985); *Rivard v. United States*, 375 F.2d 882 (5th Cir.1967). In the example discussed *supra* § 8–3, the court viewed the application of U.S. criminal law to terrorist acts abroad against two U.S. embassies as most directly related to the protective principle. *See United States v. Bin Laden*, 92 F.Supp.2d 189, 193–97 (S.D.N.Y.2000).

§ 8–10. Universality principle. A state may exercise jurisdiction over conduct outside its territory if that conduct is universally dangerous to states and their nationals. The justification for this principle is that states must be permitted to punish such acts wherever they may occur as a means of protecting the global community as a whole, even absent a link between the state and the parties or the acts in question. Universal jurisdiction traditionally was asserted over the crime of piracy on the high seas and over persons engaging in the slave trade. There is growing support today for the proposition that perpetrators of genocide, crimes against humanity, and war crimes are also subject to universal jurisdiction. *See generally* K. Randall, *Universal Jurisdiction Under International Law*, 66 Tex. L. Rev. 785 (1988); *Restatement (Third)* § 404.

In addition, various types of terrorist acts may be subject to universal jurisdiction pursuant to international treaties and perhaps even under customary international law. *See* Convention for the Suppression of Unlawful Seizure of Aircraft, Dec. 16, 1970, 22 U.S.T. 1641, 860 U.N.T.S. 105; Convention for the Suppression of Unlawful Acts Against the Safety of Civil Aviation, Sept. 23, 1971, 24 U.S.T. 565, 974 U.N.T.S. 177; Convention on the Prevention and Punishment of Crimes Against Internationally Protected Persons, Including Diplomatic Agents, Dec. 14, 1973, 28 U.S.T. 1975, 1035 U.N.T.S. 167. These agreements provide that parties are obligated either to extradite offenders or submit them to prosecution, even though such offenses are not committed within the party's territory, or committed by or against its nationals.

A close analysis of the national laws of states worldwide indicates that very few have national laws that assert jurisdiction solely on the basis of the universality principle. *See* M. Bassiouni, *Univer-*

sal Jurisdiction for International Crimes, 42 Va. J. Int'l L. 81, 136–51 (2001). On the question of whether the exercise of such jurisdiction with regard to serious international crimes is permissible under international law, see the joint separate opinion by Judges Higgins, Kooijmans and Buergenthal, and the dissenting opinion by Judge *ad hoc* Van den Wyngaert in *Arrest Warrant of 11 April 2000 (Congo v. Belg.)*, 2002 I.C.J. (Feb. 14).

§ 8–11. Combinations of jurisdictional principles. More than one jurisdictional "principle" may apply in certain cases. For instance, in *United States v. King*, 552 F.2d 833 (9th Cir.1976), the defendants were prosecuted in the United States under a U.S. law that prohibited the distribution of heroin, even though the distribution occurred in Japan. The court found that the application of the law to conduct that occurred in Japan was acceptable under international law based both on the territorial principle (because the heroin was intended for importation into the United States and thus would have effects in the United States) and on the nationality principle (the defendants were U.S. nationals). In *Chua Han Mow v. United States*, 730 F.2d 1308 (9th Cir.1984), the court found on similar facts—but for conduct occurring in Malaysia by a Malaysian national—that both the territoriality principle and the protective principle applied.

§ 8–12. Discretion to exercise permissible jurisdiction. At this point, it must be emphasized that even if international law permits the exercise by a state of jurisdiction, it is wholly within the discretion of the state whether actually to do so. For instance, international law permits a state to enact legislation prohibiting its nationals from committing crimes abroad (based on the nationality principle) and many states have enacted such laws. However, under U.S. law, criminal law is principally regulated by the laws of the several states (not federal law), which in most instances are not interpreted by state courts as applying outside the territory of the state, let alone outside the United States. Consequently, when a U.S. national commits a serious crime abroad, such as murder, normally there are no means for prosecuting that person in the United States, even though international law permits the United States to do so. In short, do not confuse the existence of the five principles present in international law as *in fact* establishing jurisdiction by a particular state over persons or conduct abroad; you must also look to national law to determine whether the state has actually exercised the discretion permitted to it under international law.

§ 8–13. **Reasonability of exercising jurisdiction**. Even if a state has enacted a statute exercising jurisdiction, and that exercise of jurisdiction is permissible under one of the principles discussed above, the exercise of jurisdiction is still unlawful under international law if it is *unreasonable*. According to the *Restatement (Third)*, various factors are to be evaluated or balanced in determining whether the regulation by a state over a person or activity is unreasonable, such as "the existence of justified expectations that might be protected or hurt by the regulation," "the extent to which another state may have an interest in regulating the activity," or "the likelihood of conflict with regulation by another state." *Restatement (Third)*

§ 403(2)(d), (g) & (h); *see Timberlane Lumber Co. v. Bank of Am.,* 549 F.2d 597 (9th Cir.1976).

This "balancing" test for ascertaining reasonableness, however, was called into question by the Supreme Court in *Hartford Fire Ins. v. California,* 509 U.S. 764 (1993). In that case, the Court upheld the application of the Sherman Antitrust Act to certain conduct by insurers located in the United Kingdom. In doing so, the Court did not engage in the type of analysis envisaged in the *Restatement (Third).* Rather, the Court simply asked whether there was any direct conflict between U.S. and U.K. law. 509 U.S. at 798–799. Finding that U.K. law did not expressly prohibit companies in the U.K. from abiding by U.S. standards of antitrust law, the Court concluded that application of U.S. law was permissible. In his dissent, Justice Scalia criticized the majority for not considering the factors outlined in the *Restatement (Third). See* 509 U.S. at 814–815.

The concept of reasonableness is closely allied to the notion of comity among states. Comity is "the recognition which one nation allows within its territory to the legislative, executive or judicial acts of another nation, having due regard both to international duty and convenience, and to the rights of its own nationals or of other persons who are under the protection of its laws." *Hilton v. Guyot,* 159 U.S. 113, 164 (1895) (refusing to enforce a French judgment on grounds that France did not enforce U.S. judgments). The practical necessity of arriving at a principled method for such accommodation was stated by Justice Jackson in *Lauritzen v. Larsen,*

345 U.S. 571, 582 (1953), where he distinguished between the existence of national power and the wisdom of its exercise.

> [International law] aims at stability and order through usages which considerations of comity, reciprocity and long-range interest have developed to define the domain which each nation will claim as its own. . . . [I]n dealing with international commerce we cannot be unmindful of the necessity for mutual forbearance if retaliations are to be avoided; nor should we forget that any contact which we hold sufficient to warrant application of our law to a foreign transaction will logically be as strong a warrant for a foreign country to apply its law to an American transaction.

The comity principle is most accurately characterized as a golden rule among nations—that each should respect the laws, policies, and interests of others as it would have others respect its own in similar circumstances. In the United States, courts have resorted to the comity principle both as a rationale for refusing to apply U.S. law to foreign persons or events in situations where concurrent jurisdiction exists, and for refusing to give effect to a foreign state's law, if that state breached its duty of comity to the United States.

§ **8–14. Concurrent jurisdiction**. International law recognizes that more than one state may have jurisdiction over a particular person or event. Concurrent jurisdiction may exist because more than one state may have legitimate interests in regulating with respect to the same events or persons. Thus, if an Algerian terrorist murders a U.S. national in France, then at least three states might have national laws extending jurisdiction over the murder. France no doubt would have a statute criminalizing murder within its territory (permissible under the territorial principle); the United States might criminalize it as an act of terrorism against its nationals abroad (passive personality principle); and Algeria might have a statute criminalizing murder by its nationals abroad (nationality principle). Most U.S. courts resort to comity to determine how to balance the exercise of concurrent authority in such circumstances.

III.   JURISDICTION TO PRESCRIBE, ADJUDICATE, AND ENFORCE

Thus far, we have focused principally on the exercise of a state's jurisdiction by means of a statute. However, states can exercise jurisdiction in different ways and, depending on what aspect of jurisdiction is being exercised, the limitations under international law may differ. The *Restatement (Third)* adopts a tri-partite characterization of jurisdiction—jurisdiction to prescribe, jurisdiction to enforce and jurisdiction to adjudicate.

§ 8–15.   Jurisdiction to prescribe. The *Restatement (Third)* § 401(a) asserts that, under international law, a state is subject to limitations on its "jurisdiction to prescribe, *i.e.*, to make its law applicable to the activities, relations, or status of persons, or the interests of persons in things, whether by legislation, by executive act or order, by administrative rule or regulation, or by determination of a court." U.S. lawyers commonly refer to this type of jurisdiction as *subject matter jurisdiction*. As the *Restatement (Third)* notes, a state might seek to regulate conduct extraterritorially through enactment of a statute, but also through some other form of rule or regulation or even extension of the law through judicial decision. Regardless of the form, the same rules discussed previously in Part II of this chapter apply. The jurisdiction must fit within one of the five "principles" and the exercise of the jurisdiction must be reasonable.

§ 8–16. Jurisdiction to adjudicate. The *Restatement (Third)* § 401(b) asserts that, under international law, a state is subject to limitations on its "jurisdiction to adjudicate, *i.e.*, to subject persons or things to the process of its court or administrative tribunals, whether in civil or in criminal proceedings, whether or not the state is a party to the proceedings." U.S. lawyers commonly refer to this type of jurisdiction as *personal jurisdiction*. International law requires that a state only exercise jurisdiction to adjudicate in situations where it is reasonable to do so. The standard of reasonableness is not the same as the standard applied for jurisdiction to prescribe. It is entirely possible that international law would regard as reasonable the exercise by a state of subject matter jurisdiction over a person, but not regard as reasonable the exercise of personal jurisdiction over that person (and vice versa).

For this type of jurisdiction, international law looks to see if there is a particular link between state and the person or thing at the time the jurisdiction is asserted. Relevant links would include (1) whether the person or thing is present in the territory of the state; (2) whether the person is a national of, or domiciled or resident in, the state; and (3) whether the person, natural or juridical, has consented to the exercise of jurisdiction or has regularly carried on business in the state. *See Restatement (Third)* § 421.

U.S. lawyers become familiar with these concepts by studying the "minimum contacts" necessary when according due process to defendants under the U.S. Constitution. *See, e.g., International Shoe Co. v. Washington*, 326 U.S. 310 (1945); *Asahi Metal Indus. Co. v. Superior Court*, 480 U.S. 102 (1987). Typically, a U.S. court will (1) consider whether the plaintiff's claim arises out of or is related to the defendant's conduct within the forum state; (2) assess the defendant's contacts with the forum state to determine whether they constitute purposeful activity, such that being haled into court there would be foreseeable; and (3) look at the "forum state's interest in adjudicating the dispute; the plaintiff's interest in obtaining convenient and effective relief, at least when that interest is not adequately protected by the plaintiff's power to choose the forum; the interstate judicial system's interest in obtaining the most efficient resolution of controversies; and the shared interest of the several States in furthering fundamental substantive social policies." *World-Wide Volkswagen Corp. v. Wood-*

son, 444 U.S. 286, 292 (1980) (internal citations omitted).

§ 8–17. Jurisdiction to enforce. The *Restatement (Third)* § 401(c) asserts that, under international law, a state is subject to limitations on its "jurisdiction to enforce, *i.e.*, to induce or compel compliance or to punish noncompliance with its laws or regulations, whether through courts or by use of executive, administrative, police or other non-judicial action." Such enforcement measures include ordering the production of documents, criminal sanctions (fines or imprisonment), or sanctions for the failure to comply with a judicial or administrative order.

Generally, the limitations set by international law provide that a state must first have jurisdiction to prescribe with respect to a matter before the state seeks to enforce its law relating to that matter, whether done through its courts or otherwise (e.g., through administrative or police action). Further, international law requires that a state only exercise jurisdiction to enforce in situations where it is reasonable to do so, by measures in proportion to the violation. Finally, a state may only employ enforcement measures against a person located outside its territory if (1) the person is given reasonable notice of the claims or charges against him, (2) the person is given an opportunity to be heard, and (3) when enforcement is through a state's courts, only if the state has jurisdiction to adjudicate. *Id.*, § 431. If enforcement is to be exercised by a state's law enforcement officers, they may only exercise their functions in the territory of another state with that state's consent. *Id.*, § 432; *but see United States v. Alvarez–Machain*, 504 U.S. 655 (1992) (upholding U.S. jurisdiction over a Mexican who was forcibly abducted from Mexico and brought to the United States through an operation sponsored by the U.S. Drug Enforcement Administration).

CHAPTER 9

IMMUNITIES FROM JURISDICTION

I. INTRODUCTION

The prior chapter discussed limitations imposed by international law on the right of a state to extend its jurisdiction over persons or events that are outside the state's territory. This chapter considers further limitations on the right of a state to exercise its jurisdiction over foreign governments and officials because of the immunities they enjoy. Part II of this chapter considers the immunities accorded to *persons*, whether they be diplomatic or consular personnel of a state, persons employed by an international organization, or heads of state. Part III of this chapter deals with the immunities enjoyed by *states* (or governments). The last part of this chapter explains the "act of state doctrine". Under the act of state doctrine, courts generally refrain from passing upon the validity of a foreign government's official acts taken within its territory.

II. DIPLOMATIC AND CONSULAR IMMUNITIES

§ **9–1. Function**. A longstanding feature of the international legal system is the immunity of

foreign diplomatic personnel and property from proceedings before national courts or other authorities.
Diplomatic immunity contributes to friendly relations among states by allowing the representatives
of states to perform their functions without the risk
of being exposed to national proceedings, which in
some instances might be a form of harassment or
retaliation. In general, once a government (the
"sending state") accredits a person as a diplomat to
another government (the "receiving state"), that
person is then immune with respect to acts or
omissions in the exercise of his or her official functions and in other circumstances in which lack of
immunity would be inconsistent with diplomatic
status. The diplomat is also immune from criminal
process and from most civil process in the receiving
state. *See* American Law Institute, *Restatement of
the Foreign Relations Law of the United States
(Third)* § 464 (1987) (*Restatement (Third)*).

§ 9–2. **Diplomatic immunities**. Customary
international law governing the treatment of diplomats and diplomatic property is codified in the
Vienna Convention on Diplomatic Relations, Apr.
18, 1961, 23 U.S.T. 3227, 500 U.N.T.S. 95 (VCDR).
The VCDR has been ratified by more than 180
states as of mid–2002, including the United States.
Under the VCDR, the "person" of the diplomat is
inviolable and the receiving state has an affirmative
duty to protect each diplomat from an attack "on
his person, freedom or dignity." VCDR, art. 29. The
receiving state may neither arrest nor detain the
diplomat, and the diplomat is immune from criminal laws as well as from civil and administrative
jurisdiction (art. 31(1)). Diplomats may not be compelled to give evidence (art. 31(2)). They are also

immune from personal service (art. 35), most taxes (art. 34), social security provisions (art. 33), and customs duties and inspections (art. 36). Diplomatic immunity also extends to the diplomat's family members (art. 37).

Diplomats are not exempt from the jurisdiction of the sending state (art. 31(4)). The sending state may also expressly waive the immunity of its diplomatic personnel. An example of such a waiver of immunity is the case of Gueorgui Makharadze, a diplomat posted at the Embassy of Georgia in Washington, D.C. In January 1997, Makharadze was speeding in his car when it crashed, killing a sixteen-year-old woman and injuring four others. After reviewing the facts, the U.S. attorney's office for the District of Columbia informed the U.S. Department of State that Makharadze could be charged with negligent homicide, involuntary manslaughter, or second-degree murder. Because of his diplomatic status, however, Makharadze was immune from U.S. criminal jurisdiction. Consequently, the U.S. Department of State requested the Georgian Embassy to waive Makharadze's immunity from criminal prosecution. The Georgian government did so under VCDR Article 32. In February 1997, Makharadze was charged with one count of involuntary manslaughter and four counts of aggravated assault. In October, he pled guilty and eventually was sentenced to seven to twenty-one years in prison. After more than a year of discussions among the U.S. Department of Justice, the U.S. Department of State, and the government of Georgia, agreement was reached for Makharadze to be sent back to Georgia to serve the remainder of his term. *See* S. Murphy, *United States Practice in International Law 1999–2001* 86–88 (2002).

The VCDR also provides for the protection of diplomatic property. Under the VCDR, the physical premises of a diplomatic "mission" (meaning the embassy and other diplomatic buildings) are inviolable (art. 22). But contrary to popular belief, they are not the sovereign territory of the sending state. The receiving state has an affirmative duty to assist the sending state in obtaining all necessary facilities (art. 25) and to protect those facilities once they are established (art. 22). Additionally, the receiving state has an affirmative obligation to allow the embassy freedom of movement (art. 26) and communication (art. 27). The archives of an embassy are also inviolable (art. 24).

An example of the protection diplomatic missions enjoy is provided by a case in which a landlord sued a diplomatic mission that had fallen into arrears on its rent. Here a federal court of appeals denied the landlord the right to evict the diplomatic mission from the premises because doing so would transgress the mission's inviolability. To quote the court:

> Enforcement of an owner's common law right to obtain possession of its premises upon the tenant's non-payment of rent may not override an established rule of international law. Nor under the guise of local concepts of fairness may a court upset international treaty provisions to

which the United States is a party. The reason for this is not a blind adherence to a rule of law in an international treaty, uncaring of justice at home, but that by upsetting existing treaty relationships American diplomats abroad may well be denied lawful protection of their lives and property to which they would otherwise be entitled.

767 Third Avenue Assoc. v. Zaire, 988 F.2d 295, 296 (2d Cir.1993).

An authoritative statement of the international law on diplomatic immunity can be found in *United States Diplomatic and Consular Staff in Tehran (U.S. v. Iran)*, 1980 I.C.J. 3 (May 24). In that case, the United States accused the Iranian government of seizing the U.S. embassy and consulates in Iran and of unlawfully detaining U.S. diplomats and consular officers as hostages. In its opinion, the Court stressed repeatedly that Iran had clearly breached its obligations to the United States, under both international treaties and general international law. *Id.*, at 30–1, 37–41. Further, the Court emphasized the fundamental importance of the rules on diplomatic immunity, which could not be altered by alleged extenuating circumstances, such as Iran's claims of past U.S. wrongdoing. *Id.* at 41–42.

§ 9–3. Consular immunities. Customary international law governing the treatment of consular officers and consulates is codified in the Vienna Convention on Consular Relations, Apr. 24, 1963, 21 U.S.T. 77, 596 U.N.T.S. 261 (VCCR). The VCCR has been ratified by more than 165 states as of mid–

2002, including the United States. The VCCR prohibits the arrest or detention of consular officers except for grave crimes and under court order (art. 41). Consular officers are not subject to judicial jurisdiction "in respect of acts performed in the exercise of their consular functions" (art. 43), although they may be required to give evidence (art. 44). These privileges may be waived by the sending state (art. 45). *See Restatement (Third)* § 465 (1987).

§ **9–4. International civil servant immunities**. International civil servants employed by international organizations typically enjoy a variety of immunities. For the United Nations, the relevant multilateral treaty is the Convention on the Privileges and Immunities of the United Nations, Feb. 13, 1946, 21 U.S.T. 1418, 1 U.N.T.S. 16. That convention provides generally for immunity from personal arrest and protects papers, documents and courier bags. International civil servants are usually exempted from alien registration acts and generally have personal immunities similar to those accorded diplomats and consuls. Since the U.N. headquarters is in the United States, certain privileges and immunities are accorded by the United States pursuant to a bilateral U.S.-U.N. agreement. *See* Agreement Relating to the Headquarters of the United Nations, June 26, 1947, U.S.-U.N., 61 Stat. 3416, 11 U.N.T.S. 11 (subsequently supplemented and amended).

The International Court of Justice recently addressed the immunity of an international civil servant. In March 1994, the Chairman of the U.N. Commission on Human Rights appointed a Malaysian national, Dato' Param Cumaraswamy, as Special Rapporteur on the Independence of Judges and Lawyers. The Commission charged the Special Rapporteur with, among other things, investigating, reporting, and making recommendations concerning allegations of attacks on the independence of judges, lawyers, and court officials worldwide. As a part of this mandate, Cumaraswamy initiated an investigation into alleged judicial dependence in numerous states, including Malaysia. In November 1995, Cumaraswamy's views regarding the independence of Malaysian judges were quoted in a British magazine. Thereafter, several law suits were filed by Malaysian nationals against Cumaraswamy in Malaysian courts alleging defamation and seeking compensation. The U.N. Secretary–General informed the government of Malaysia in March 1997 that Cumaraswamy's statements were made in the course of his mission, which ensured his immunity from legal process in Malaysian courts with respect to those statements. Nevertheless, Cumaraswamy's claim to immunity was rejected by those courts. In August 1998, the U.N. Economic and Social Council requested an advisory opinion on the matter from the International Court. The Court determined that the Secretary–General had correctly found that Cumaraswamy, when providing the interview, was acting in the performance of his mission as Special Rapporteur, and was therefore immune from legal process under the Convention on the Privileges and Immunities of the United Nations. The Court further found that Malaysia had failed in its obligation under the U.N. Charter and the Convention to inform its courts of the position taken by the Secretary–General. *See Advisory Opinion on Difference Relating to Immunity from Legal Process of a Special Rapporteur of the Commission on Human Rights*, 1999 I.C.J. 62 (Apr. 29).

§ 9–5. U.S. statutory law. The United States has enacted the VCDR into federal statutory law, 22 U.S.C. § 254a–e (1994), which extends the privileges and immunities of the Convention to *all* diplomats regardless of whether the sending state is a Convention party. *Id.*, § 254b. Under the statute, the President may, on the basis of reciprocity, specify privileges and immunities for diplomats which are either more or less favorable than those specified by the Convention. *Id.*, § 254c. The United States may also require diplomatic missions to insure themselves against liability for the benefit of parties injured by diplomats. Purchasing liability insurance does not constitute a waiver of immunity under the Convention. *Id.* § 254(e). The United States implemented the provisions of the Convention on the Prevention and Punishment of Crimes Against Internationally Protected Persons, Including Diplomatic Agents in 18 U.S.C. § 112 (1994), making an attack upon diplomats a federal offense. Both statutes cover consular officials as well. The International Organizations Immunities Act, 22 U.S.C.A. §§ 288–288k (West Supp. 2001), provides protection for international civil servants and certain other persons in the United States.

§ 9–6. Head of state immunity. Separate from the immunities accorded to diplomats, consular officials, and international civil servants, international law has developed the concept of "head of state" immunity. In the United States, head of state immunity is a part of federal common law. When senior foreign officials are sued or prosecuted in U.S. courts, they will often raise head of state immunity as a defense. *See, e.g., United States v. Noriega*, 117 F.3d 1206, 1212 (11th Cir.1997) (rejecting head of state immunity for Panamanian military leader being prosecuted on drug charges); *Kadic v. Karadzic*, 70 F.3d 232, 248 (2d Cir.1995) (rejecting head of state immunity for civilian leader of Serbs in Bosnia). U.S. courts will typically defer to the executive branch's position on whether head of state immunity should be accorded. *See Noriega*, 117 F.3d at 1212. Further, such immunity may be waived by the individual's government. *See, e.g., Doe v. United States*, 860 F.2d 40, 44–46 (2d Cir. 1988) (finding no head of state immunity for former Philippine leader and his wife due to waiver by the Philippine government).

For example, several Zimbabwe nationals filed a civil action in 2000 before a New York federal court under the Torture Victim Protection Act (TVPA), 28 U.S.C. § 1350 note (1994), seeking compensatory and punitive damages. The various defendants included Zimbabwean President Robert Mugabe and Foreign Minister Stan Mudenge. The plaintiffs alleged that they or their deceased relatives had been subject to murder, torture, or other acts of violence under orders from President Mugabe as part of a widespread campaign to intimidate his political opponents. The U.S. Department of State appeared in the case and argued that Mugabe, as the head of a foreign state, was immune from the Court's jurisdiction. As precedent, the Department cited to *First Am. Corp. v. Sheikh Zayed Bin Sultan Al–Nahyan*, 948 F.Supp. 1107, 1119 (D.D.C.1996); *Alicog v. Saudi Arabia*, 860 F.Supp. 379, 382 (S.D.Tex.1994), *aff'd*, 79 F.3d 1145 (5th Cir.1996); *Lafontant v. Aristide*, 844 F.Supp. 128, 132 (E.D.N.Y.1994). The Department also asserted that Mudenge was immune from the court's jurisdiction, citing to *The Schooner Exchange v. M'Faddon*, 11 U.S. (7 Cranch) 116, 138 (1812) (Marshall, C.J.) (recognizing that, under customary international law, "the immunity which all civilized nations allow to foreign ministers" is coextensive with the immunity of the sovereign). The district court accepted the Department of State's suggestion of immunity and dismissed the action as against the two defendants. *See Tachiona v. Mugabe*, 169 F. Supp.2d 259 (S.D.N.Y.2001).

On October 16, 1998, General Augusto Pinochet, the former President of Chile, was arrested in London by U.K. authorities after a Spanish magistrate issued an international warrant seeking his detention. Spain requested the detention and sought extradition on grounds that Pinochet allegedly directed a widespread conspiracy from 1973 to 1990 to take over the government of Chile by coup and, thereafter, to reduce the state to submission through genocide, murder, torture, and the taking of hostages, primarily in Chile but elsewhere as well. On October 28, a lower U.K. court ruled that Pinochet was immune from arrest because he was a head of state at the time the alleged crimes were committed (Pinochet was in power from 1973 to 1990). *See* 38 I.L.M. 68 (1999); *see* In re *Pinochet*, 93 Am. J. Int'l L. 690 (1998). On November 25, however, the House of Lords ruled that Pinochet was not immune on such grounds, given the nature of the crimes he had allegedly committed. *See* 37 I.L.M. 1302 (1998). Thereafter, the U.K. Home Secretary certified that most of the crimes set forth in the Spanish request were extraditable crimes under the U.K. Extradition Act of 1989 (not, however, the charges of genocide), paving the way for the extradition to proceed. *See* 38 I.L.M. 489 (1999). On March 24, 1999, however, the House of Lords found that acts of torture (as well as conspiracy to commit torture) are "extraditable offenses" under the U.K. Extradition Act of 1989, only so long as they occurred after September 29, 1988, when the U.K. Criminal Justice Act entered into force establishing the crime of torture within the United Kingdom. *See* 38 I.L.M. 581 (1999). Although the seven different decisions by the judges vary in their treatment of the issues, in essence the House of Lords found that Pinochet could not be extradited for conduct that was not criminal under U.K. law at the time it occurred. Further, the House of Lords found that while Pinochet could not invoke as "official acts" under the U.K. State Immunity Act of 1978 those acts regarded as criminal under international law (such as torture), he was entitled to immunity for acts regarded as criminal only under national law. This decision significantly reduced the scope of the charges for which Pinochet could be extradited.

Ultimately, in March 2000, Pinochet was permitted to fly home to Chile because his health had deteriorated.

In October 2000, the Democratic Republic of Congo sued Belgium in the International Court of Justice, seeking the annulment of a Belgian judge's "international arrest warrant" issued for "serious violations of international humanitarian law" against Mr. Abdulaye Yerodia Ndombasi, Congo's then-Minister for Foreign Affairs. Congo asserted that a sitting foreign minister was immune from such process. In a decision issued in February 2002, the Court found that, while in office, a Minister for Foreign Affairs traveling abroad enjoys full immunity from criminal jurisdiction and inviolability. That immunity and inviolability protect the Minister against any act of authority of another State which would hinder the Minister in the performance the Minister's duties. The Court found that this rule applied even if the Minister is suspected of having committed war crimes or crimes against humanity. Consequently, the Court held that the issuance of the arrest warrant and its international circulation constituted violations of Belgium's legal obligation towards the Congo to respect such immunity. *See Arrest Warrant of 11 April 2000* (Congo v. Belg.), 2002 I.C.J. (Feb. 14), *available at* <http://www.icj-cij.org>.

III. STATE IMMUNITIES

§ 9–7. Function. As in the case of diplomatic immunities, immunities for *states* (or governments) reflect the proposition that where one sovereign has jurisdiction over the acts of another, the interests of international harmony dictate restraint by national courts and other authorities. The doctrine of sovereign immunity emerged as one of the earliest principles of international law, but there is no global treaty codifying customary international law in this area. Consequently, one must look to the national law of each state to ascertain how the principle of sovereign immunity has been implemented. Here we will focus on U.S. law dealing with this subject.

§ 9–8. **Historical development**. In the *The Schooner Exchange v. M'Faddon*, 11 U.S. (7 Cranch) 116 (1812), the U.S. Supreme Court found that a French warship in a U.S. port was immune from the jurisdiction of U.S. courts, even though the plaintiffs charged that the vessel had been illegally seized from them by France. Chief Justice John Marshall concluded that no foreign sovereign would subject itself to the absolute and exclusive power of another without an implied understanding that entry into the foreign territory included a grant of immunity from the territorial sovereign's power. This doctrine of "absolute immunity," which had its basis in principles of state sovereignty, was for centuries deemed to reflect customary international law. *See Berizzi Bros. v. Steamship Pesaro*, 271 U.S. 562 (1926).

By the 1940's, however, U.S. courts began considering situations where foreign sovereign immunity should be restricted. To ascertain the boundaries of foreign sovereign immunity, U.S. courts typically would seek a recommendation from the U.S. Department of State or, when no such recommendation was forthcoming, decide the matter based on past Department of State practice. *See, e.g., Mexico v. Hoffman*, 324 U.S. 30 (1945). The Department's views, however, were often unclear or contradictory. In an effort to regularize the Department's views, the Department's Legal Adviser in 1952 informed the Department of Justice that henceforth the Department of State would favor the theory of "restrictive" sovereign immunity (such a theory had already gained currency in various foreign states). *See The Tate Letter*, 26 State Dept. Bull. 984 (1952). Under that theory, the Department would recommend immunity only when a case involved the public acts of a foreign government (*jure imperii*), not when it involved the commercial acts of a foreign government, which could have equally been carried on by private parties (*jure gestionis*). If the State Department made no recommendation of immunity the characterization of an act as "governmental" or "commercial" was to be determined by the courts. *See, e.g., National City Bank of New York v. China*, 348 U.S. 356 (1955).

For example, in *Victory Transport, Inc. v. Comisaria General*, 336 F.2d 354 (2d Cir.1964), the Second Circuit held that the Spanish government's chartering of a ship to move surplus grain from the United States to Spain for distribution to the Spanish people was a private commercial act. Consequently, the defendant was not immune from suit to compel arbitration as required by the charter party, although it was an arm of the Spanish government. In reaching its conclusion, the court identified five categories of acts generally treated as being governmental in nature: (a) internal administrative acts, such as expulsion of an alien; (b) legislative acts, such as nationalization; (c) acts concerning the armed forces; (d) acts concerning diplomatic activity; and (e) public loans. *Id.* at 360.

Given the diplomatic pressures brought to bear on the State Department to recommend immunity in cases involving foreign sovereigns, and the political difficulties that arose when such recommendations were not made, it was virtually impossible for the Department to follow the restrictive theory consistently in determining whether to recommend immunity in specific cases. *See, e.g., Rich v. Naviera Vacuba, S.A.*, 295 F.2d 24 (4th Cir.1961). Efforts to hold administrative-style hearings to determine immunity did not alleviate the problem. Consequently, the Foreign Sovereign Immunities Act of 1976, 28 U.S.C. §§ 1330, 1332, 1391(f), 1441 (d), 1602–1611 (1994) (FSIA) was enacted to eliminate the State Department's extensive role in sovereign immunity cases in favor of the judiciary determining immunity on the basis of codified rules of law.

§ 9–9. Foreign Sovereign Immunities Act (FSIA). The FSIA provides the sole basis for obtaining jurisdiction over a foreign state in U.S. courts. *See Argentine Republic v. Amerada Hess Shipping Corp.*, 488 U.S. 428 (1989). Considerations related to subject-matter jurisdiction and personal jurisdiction are merged under the FSIA. The FSIA grants subject matter jurisdiction for "any nonjury civil action against a foreign state" in which the foreign state is not entitled to immunity (§ 1330(a)). The FSIA also grants personal jurisdiction if the court has jurisdiction under § 1330(a) and service of process has been made in accordance with the FSIA (§§ 1330(b), 1608). Actions under the FSIA may be brought initially in either state or federal court, but a foreign state is guaranteed the right to remove a civil action from state to federal courts (§ 1441). *See, e.g., Delgado v. Shell Oil Co.,* 231 F.3d 165, 176–77 (5th Cir.2000); *Davis v. McCourt,* 226 F.3d 506 (6th Cir.2000).

The definition of a "foreign state" under the FSIA includes any of its political subdivisions, agencies, or instrumentalities (§ 1603(a)). Agencies and instrumentalities are defined as any entity which is "a separate legal person, corporate or otherwise," which is either an organ of or owned by a foreign state and which is neither a national of the United States or of any third state (§ 1603(b)). *See First Nat'l City Bank v. Banco Para El Comercio Exterior de Cuba,* 462 U.S. 611, 619 (1983). However, while an agency or instrumentality may be regarded as governmental for purposes of application of the FSIA, U.S. courts nevertheless maintain a presumption of separateness between the agency/instrumentality and the government, such that the acts of the former cannot automatically be imputed to the latter. Thus, if a judgment is obtained against an instrumentality, the judgment normally can only be satisfied against the assets of that instrumentality, not against the assets of the government as a whole. Further, if sustaining a claim requires showing conduct by a government (e.g., an act of expropriation;

see infra § 9–12), then simply showing that an instrumentality engaged in the conduct will not be sufficient.

As a general matter, the FSIA recognizes immunity from U.S. jurisdiction for all foreign sovereigns (§ 1604). However, the FSIA sets forth a series of exceptions to that immunity, which are discussed below. Once a defendant presents a *prima facie* case that it is a foreign sovereign, the plaintiff has the burden of showing that, under the exceptions to the FSIA, immunity should not be granted. *See, e.g., Cabiri v. Ghana*, 165 F.3d 193 (2d Cir.1999). Further, it must be noted that the FSIA operates "subject to existing international agreements to which the United States is a party" (§ 1609). This means that the diplomatic and consular immunities of foreign states recognized under treaties such as the VCDR and VCCR (discussed *supra* sec. II) remain unaltered by the FSIA.

§ **9–10. Exception based on waiver.** A foreign state will be subject to U.S. jurisdiction if it has either impliedly or expressly waived its immunity (§ 1605(a)(1)). Once a waiver is made, it cannot be withdrawn except in a manner consistent with the terms of the waiver. An explicit waiver of immunity occurs when a foreign state waives immunity by treaty, by a contract with a private party, or by a statement by an authorized official after a dispute arises. *See, e.g., Aquamar v. Del Monte Fresh Produce*, 179 F.3d 1279 (11th Cir.1999) (giving effect to an express waiver by Ecuador's ambassador to the United States). An implicit waiver may occur when a foreign state agrees to arbitration in another state knowing that U.S. courts can compel or enforce such arbitration, or agrees that the law of another state will govern a contract. Sovereign immunity may also be waived by a failure to raise it as a defense in the first responsive pleading. *But see S & Davis Int'l v. Yemen*, 218 F.3d 1292 (11th Cir.2000) (finding that Yemen's agreement to arbitrate did not demonstrate the requisite intent to waive its sovereign immunity to suit in U.S. court).

§ 9–11. Commercial activity exception. Under the FSIA, a foreign state is not immune from the jurisdiction of U.S. courts where the plaintiff's "action is based upon a commercial activity," so long as it is carried out in, or has a direct effect in, the United States (§ 1605(a)(2)).

A "commercial" activity may be regular conduct or an individual transaction, so long as its nature, rather than its purpose, is the determining factor (§ 1603(d)). Here courts look to whether the foreign government was acting as a regulator of a market, in which case the action is not commercial, or whether it was acting in the manner of a private player within the market, in which case the action is commercial. *See Argentina v. Weltover, Inc.*, 504 U.S. 607, 614 (1992). The claim must be based on the commercial activity, rather than being merely related to it. *See, e.g., Saudi Arabia v. Nelson*, 507 U.S. 349 (1993) (finding that a government's imprisonment and alleged torture of a U.S. national is not a "commercial activity", even though the national's presence in Saudi Arabia was pursuant to an employment contract).

As for satisfaction of the "direct effect" requirement, Congress explicitly left this issue to judicial discretion on a case-by-base basis, but in a committee report offered examples of such effects: commercial transactions performed, in whole or in part, in the United States; import-export transactions involving sales to, or purchases from, concerns in the United States; business torts occurring in the United States; and an indebtedness incurred by a foreign state which negotiates or executes a loan agreement in the United States. *See H.R. Rep.* 94–1487, at 15 (1976).

For example, in *Lyon v. Agusta S.P.A.*, 252 F.3d 1078 (9th Cir.2001), two U.S. nationals were killed in 1993 when an airplane designed, manufactured, or owned by certain Italian companies—which were instrumentalities of the government of Italy—crashed in Santa Monica, California. When their survivors brought suit, the Italian companies moved to dismiss the action on the basis of immunity under the FSIA. The Ninth Circuit Court of Appeals found that the companies' acts of designing, manufacturing and owning the airplanes was in connection with a commercial activity, and while that activity was outside the territory of the United States, it caused a direct effect in the United States by resulting in an accident. As such, the requirements of the FSIA exception were met, and the case should not be dismissed.

By contrast, in *Butters v. Vance Int'l, Inc.*, 225 F.3d 462 (4th Cir.2000), a female former employee of a U.S. security corporation sued the corporation

for gender discrimination, principally on grounds
that she was denied a promotion as a security guard
for a Saudi princess because she was not allowed to
serve a full rotation at a particular command post.
Apparently, Saudi officials instructed the U.S. security corporation that such a rotation was unaccepta-
ble under Islamic law and that it was inappropriate
for male officers to spend long periods of time in a
command post with a woman present. The Fourth
Circuit Court of Appeals found that since the U.S.
corporation was following Saudi government orders,
the corporation was "entitled to derivative immunity under the FSIA." *Id.* at 466. The plaintiff invoked the commercial activity exception, but the
court found that "a foreign sovereign's decision as
to how best to secure the safety of its leaders ... is
quintessentially an act 'peculiar to sovereigns'"
and thus not commercial in nature. *Id.* at 465.
Other acts characterized as governmental include
the granting and revocation of a license to export a
natural resource, *see MOL, Inc. v. Bangladesh*, 736
F.2d 1326 (9th Cir.1984), and the supervision of an
office and personnel by an international health organization. *See Tuck v. Pan Am. Health Org.*, 668
F.2d 547 (D.C.Cir.1981).

§ 9–12. Expropriation exception. A foreign state is not immune from the jurisdiction of
U.S. courts in an action "in which rights in property taken in violation of international law are at
issue and that property ... is present in the United
States in connection with a commercial activity
carried on in the United States by the foreign
state" (§ 1605(a)(3)). Thus, this exception contem-

plates suits involving property that was nationalized or expropriated by a foreign government without compensation, so long as there is a nexus with a commercial activity in the United States.

An example of this exception is provided by *Zappia Middle East Constr. Co. v. Abu Dhabi*, 215 F.3d 247 (2d Cir.2000). From 1979 to 1982, Zappia Middle East Construction Company (ZMEC) entered into eight public works construction contracts with an instrumentality of the emirate of Abu Dhabi (of the United Arab Emirates) that required periodic payments by the emirate. Ultimately, ZMEC filed suit in U.S. court alleging that the emirate forced ZMEC to "perform work outside the contracts ... and delayed making payments," requiring ZMEC to borrow funds from the Emirates Commercial Bank on unfavorable terms. Moreover, ZMEC alleged that the emirate would not allow ZMEC employees to leave the emirate, and threatened ZMEC's owner with imprisonment. ZMEC asserted that the U.S. court had jurisdiction under the expropriation exception to sovereign immunity contained in the FSIA.

The Second Circuit Court of Appeals noted that to satisfy the expropriation exception, a plaintiff must show that: (1) rights in the property are in issue; (2) the property was "taken"; (3) the taking was in violation of international law; and (4) the entity that took the property was a foreign government. The court then rejected ZMEC's argument, finding that, while the acts alleged were taken by the emirate's instrumentality, there is a presumption of separateness between the instrumentality and the emirate such that the acts of the former cannot automatically be imputed to the latter (*see supra* § 9–9). Since the plaintiff had failed to overcome this presumption, there could be no expropriation by the emirate's instrumentality. The emirate's refusal to pay ZMEC under the construction contracts did not constitute expropriation because "breach of a commercial contract alone does not constitute a taking pursuant to international law." *Id.* at 252. With respect to whether the emirate itself engaged in expropriation, the court noted that the government at no point seized control of ZMEC.

§ **9–13. Tort exception**. A state is not immune from tort actions involving money damages where the tort occurred in the United States, including actions for personal injury, death, and loss or damage to property caused by a tortious act or omission of the foreign state or its agents (§ 1605(a)(5)). A state will remain immune, however, if the tort claim is based upon the discharge of a discretionary function, or if it arises from "malicious prosecution, abuse of process, libel, slander, misrepresentation, deceit or interference with contract rights" (§ 1605(a)(5)(A) & (B)). Although the exception is cast in terms sufficiently general to make it applicable to a variety of situations, the legislative history suggests that the provision was intended to address traffic accidents caused by automobiles operated by foreign embassy personnel. *See Persinger v. Iran*, 729 F.2d 835, 840 (D.C.Cir.1984).

It must be stressed that the exception "is limited by its terms ... to those cases in which the damage to or loss of property occurs *in the United States.*" *Argentine Republic v. Amerada Hess Shipping Corp.,* 488 U.S. 428, 439 (1989) (emphasis in original). The "United States" includes "all territories and waters, continental or insular, subject to the jurisdiction of the United States" (§ 1603(c)). U.S. embassies located abroad are not within this exception because the ground on which an embassy stands remains the territory of the receiving state. *See McKeel v. Iran,* 722 F.2d 582, 588 (9th Cir. 1983).

§ **9–14. Exception for arbitration**. A foreign state is not immune from the jurisdiction of U.S. courts in any case where the action is brought to enforce an agreement made by the foreign state with a private party to submit to arbitration differences which may arise with respect to a defined legal relationship, whether contractual or not, concerning a subject matter capable of settlement by arbitration under U.S. law, or to confirm an award made pursuant to such an arbitration (§ 1605 (a)(6)). *See, e.g., Creighton Ltd. v. Qatar,* 181 F.3d 118 (D.C.Cir.1999).

§ **9–15. Terrorist state exception**. This exception to immunity permits civil suits for monetary damages against foreign states that cause personal injury or death "by an act of torture, extrajudicial killing, aircraft sabotage, hostage taking, or the provision of material support or resources . . . for such an act" (§ 1605 (a)(7)). Under this exception, the claimant or victim must have been a U.S. national when the terrorist act occurred and the state must be one designated by the Secretary of State as a sponsor of terrorism. As of mid–2002, the State Department had designated Cuba, Iran, Iraq, Libya, North Korea, Syria, and Sudan as terrorist states. When enacting this exception, Congress also passed a civil liability statute creating a cause of action against an agent of a foreign state that acts under the conditions specified in the new FSIA exception. *See* 28 U.S.C.A. § 1605 note (Law Co-op. Supp. 1999). The civil liability statute provided that the agent shall be liable for "money damages which may include economic damages, solatium, pain and suffering, and punitive damages."

Since enactment of this exception in 1996, numerous cases have been filed by U.S. nationals against terrorist-listed states. For example, on April 9, 1995, a suicide bomber drove a van loaded with explosives into a bus passing through the Gaza Strip, killing seven Israeli soldiers and one U.S. national, a twenty-year-old college student spending a semester abroad in Israel. The Shaqaqi faction of Palestine Islamic Jihad—a terrorist group funded by the government of Iran—claimed responsibility for the explosion. The deceased's father, Stephen M. Flatow, sued Iran, invoking the FSIA terrorist-state exception. On March 11, 1998, a U.S. court found that Iran was not immune from suit and was responsible for the death of Michelle Flatow. The district court held the Iran and its officials jointly and severally liable for compensatory and punitive damages in an amount of US $247 million. *See Flatow v. Iran*, 999 F.Supp. 1 (D.D.C.1998); *see also Alejandre v. Cuba*, 996 F.Supp. 1239, 1253 (S.D.Fla.

1997); *Daliberti v. Iraq*, 97 F. Supp.2d 38 (D.D.C. 2000).

§ 9–16. Counterclaims exception. If a foreign state brings an action in U.S. court, the foreign state is not immune from the jurisdiction of U.S. courts for any counterclaim arising out of the same transaction or occurrence that is the subject of its own claim, to the extent that the counterclaim does not seek relief exceeding the amount sought by the foreign state (§ 1607). For example, in *Cabiri v. Ghana*, 165 F.3d 193 (2d Cir.1999), the government of Ghana sued in U.S. court to evict the family of Bawol Cabiri (a former Ghana government employee) from their New York home, which they had obtained as part of his employment contract. Cabiri counterclaimed for, among other things, breach of his employment contract. The government of Ghana asserted that it was immune from suit under the FSIA. The Second Circuit Court of Appeals, however, held that Cabiri's breach of contract claim was permissible since "the breach of contract claim arises out of the same transactions as the eviction proceeding: Cabiri's employment contract and his termination." *Id.* at 196. As such, the government of Ghana was not immune from suit.

§ 9–17. Extent of liability. If a foreign state is not entitled to immunity from jurisdiction, it is generally liable to the same extent as if it were a private party (§ 1606). *See State Bank of India v. NLRB*, 808 F.2d 526 (7th Cir.1986). However, a foreign state will only be subject to punitive damages in two circumstances. First, punitive damages may be awarded for cases falling under the terrorist-state exception. Second, punitive damages may be awarded in a wrongful death action where the law of the state in which the act occurred provides only punitive damages. *See, e.g., Harris v. Polskie Linie Lotnicze*, 820 F.2d 1000 (9th Cir.1987).

§ 9–18. Attachment and execution. Even if a foreign state is not immune from suit in U.S. courts, its assets are generally presumed to be immune from attachment or execution (§ 1609), unless two conditions are met. First, the property must be in use for commercial purposes. Thus, diplomatic and consular properties are generally immune from attachment and execution. *See City of Englewood v. Libya*, 773 F.2d 31, 36–37 (3d Cir. 1985) (finding that although the purchase of certain property was a commercial transaction, its use as a diplomatic residence "as a matter of law . . . is not commercial activity"). Second, the attachment and execution must fit within one of several secondary requirements contained in FSIA § 1610. Those requirements largely parallel the exceptions to immunity contained in § 1605. Thus, a claimant may attach or execute against property of a foreign government if that government has waived its immunity from attachment or execution, *see, e.g., Venus Lines Agency v. CVG Industria Venezolana De Aluminio*, 210 F.3d 1309 (11th Cir.2000), or if the attachment and execution is based upon an order confirming an arbitral award. *See, e.g., Lloyd's Underwriters v. AO Gazsnabtranzit*, 2000 WL 1719493, at *1 (N.D.Ga.2000). Further, legislation enacted in October 2000 provides special opportunities for certain claimants holding judgments against terrorist states, allowing those claimants to execute against certain assets of the foreign state, but also to obtain compensation from the U.S. Treasury in the event that such assets are not available. *See* Pub. L. No. 106–386, § 2002, 114 Stat. 1464, 1541–43 (2000).

However, even if the property is used for commercial purposes and one of the secondary requirements is met, the property still remains immune if it is used for the purposes of the government's central bank or its military (§ 1611). *See, e.g., Olympic Chartering v. Ministry of Indus. & Trade of Jordan,* 134 F. Supp.2d 528 (S.D.N.Y.2001).

IV.   ACT OF STATE DOCTRINE

§ 9–19.   Act of state doctrine generally. The act of state doctrine is essentially a rule of judicial self-restraint that has developed in the United States and in many other states in one form or another. *See Restatement (Third)* § 443, rptrs. n. 12. Under this rule, U.S. courts generally decline to "sit in judgment" on the acts of a foreign government when those acts are taken within the foreign government's territory. The principal motivation for this self-restraint appears to be a desire that disputes involving the acts of foreign governments in their own territories are best resolved through diplomatic means, not through litigation in national courts. *See generally Oppenheim's International Law* 365–71 (9th ed., R. Jennings & A. Watts, eds., 1992).

An early application of this doctrine in the United States is *Underhill v. Hernandez,* 168 U.S. 250 (1897). In 1982, revolution broke out in Venezuela, during which one of the revolutionary leaders, General Hernandez, assumed control of the city of Bolivar (eventually the revolution succeeded in setting up a new Venezuelan government recognized by the United States). A U.S. national, Underhill, wished to leave the city, but was prevented by Hernandez because Underhill had constructed the city's waterworks and was needed to help operate the system. Eventually Underhill was able to leave Venezuela. Upon his return to the United States, he sued Hernandez in the United States for violations of Venezuelan tort law. The U.S. Supreme Court affirmed dismissal of the case based on the act of state doctrine.

> Every sovereign state is bound to respect the independence of every other sovereign state, and the courts of one country will not sit in judgment on the acts of the government of another done within its own territory. Redress of grievances by reason of such acts must be obtained through the means open to be availed of by sovereign powers as between themselves.

Id. at 252. Later cases either suggested that the doctrine was required by principles of comity, *see, e.g., Oetjen v. Central Leather Co.*, 246 U.S. 297 (1918); *Ricaud v. American Metal Co.*, 246 U.S. 304 (1918), or treated it as a special choice of law rule. *See, e.g., American Banana Co. v. United Fruit Co.*, 213 U.S. 347 (1909).

Since the act of state doctrine is frequently involved in cases involving foreign governments in U.S. courts, discussion of the doctrine is often grouped with discussion of sovereign immunity. It must be emphasized, however, that the act of state doctrine can be relevant in *any case* where the validity of a foreign government's act, taken in its own territory, is at issue. Such cases may arise when the foreign government itself is not a party. Thus, if a foreign government issues a decree ordering that certain property be transferred within its territory from John to Jane, if John sues Jane in a U.S. court to recover the property, Jane may raise as one of her defenses the act of state doctrine. By contrast, sovereign immunity issues arise only in cases in which one of the parties is alleged to be a foreign government or one of its instrumentalities.

§ **9–20.** *Sabbatino* **case**. A landmark decision in the U.S. Supreme Court on the act of state doctrine is *Banco Nacional de Cuba v. Sabbatino*, 376 U.S. 398 (1964). In that case, the Cuban government had nationalized a company in which U.S. investors had an interest. A U.S. commodities broker had contracted to purchase a shipload of sugar from the company. After the nationalization, the broker entered into a new agreement to buy the sugar from the Cuban government. After gaining possession of the shipping documents (and thus of the sugar), the broker made payment not to the Cuban government, but to the U.S. investors. Banco Nacional de Cuba sued in U.S. court to obtain possession of the funds. The broker defended on the grounds that title to the sugar never passed to Cuba because the expropriation violated international law.

While lower U.S. courts held that the act of state doctrine did not apply because the taking was in violation of international law, the Supreme Court stated that the adjudication of this claim risked serious embarrassment to the executive branch because the international law concerning the compensation for expropriation was unclear. Justice Harlan summarized the holding as follows:

> . . . [w]e decide only that the Judicial Branch will not examine the validity of a taking of property within its own territory by a foreign sovereign government, extant and recognized by this country at the time of suit, in the absence of a treaty or other unambiguous agreement regarding controlling legal principles, even if the complaint alleges that the taking violated customary international law.

376 U.S. at 428; *see Restatement (Third)* § 443 (1987).

§ 9–21. Exceptions to the doctrine. Since the act of state doctrine has evolved in the United States principally through judicial decisions, the exact contours of the doctrine are not clear. In several cases, the courts have declared that there are certain situations where the act of state doctrine should not be applied. It must be noted, however, that U.S. decisions are not consistent in interpreting and applying these exceptions. *See generally* M. Ramsey, *Acts of State and Foreign Sovereign Obligations*, 39 Harv. Int'l L.J. 1 (1998); M. Bazyler, *Abolishing the Act of State Doctrine*, 134 U. Pa. L. Rev. 325 (1986).

§ 9–22. Exception when Congress so directs. U.S. courts will not apply the act of state doctrine when they are directed by statute not to do so. Shortly after the Supreme Court's decision in *Sabbatino*, Congress passed the "Second Hickenlooper Amendment" to the Foreign Assistance Act of 1964, 22 U.S.C. § 2370(e)(2) (1994), which provides:

> [N]o court in the United States shall decline on the ground of the federal act of state doctrine to make a determination on the merits giving effect to principles of international law in a case in which a claim of title or other rights to property is asserted by any party including a foreign state ... based upon ... a confiscation or other taking after January 1, 1959, by an act of that state in violation of the principles of international law....

This statute in effect reversed the Supreme Court's decision in *Sabbatino*, with the result that on remand the lower court found the Cuban taking to be invalid. *See Banco Nacional de Cuba v. Farr*, 383 F.2d 166 (2d Cir.1967). Subsequent cases have construed the *Sabbatino* Amendment narrowly to limit its effect to situations where the property whose title is in dispute is physically present in the United States (e.g., the funds from the sale of the sugar). Congress has also directed that the act of state doctrine not be applied to refuse the enforcement of arbitral agreements, the confirmation of arbitral awards, or the execution upon judgments based on orders confirming arbitral awards. *See* 9 U.S.C. § 15 (1994).

§ 9–23. Exception when State Department so advises. In *Bernstein v. Van Heyghen*

Freres, 163 F.2d 246 (2d Cir.1947), Judge Learned Hand applied the act of state doctrine so as not to pass upon the validity of the coercive taking of property from the Jewish plaintiff by Nazi officials (even though the war against Germany was over and the Nazis were no longer in power). In a later identical case, the State Department informed the court by letter that U.S. foreign relations did not require judicial abstention in cases involving Nazi confiscations. Consequently, the court did not apply the act of state doctrine. *See Bernstein v. Nederlandsche–Amerikaansche Stoomvaart–Maatschappij*, 210 F.2d 375 (2d Cir.1954). Under this so-called "*Bernstein* exception," the act of state doctrine is not applied when the State Department explicitly indicates to the court that such application is not required for the conduct of U.S. foreign relations. Whether the *Bernstein* exception is fully accepted by the U.S. Supreme Court, however, is unclear. In *First Nat'l City Bank v. Banco Nacional de Cuba*, 406 U.S. 759 (1972), the Supreme Court considered whether to adjudicate the validity of a Cuban taking of Citibank's property as part of a counterclaim. The Department of State wrote to the Court that the act of state doctrine need not apply. While a majority of the Court found the doctrine inapplicable, only a minority was willing to recognize the *Bernstein* exception and to regard the Executive's statement as conclusive on the matter. *See also Alfred Dunhill of London, Inc. v. Republic of Cuba*, 425 U.S. 682 (1976).

§ **9–24. Treaty exception**. In *Kalamazoo Spice Extraction Co. v. Ethiopia*, 729 F.2d 422 (6th Cir.1984), the court was asked to decide a counterclaim by a U.S. defendant for the expropriation of his property by the revolutionary government of Ethiopia. The Treaty of Amity and Economic Relations, Sept. 7, 1951, U.S.-Eth., 4 U.S.T. 2134, 206 U.N.T.S. 41, included a standard of "prompt payment of just and effective compensation" in the event that one party expropriated property belonging to nationals of the other. The district court applied the act of state doctrine and dismissed the case. Before the appeal was heard, the Department of State transmitted a letter to the Sixth Circuit stating: "When, as in this case, there is a controlling legal standard for compensation, we believe that adjudication would not be inconsistent with foreign policy interests under the Act of State Doctrine." On appeal, the Sixth Circuit accepted the position expressed in the letter that the treaty exception applied. It is not clear whether the courts will apply the "treaty exception" without first receiving the government's position. This exception appears to reflect the proposition advanced in *Sabbatino* that the act of state doctrine is appropriate when there is insufficient consensus on the applicable international law rule, but not appropriate where such consensus exists, for example, in a treaty.

§ 9–25. Exception for extraterritorial government action. The act of state doctrine does not apply where the foreign government act seeks to affect property located outside the government's territory. *See Iraq v. First Nat'l City Bank*, 353 F.2d 47 (2d Cir.1965). Situs questions become particularly important in cases involving actions against intangibles, such as credits, debts or securities.

§ **9–26. Exception for commercial activities**. In *Alfred Dunhill of London, Inc. v. Republic of Cuba*, 425 U.S. 682 (1976), three justices argued that the act of state doctrine did not apply to a foreign sovereign's commercial acts, even though those acts were done within its own territory. According to those justices, such acts are incapable of examination in U.S. courts only if U.S. jurisdiction over the conduct is limited under international jurisdictional principles. *See supra* ch. 8.

§ **9–27. Exception where validity of act is not in question**. In *W.S. Kirkpatrick & Co., Inc. v. Environmental Tectonics Corp.*, 493 U.S. 400 (1990), the plaintiff was an unsuccessful bidder on a contract with the government of Nigeria. The defendant was the successful bidder, who had allegedly bribed a government of Nigeria official in order to get the contract, in violation of U.S. law. The Supreme Court declined to apply the act of state doctrine, saying that the question before it was not whether to "declare invalid the official act of a foreign sovereign performed within its own territory." Rather, the issue before the court was whether an unlawful motivation could be imputed to a foreign official in the performance of his duties so as to satisfy U.S. requirements for a civil recovery by the plaintiff against the defendant. *Id.* at 405.

§ **9–28. Exception for counterclaims**. In *First Nat'l City Bank v. Banco Nacional de Cuba*, 406 U.S. 759 (1972), noted *supra* § 9–23, the foreign government had filed a claim and a U.S. national had responded with a counterclaim. The foreign government raised the act of state doctrine as a defense to the counterclaim. The Supreme Court declined to apply the doctrine. One justice, Justice Douglas, took the position that the act of state doctrine should not be applied to counterclaims. *Id.* at 773–74 (citing to *National City Bank v. China*, 348 U.S. 356 (1955)). None of the other justices, however, found that issue dispositive.

§ 9–29. Exception for human rights cases. U.S. courts usually do not apply the act of state doctrine so as to dismiss cases alleging human rights violations by a foreign government in its territory. *See, e.g., Forti v. Suarez–Mason*, 672 F.Supp. 1531, 1544–47 (N.D.Cal.1987) (finding that the act of state doctrine does not bar an action for torture abroad brought under the Alien Tort Claims Act, 28 U.S.C. § 1350 (1994)). When enacting the Torture Victim Protection Act, 28 U.S.C. § 1350 note (1994)—which provides a civil remedy to persons who suffer torture or extrajudicial killing by, or under authority of, a foreign government—a Congressional committee indicated that it did not intend the act of state doctrine to apply to such claims. *S. Rep. No.* 102–249, at 8 (1991).

CHAPTER 10

LAW OF THE SEA

I. INTRODUCTION

Until the 1950's, the basic principles of the law of the sea had their source in customary international law. In 1958, the United Nations convened the first U.N. Conference on the Law of the Sea (UNCLOS I), which succeeded in adopting four conventions on: (1) the territorial sea and contiguous zone; (2) the high seas; (3) the continental shelf; and (4) fishing and conservation of living resources of the high seas. While the first three conventions were ratified by numerous states (including the United States) and have come to be regarded as reflecting customary international law, the fourth convention (as well as an optional protocol on dispute settlement) obtained much less adherence.

UNCLOS I was a considerable success, but it failed to resolve certain very important issues concerning the law of the sea, such as the breadth of the territorial sea. Consequently, the United Nations convened a second conference (UNCLOS II) in 1960, but insufficient time had passed to allow states to resolve their differences, and the conference failed.

In 1973, the third U.N. Conference on the Law of the Sea (UNCLOS III) was convened. In 1982, the conference adopted the U.N. Convention on the Law of the Sea (LOSC). During the two-year period that it was open for signature, 159 states signed the convention, but several major industrialized states (including Germany, the United Kingdom, and the United States) did not. Those states were principally concerned with provisions in Part XI of the convention for administering the resources of the deep sea-bed (discussed *infra* § 10–7). After a 1994 "implementation" agreement radically modified Part XI, most industrialized states ratified the LOSC. As of mid–2002, the U.S. Senate had not yet granted advice and consent to ratification. The United States, however, has indicated that many of the LOSC's provisions reflect customary international law. For the transmittal by the President to the Senate of the convention and the agreement relating to Part XI, see *S. Treaty Doc.* 103–39 (1994).

Under the LOSC, and associated customary rules, the law of the sea is largely organized based on certain major maritime zones (part II below), as well as on certain functional uses of the sea (part III). For further background on the history and development of the law of the sea, see D. O'Connell, *The International Law of the Sea* (1982) (two vols.); R. Churchill & A. Lowe, *The Law of the Sea* (3d ed. 1999).

II. MAJOR MARITIME ZONES

The seas cover about seventy percent of the Earth's surface. Much of the contemporary law of the sea can be understood through reference to rules that apply within certain maritime zones. As a general matter, zones closer to the state's coast envisage higher levels of coastal state sovereignty or control over activities within the zone, whereas zones further from coast envisage lesser coastal state control.

§ 10–1. Baselines and internal waters. The starting point for establishing the maritime zones are the "baselines." The baselines of a state serve dual functions. They demarcate the state's internal waters from external waters. They also provide the lines from which the outer limits of maritime zones will be measured. Thus, all waters of a state that are landward of its baselines are internal waters and are treated virtually as if they were part of the state's land territory. Waters seaward of a state's baselines are subject to the law of the sea.

LOSC Article 5 provides that "the normal baseline for measuring the breadth of the territorial sea is the low-water line along the coast as marked on large-scale charts officially recognized by the coastal State." This general rule works well for coasts that are relatively smooth. However, the general rule is less useful for states that have extensive indentations in their coasts or that are fringed with islands, because it is very cumbersome and confusing to ascertain the location of the maritime zones measured from those highly irregular features. More-over, the general rule is unhelpful in dealing with natural features commonly found along coasts, such as bays, river mouths, islands, low-tide elevations, or reefs. The LOSC has developed special rules for drawing baselines with respect to those natural features, as well as artificial harbors.

For instance, to handle coasts that are deeply indented, the LOSC allows a state to draw a series of straight lines using the outermost points along the coast. However, there are limits to how a state may draw such "straight baselines." LOSC Article 7(3) provides that these straight baselines "must not depart to any appreciable extent from the general direction of the coast, and the sea areas lying within the lines must be sufficiently closely linked to the land domain to be subject to the régime of internal waters." Further, Article 7(4) provides that straight baselines "shall not be drawn to and from low-tide elevations, unless lighthouses or similar installations which are permanently above sea level have been built upon them" or where doing so has received "general international recognition." Article 7(5) provides that "account may be taken ... of economic interests peculiar to the region concerned, the reality and the importance of which are clearly evidenced by long usage." These rules emerged in large part from the International Court of Justice's decision in *Fisheries Case* (U.K. v. Nor.), 1951 I.C.J. 116 (Dec. 18). *See* C. Waldock, *The Anglo–Norwegian Fisheries Case*, 28 Brit. Y.B. Int'l L. 114 (1951). Such rules, however, are inherently flexible, allowing states considerable latitude when drawing straight baselines. *See generally* J. Roach & R. Smith, *United States Responses to Excessive Maritime Claims* (2d. ed. 1996).

As noted above, once baselines are established, the waters landward of the baselines are internal waters. The coastal state enjoys full territorial sovereignty over its internal waters, with the exception that there is a right of innocent passage (*see infra* § 10–2) through waters enclosed by a straight baseline that previously had not been considered internal waters. LOSC, art. 8(2). There is no right generally under international law for foreign vessels to enter a state's internal waters. *See Military and Paramilitary Activities in and Against Nicaragua* (Nicar. v. U.S.), 1986 I.C.J. 14, para. 213 (June 27). At the same time, the international ports of a state are presumed to be open to international non-military vessels, subject to whatever conditions for entry that may be set by the state. Further, customary international law and various treaties (such as treaties of friendship, commerce, and navigation) contemplate a right of entry to a port when a vessel is in distress.

Once a foreign vessel is in a state's internal waters, it is exposed to that state's criminal and civil jurisdiction. Thus, a merchant vessel visiting at a port may be seized for customs violations and is exposed to actions *in rem* against the ship. In practice, coastal states do not exercise jurisdiction over matters that concern a foreign vessel's internal activities (such as the theft by one crew member from another) but, rather, leave such matters to authorities on the vessel or of the state which granted the vessel the right to sail under its flag (the "flag state"). *See supra* § 8–7. Coastal states will exercise their jurisdiction, however, when requested by the captain or the flag state, or over matters that affect the peace or good order of the port. *See Wildenhus's Case*, 120 U.S. 1 (1886). On the subject generally, see V. Degan, *Internal Waters*, 17 Neth. Y.B. Int'l L. 3 (1986).

§ **10–2. Territorial sea**. When the law of the sea first emerged, there were disagreements about whether the high seas should be subject to state sovereignty or should be free to navigation and use by all. Yet, even then, there was a general consensus that coastal states enjoyed some rights to regulate activities in seas immediately adjacent to their coasts. Differences of view concerning this "territorial sea" zone focused not on its existence, but on (1) its breadth, (2) the nature of coastal state's rights in the zone, and (3) the right of the vessels of other states to pass through the zone. With the LOSC, considerable consensus has formed on these three points.

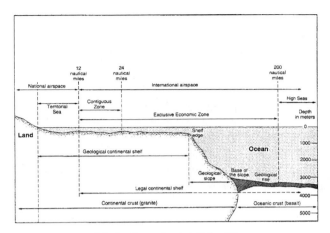

Law of the Sea Convention Jurisdictional Zones

With respect to the breadth of the territorial sea, many states initially advocated that the territorial sea extend up to a point at which the sea could be controlled by shore-based cannons, which was a distance of approximately three nautical miles. This "cannon-shot" rule garnered widespread but never uniform acceptance; Scandinavian states, for example, consistently maintained that their territorial sea extended four nautical miles. By the final stages of the LOSC negotiations, states were able to reach consensus on a wider breath for a territorial sea, driven in large part by a desire of all states to have full sovereign control over fishing and pollution occurring near their coasts. LOSC Article 3 provides that a coastal state may claim a territorial sea extending no more than twelve nautical miles from its baselines. President Ronald Reagan proclaimed such a zone for the United States in 1988. *See*

Proclamation 5928 of December 27, 1988, 54 Fed. Reg. 777 (Jan. 9, 1989).

With respect to the coastal state's rights in the territorial sea, the LOSC provides that its sovereignty extends beyond its land territory and internal waters to the territorial sea, subject to the provisions of the LOSC and other rules of international law, such as rules on sovereign and diplomatic immunities. LOSC, arts. 2(1) & (3). The coastal state's sovereignty extends not just to the waters, but also to the airspace above the waters and to the sea-bed and subsoil below the waters (art. 2(2)). While the coastal state has extensive control over the territorial sea, it may not (1) legislate so as to hamper or levy charges on vessels engaged in "innocent passage" (art. 24(1)); (2) enforce its laws over crimes committed on a vessel except in limited circumstances (art. 27); and (3) arrest a vessel in connection with liabilities not incurred in connection with its voyage through the territorial sea (art. 28). Further, while the coastal state has extensive rights in the territorial sea, it also has duties to foreign vessels which enter the territorial sea, such as to buoy and mark channels, to keep navigable waters clear, and to provide rescue services (arts. 22(1) & 24(2)). *See Fisheries Jurisdiction* (U.K. v. Ice.), 1973 I.C.J. 3, 24 at para. 8, n. 8 (separate opinion of Judge Fitzmaurice).

With respect to the entry by foreign vessels into the territorial sea, a right of "innocent passage" was generally accepted early in the development of the law of the sea. As codified in the LOSC, "passage" means passing through the territorial sea in a continuous and expeditious manner. Such passage, however, includes stopping and anchoring when doing so is incidental to ordinary navigation or is compelled by distress (art. 18). The LOSC provides furthermore that "innocent" passage means passage that "is not prejudicial to the peace, good order or security of the coastal state" (art. 19(1)). At the same time, the LOSC enumerates a series of activities that are considered not to be innocent, such as engaging in weapons practice, spying, propaganda, wilful and serious pollution, fishing, and "any other activity not having a direct bearing on passage" (art. 19(2)). This list suggests a more objective standard, whereby the specific activity serves as the touchstone for innocence, and not the coastal state's interpretation of that activity. At the same time, the final item in the list appears to sweep within it all activities not having a "direct bearing on passage," even if that activity is not prejudicial to the coastal state, thus potentially severely diminishing the right of innocent passage. In an effort to avoid such implication, the United States and the Soviet Union in 1989 issued a "uniform interpretation" of international law governing innocent passage in which they stated that the LOSC sets out "an exhaustive list of activities that would render passage not innocent." 28 I.L.M. 1444, para. 3 (1989).

Vessels not engaged in innocent passage may be excluded from a state's territorial sea. Further, "[t]he coastal State may, without discrimination ... among foreign ships, suspend temporarily in specified areas of its territorial sea the innocent passage of foreign ships if such suspension is essential for the protection of its security, including weapons exercises" (art. 25(3)). The LOSC does not *expressly* address the issue of innocent passage by warships through the territorial sea. The Convention grants a right of innocent passage to the "ships of all States" without distinction between military and non-military vessels (art. 17), and it contemplates specific rules relating to innocent passage by submarines (which are presently all warships) (art. 20). Nevertheless, some forty states require foreign warships to obtain authorization before entering their territorial sea. In the U.S.-Soviet "uniform interpretation" referred to above, those two states agreed that all ships, including warships, enjoy the right of innocent passage. 28 I.L.M. 1444, para. 2 (1989).

§ **10–3. Contiguous zone**. Prior to the modern law of the sea codification, some states claimed a jurisdictional zone outside their territorial sea, usually for customs and security purposes. For example, during the alcohol prohibition era in the United States (1920–33), the United States enforced its prohibition laws against foreign vessels hovering just outside the U.S. territorial sea, as a means of preventing them from "running whiskey" into the United States at night or when the "coast was clear". *See Schroeder v. Bissell*, 5 F.2d 838 (D.Conn. 1925) ("Over the Top" case). Other states, such as the United Kingdom, asserted that international law provided for no such contiguous zone.

As codified in LOSC Article 33, a coastal state may exercise control over a contiguous zone extending no more than twenty-four nautical miles from the baselines, as necessary to:

    (a) prevent infringement of its customs, fiscal, immigration or sanitary laws and regulations within its territory or territorial sea;

    (b) punish infringement of the above laws and regulations committed within its territory or territorial sea.

Thus, the coastal state may undertake enforcement action against vessels in the contiguous zone for certain offenses committed within its territory or territorial sea, but not for any actions occurring in the contiguous zone itself. The enforcement action may include stopping and boarding the vessel, and then seizing the vessel and bringing it into port if evidence of an offense or likely offense is uncovered. *See generally* A. Lowe, *The Development of the Concept of the Contiguous Zone*, 52 Brit. Y.B. Int'l L. 109 (1981).

States are not obligated to declare a contiguous zone. Indeed, only about one-third of all coastal states have declared such zones. The United States has declared such a zone. *See* Proclamation No. 7219 of September 2, 1999, 64 Fed. Reg. 48,701 (Sept. 8, 1999).

    § 10–4. Continental shelf. Geologically, the sea-bed that slopes away from the coast typically consists of first a gradual slope (the continental shelf proper), then a steep slope (the continental slope), and then a more gradual slope leading to the deep sea-bed floor. These three areas—collectively known as the "continental margin"—are rich in natural resources, including oil, natural gas, and certain minerals.

In 1945, President Harry Truman issued a proclamation declaring that the United States "regards the natural resources of the subsoil and sea-bed of the continental shelf beneath the high seas but contiguous to the coasts of the United States as appertaining to the United States, subject to its jurisdiction and control." Proclamation No. 2667 of October 1, 1945, 10 Fed. Reg. 12,303 (Oct. 2, 1945). Thereafter, several other states advanced similar claims and, in 1969, the International Court proclaimed:

> [T]he rights of the coastal State in respect of the area of continental shelf that constitutes a natural prolongation of its land territory into and under the sea exist *ipso facto* and *ab initio*, by virtue of its sovereignty over the land, and as an extension of it in an exercise of sovereign rights for the purpose of exploring the seabed and exploiting its natural resources.

North Sea Continental Shelf (FRG v. Den.; FRG v. Neth.), 1969 I.C.J. 3, at para. 19 (Feb. 20).

In the LOSC, the "continental shelf" is legally defined as comprising the sea-bed and subsoil of the submarine areas that extend beyond the territorial sea throughout the natural prolongation of the land territory to the continental margin's outer edge (art. 76(1)). If that natural prolongation falls short of 200 nautical miles from the baselines, the legal "continental shelf" is regarded as nevertheless continuing up to 200 nautical miles from the baselines. If the natural prolongation exceeds 200 nautical miles from the baselines, the coastal state's "continental shelf" continues until the natural prolongation ends, but under no circumstances may it exceed either (1) 350 nautical miles from the baselines or (2) 100 nautical miles beyond the 2,500 meter isobath (a line connecting the depth of 2,500 meters) (art. 76(4)–(6)).

The coastal state has sovereign rights over the natural resources of its continental shelf. Those resources consist of:

> the mineral and other non-living resources of the sea-bed and subsoil together with living organisms belonging to sedentary species, that is to say, organisms which, at the harvestable stage, either are immobile on or under the sea-bed or are unable to move except in constant physical contact with the sea-bed or the subsoil.

LOSC, art. 77(4). *See generally* E. Brown, *Sea-Bed Energy and Minerals: The International Legal Regime* (1992).

§ 10–5. Exclusive economic zone. Even before the LOSC was adopted, many states, including the United States, declared fishery conservation zones extending outside their territorial seas. *See* Proclamation No. 2668 of October 1, 1945, 10 Fed. Reg. 12,304 (Oct. 2, 1945). Thus, it was no surprise that states agreed in the LOSC to permit a coastal state to claim an "exclusive economic zone" (EEZ) of up to 200 nautical miles from its baselines within which it may exercise extensive rights in relation to natural resources. Shortly after the LOSC's adoption, President Reagan proclaimed an EEZ for the United States within 200 nautical miles of its coast even though the United States did not sign the LOSC. *See* Proclamation No. 5030 of March 10, 1983, 48 Fed. Reg. 10605 (Mar. 14, 1983). The rapid acceptance by states of this concept may be seen in the International Court of Justice's observation in 1985 (before the LOSC entered into force) that it was "incontestable that ... the exclusive economic zone ... is shown by the practice of States to have become part of customary law." *Continental Shelf* (Libya/Malta), 1985 I.C.J. 13, at para. 34 (June 3).

Under LOSC Article 56(1)(a), the coastal state in the EEZ has "sovereign rights for the purpose of exploring and exploiting, conserving and managing" both the living and non-living natural resources of the sea-bed, its subsoil, and superadjacent waters (these rights in part duplicate the coastal state's rights in the continental shelf). As such, the coastal state has extensive control over fishing activities in the EEZ, which will be discussed *infra* § 10–12. Further, Article 56(1)(a) accords the coastal state sovereign rights with regard to other activities for economic exploitation and exploration of the zone, such as "the production of energy from the water, current and winds". The coastal state has jurisdiction in the EEZ over artificial islands, installations and structures (art. 56(b); *see also* art. 60), marine scientific research (*see also* art. 246), and the protection and preservation of the marine environment (*see also infra* § 10.11).

Other states, however, also have rights in the EEZ, which must be respected by the coastal state (art. 56(2)). Vessels of other states generally enjoy in the EEZ the same navigational freedoms that they have on the high seas (arts. 58(1) & 87), but they are subject to the powers accorded the coastal state in its contiguous zone, and the coastal state's regulations regarding pollution control throughout the EEZ. Other states' aircraft generally enjoy over-flight freedom in the EEZ, again subject to the coastal state's powers on matters such as the dumping of wastes. Other states enjoy the freedom to lay submarine cables and pipelines in the EEZ, subject to certain provisions relating to those cable or pipelines being broken or damaged (arts. 112–15), and a provision on obtaining coastal state consent to the route of the pipelines (art. 79(3)). Finally, in exercising their rights in the EEZ, other states must have due regard to the rights and duties of the coastal state (art. 58(3).

All land territory, including islands, can generate both a continental shelf and an EEZ. However, "[r]ocks which cannot sustain human habitation or economic life of their own shall have no exclusive economic zone or continental shelf" (art. 121(3)).

If all coastal states were to establish 200 nautical mile EEZs, they would cover just over one-third of the total area of the sea. Yet within those EEZs would be found more than ninety percent of all fish stocks that are presently commercially exploitable. *See generally* D. Attard, *The Exclusive Economic Zone in International Law* (1987); F. Vicuña, *The Exclusive Economic Zone: Regime and Legal Nature Under International Law* (1989).

§ **10–6.** **High seas**. With the gradual expansion of coastal state control over waters adjacent to their coasts, the area of the high seas has been significantly diminished. Under the contemporary law of the sea, the high seas are defined as "all parts of the sea that are not included in the exclusive economic zone, in the territorial sea or in the internal waters of a State, or in the archipelagic waters of an archipelagic state" (art. 86).

In general, the high seas are open to all states. The LOSC provides a non-exhaustive list of the freedoms all states enjoy on the high seas: freedoms of navigation, overflight, fishing, laying and maintenance of submarine cables and pipelines, scientific research, and artificial installation construction (art. 87). A state is generally obligated to have "due regard for the interests of other states" in exercising these high seas rights and rights relating to the sea-bed area (art. 87(2)). Further, states have certain specific duties, such as to negotiate and agree upon measures necessary for the conservation of high seas fisheries (*see infra* § 10.12). The high seas are to "be reserved for peaceful purposes" (art. 88).

As a general matter, the flag state has the exclusive right to exercise jurisdiction over its vessels on the high seas. Thus, penal and disciplinary proceedings against a person for causing a collision on the high seas rest either with the flag state or the state of the person's nationality (art. 97). (This rule reversed the Permanent Court of Justice's ruling in the *S.S. "Lotus" Case* (Fr. v. Turk.), 1927 P.C.I.J. (ser. A) No. 10 (Sept. 7), which held that the state whose vessel was harmed had concurrent jurisdiction.)

There are some exceptions to the exclusivity of the flag state's jurisdiction. All states may exercise jurisdiction over pirate vessels, with piracy defined as acts of violence, detention or depredation committed for private ends by the crew or passengers of a private ship (or aircraft) against another ship (or aircraft) or persons or property on board it, on (or over) the high seas (art. 101). *See* A. Rubin, *The Law Of Piracy* (1988). All states may also exercise jurisdiction over unlicensed broadcasting on the high seas (art. 109) and warships may board vessels suspected of engaging in piracy, slave trade, and certain other acts (art. 110).

§ 10–7. International sea-bed area. The sea-bed "area" consists of the "sea-bed and ocean floor and subsoil thereof, beyond the limits of national jurisdiction" (art. 1(1)(1)), and thus is the area outside the areas of "continental shelf" controlled by coastal states. The LOSC's principal focus regarding the sea-bed area relates to equitable exploitation of its mineral rich resources, which include baseball-size nodules lying on the sea-bed floor formed by processes of accretion, and containing cobalt, copper, iron, manganese, and nickel.

At the time the LOSC negotiations began, the developing states thought that sea-bed mining might bring immense profits and should be exploited only under the auspices of a U.N. organization as part of the "common heritage of mankind", rather than by private firms (predominantly from the developed states) acting on their own. *See* Declaration of Principles Governing the Sea–Bed and Ocean Floor, and the Subsoil Thereof, beyond the Limits of National Jurisdiction, G.A. Res. 2749, 10 I.L.M. 220 (1971). The provisions of Part XI of the LOSC, therefore, called for the establishment of an "International Sea–Bed Authority" that would control access by private entities to sea-bed mining sites, and would limit the amount of extraction so as not to impinge excessively on land-based mining. The private entities would be taxed and the proceeds distributed to all states. Moreover, the Sea–Bed Authority itself could engage in mining through the establishment of a new entity called the "Enterprise." Private entities seeking access to a mining site would have to identify two sites, one for itself and one for exploitation by the Sea–Bed Authority either through the Enterprise or by some association with developing states. Finally, the Sea–Bed Authority would have the ability to compel states to transfer to it, on "fair commercial terms," mining technology that was not available on the open market.

The industrialized states viewed such an International Sea–Bed Authority as irrational, expensive and inefficient, and declined to sign the convention after it was adopted. After the sixtieth ratification was deposited in November 1993, the convention by its terms was set to enter into force in November 1994. At the same time, it had become increasingly clear that extraction of deep sea-bed resources was not commercially feasible using existing technology. Consequently, in an effort to bring the major industrialized states into the regime, further negotiations were conducted leading to a 1994 agreement on the implementation of Part XI of the convention. *See Law of the Sea Forum: The 1994 Agreement on Implementation of the Seabed Provisions of the Convention on the Law of the Sea*, 88 Am. J. Int'l L. 687 (1994).

The 1994 implementing agreement retained the framework for sea-bed mining, but with radical changes. As a result, only a skeletal Sea–Bed Authority based in Jamaica exists and will only further develop in response to changing circumstances. The Sea–Bed Authority has three principal organs: a plenary Assembly; a thirty-six state Council; and a Secretariat (art. 158). The 1994 implementing agreement restructures the decision-making processes of the Sea–Bed Authority, so that all important decisions are to be made by the Council (the Assembly can only refuse to confirm the Council's decisions). Further, important Council decisions now require consensus on certain issues and a super-majority vote on other issues. The latter process involves a four-chamber system that protects the interests of different factions, including the industrialized states.

Since there is currently no planned commercial mining in the sea-bed area, the 1994 implementing agreement provides that the Enterprise not be established as yet. The Enterprise is to begin operating only when the Council decides that it should. Moreover, once it is established, the Enterprise will be required to conduct its initial mining operations through joint ventures and will not operate independently. *See generally* L. Nelson, *The New Deep Sea–Bed Mining Regime*, 10 Int'l J. Mar. & Coastal L. 189 (1995).

§ 10–8. Straits and archipelagos. A strait is a narrow stretch of water connecting two larger bodies of water. The International Court has recognized a customary rule of international law that innocent passage could not be suspended by a coastal state in straits used for international navigation between one part of the high seas and another. *See Corfu Channel* (U.K. v. Alb.), 1949 I.C.J. 4, 28 (Apr. 9). In the LOSC, detailed rules were developed for "transit passage" through straits that contain no high seas route or EEZ route. The LOSC recognizes the coastal states' interests in their expanded territorial seas, but at the same time protects the interests of the major maritime states in passage through straits. "Transit passage" provides vessels with the freedom of navigation and overflight solely for the continuous and expeditious passage through the strait (art. 38(2)). When engaging in such passage, vessels must refrain from the threat or use of force and must comply with internationally accepted regulations and practices on safety and pollution (art. 39(1) & (2)). While the coastal state may legislate on certain matters regarding the passage of vessels through the strait (art. 42(1)), it may not suspend transit passage for security or any other reasons (art. 44).

An archipelagos is a group of closely interrelated islands that form an intrinsic geographical, economic, and political entity (art. 46). Where an archipelagos forms a single state, the LOSC allows the archipelagic state to draw "archipelagic baselines" around the state, joining the outermost points of its outermost islands or reefs (art. 47(1)), rather than create separate maritime zones for each island. The LOSC sets certain limits on the state's ability to draw archipelagic baselines, such as maintaining a ratio of land to water within the baselines of no less than one-to-one and no more than one-to-nine (*id.*) The archipelagic state may then claim maritime zones over the waters seaward of these baselines (territorial sea, contiguous zone, EEZ, etc.). The waters landward of these baselines are "archipelagic waters;" they are not territorial waters, but nor are they internal waters unless they fall landward of closing lines across river mouths, bays or harbors of individual islands that are drawn in accordance with LOSC rules on normal baselines (*see* art. 50). An archipelagic state must recognize other states' rights in the archipelagic waters as may exist in other agreements, and must recognize traditional fishing rights of neighboring states (art. 51(1)). Further, LOSC provides that vessels enjoy the same right of innocent passage through these archipelagic waters that they enjoy through territorial seas; rights which may only be suspended in limited circumstances (art. 52). Several states—such as the Bahamas, Indonesia, and the Philippines—have elected to draw archipelagic baselines.

§ 10–9. Delimitation of maritime boundaries. As the law of the sea maritime zones pushed sovereign control further out from the baselines, states began more frequently to encounter overlapping claims to areas of the sea and continental shelf. Thus, states adjacent to each other along the same stretch of a coast, or states bordering opposite sides of a strait or small sea, could encounter conflicting claims to their territorial seas, exclusive economic zones, or continental shelves. To resolve such claims, states typically have entered into bilateral agreements (or multilateral agreements if more than two states are involved). For instance, the United States has concluded three bilateral agreements with Mexico regarding maritime boundaries. *See, e.g.,* Treaty with Mexico on Delimitation of Continental Shelf, June 9, 2000, U.S.-Mex., *S. Treaty Doc. No.* 106–39 (2000). Where such claims cannot be resolved by agreement, they have sometimes been submitted to international dispute resolution, such as before the International Court of Justice. *See, e.g., Delimitation of the Maritime Boundary of the Gulf of Maine Area* (Can./U.S.), 1984 I.C.J. 246 (Oct. 12); *Maritime Delimitation & Territorial Questions between Qatar & Bahrain* (Qatar v. Bahr.), 2001 I.C.J. (Mar. 16), *reprinted in* 40 I.L.M. 847 (2001).

When resolving these claims, states look to certain general rules embodied in the LOSC and customary international law. For territorial sea delimitation of states opposite to each other, the normal practice is to use a median line (a line equidistant from the closest points of the two states' coasts). For territorial sea delimitation of states adjacent to each other, sometimes a median line is drawn outwards from the coast, while other times a simple perpendicular line is used. In either type of delimitation, special circumstances may be taken into account. LOSC Article 15 provides:

> Where the coasts of two States are opposite or adjacent to each other, neither of the two States is entitled, failing agreement between them to the contrary, to extend its territorial sea beyond the median line every point of which is equidistant from the nearest points on the baselines from which the breadth of the territorial seas of each of the two States is measured. The above provision does not apply, however, where it is necessary by reason of historic title or other special circumstances to delimit the territorial seas of the two States in a way which is at variance therewith.

LOSC Article 83(1) provides somewhat less guidance for the delimitation of the continental shelf. It states:

> The delimitation of the continental shelf between States with opposite or adjacent coasts shall be effected by agreement on the basis of international law, as referred to in Article 38 of the Statute of the International Court of Justice, in order to achieve an equitable solution.

In practice, states and international tribunals have been unwilling to apply automatically an equidistance principle for delimiting the continental shelf. In the *North Sea Continental Shelf* cases, application of the equidistance principle would have resulted in a very small continental shelf for Germany (compared with Denmark and the Netherlands) due to the concave coastline of the three states along the North Sea. Instead, the Court stated that:

> delimitation is to be effected by agreement in accordance with equitable principles, and taking account of all the relevant circumstances, in such a way as to leave as much as possible to each Party all those parts of the continental shelf that constitute a natural prolongation of its land territory into and under the sea, without encroachment on the natural prolongation of the land territory of the other.

North Sea Continental Shelf (F.R.G. v. Den.; F.R.G. v. Neth.), 1969 I.C.J. 3, at para. 101 (Feb. 20). "Relevant circumstances" that have been taken into account by dispute fora include the overall coastal configuration, the lengths of the parties' coasts, the presence of islands, and the parties' prior conduct (such as agreement on a provisional boundary line).

§ 10–10. Hot pursuit across maritime zones. For centuries, states have recognized a customary right for a state's military vessel to engage in "hot pursuit" of a foreign vessel which has violated the state's laws within its internal waters or territorial sea, even if the arrest is ultimately made on the high seas. The LOSC maintains this concept with respect to pursuit that begins not just in internal waters or the territorial sea, but also in the contiguous zone, the EEZ, or archipelagic waters, or in waters above the continental shelf, with respect to offenses associated within those zones. The pursuit may use necessary and reasonable force to affect an arrest, but the pursuit must be continuous and must end as soon as the vessel enters another state's territorial sea (art. 111). For an example, see W. Gilmore, *Hot Pursuit: The Case of R. v. Mills and Others*, 44 Int'l & Comp. L.Q. 949 (1995).

III.   REGULATION OF CERTAIN USES OF THE SEA

§ **10–11.   Maritime pollution**. Vessels that transport goods across the seas are among the principal sources of pollution of the marine environment. Such pollution may derive from emissions caused by the propulsion of the vessel, from the vessel's discharge of garbage or sewage, or from the accidental or deliberate spillage of cargo. For instance, for many years oil tankers used sea water to clean their oil tanks (or to serve as ballast water in the oil tanks), and then discharged the oily sea water back into the sea. *See* R. Clark, *Marine Pollution* (5th ed. 2001).

Various types of global, regional, and bilateral treaties have sought to mitigate this marine pollution. On the global level, the International Maritime Organization (IMO) in 1973 developed the Convention for the Prevention of Pollution from Ships,

Nov. 2, 1973, 12 I.L.M. 1319, 1340 U.N.T.S. 184 (MARPOL Convention) to deal with all forms of intentional pollution of the sea from vessels, other than dumping. Along with a protocol adopted in 1978, 17 I.L.M. 546, 1341 U.N.T.S. 3 (thus creating the MARPOL 73/78 Convention) and other amendments, the convention has established complex, detailed pollution standards for vessels in annexes addressing the transport of oil and of noxious substances in bulk, which have been widely adhered to by states. States have adhered less widely to other annexes addressing transport of harmful substances in packages, sewage, garbage, and air pollution.

To address the deliberate dumping of wastes at sea by vessels and aircraft (other than disposal of wastes incidental to the normal operation of such vessels and aircraft), states adopted the Convention on the Prevention of Marine Pollution by Dumping of Wastes and Other Matter, Dec. 29, 1972, 26 U.S.T. 2403, 1046 U.N.T.S. 120, as amended (London Convention). The London Convention (1) lists certain substances, such as mercury, that may not be dumped at sea (the "black list"); (2) lists other substances, such as pesticides, that may be dumped only if authorized by a special permit issued by a party to the convention (the "grey list"); and (3) allows dumping of all other substances and wastes only if authorized by a general permit issued by a party to the convention, which may be conditioned on factors such as the method of disposal and the disposal site. Once it enters into force, a 1996 protocol to the London Convention will severely restrict the types of substances that may be dumped. *See* 36 I.L.M. 7 (1997).

The most important source of marine pollution is from land-based activities. Several regional treaties have developed that address this issue. *See, e.g.*, M. Fitzmaurice, *International Legal Problems of the Environmental Protection of the Baltic* (1992). However, as yet no global convention exists to regulate land-based sources of marine pollution. Its absence no doubt reflects the difficulty of regulating on a global level activities falling squarely within the territorial sovereignty of states.

The LOSC reinforces these standards on marine pollution by placing an obligation on all states to adopt laws and regulations that give effect to generally accepted international rules and standards (arts. 207–12). Moreover, flag states are obligated to enforce such laws and regulations against its vessels (art. 217). When a vessel enters a port, the port state may also pursue enforcement actions (art. 218). A coastal state may also enforce laws and regulations on maritime pollution within maritime zones under its authority subject to certain constraints, such as being non-discriminatory and not hampering innocent passage (art. 220).

§ **10–12. Fishing**. Historically, fish outside territorial waters have been open to exploitation by fishing vessels from any state. With modern technological advances in locating, harvesting, and storing fish (such as the use of drift nets that are thirty feet in depth and up to thirty miles in length), fish stocks worldwide have suffered from biologically unsustainable exploitation. The modern law of the sea, therefore, has sought to regulate access to fishery resources, both in the EEZ and on the high seas.

As noted *supra* § 10–5, the coastal state in the EEZ has "sovereign rights for the purpose of exploring and exploiting, conserving and managing" the living and non-living natural resources of the sea-bed, its subsoil, and superadjacent waters (art. 56(1)(a)). At the same time, the coastal state must ensure that the EEZ living resources are maintained at or restored to "levels which can produce the maximum sustainable yield, as qualified by relevant environmental and economic factors ... and taking into account fishing patterns, the interdependence of stocks and any generally recommended international minimum standards" (art. 61(3)). Further, in fulfilling an obligation to promote the optimum utilization of the EEZ living resources, the coastal state must establish the total allowable catch and must either itself harvest that catch or allow the fishing vessels of other states to do so (arts. 61–62, 69–70). Where a coastal state has permitted access to its EEZ for foreign fishing vessels, it may enforce its regulations against those vessels by "boarding, inspection, arrest and judicial proceedings" (art. 73(1)).

Fish do not confine themselves to the EEZ of a particular coastal state. They may migrate among EEZs (shared fish stocks) and between EEZs and the high seas (straddling fish stocks), whereas some fish spend their entire life cycle on the high seas.

LOSC Article 63(1) merely calls upon states with shared fish stocks to seek "to agree upon the measures necessary to co-ordinate and ensure the conservation and development of such stocks." To that end, many states have agreed upon cooperative arrangements for managing shared stocks. *See, e.g.*, Treaty Concerning Pacific Salmon, Jan. 28, 1985, U.S.-Can., T.I.A.S. 11091, 1469 U.N.T.S. 357 (further amended in June 1999). With respect to straddling fish stocks, and fish stocks that spend their entire life cycle on the high seas, LOSC Articles 117–20 impose a duty on interested states to cooperate in the management and conservation of high seas living resources, making use where appropriate of international fishery commissions. In furtherance of that cooperation, states concluded a U.N. convention on the conservation and management of straddling fish stocks and highly migratory fish stocks, Aug. 4, 1995, 34 I.L.M. 1542, which entered into force in 2001. The straddling fish stocks convention sets out detailed principles to be followed both by a coastal state within its EEZ and by all states on the high seas. Where a regional organization or arrangement exists to implement these principles, the straddling fish stocks convention obligates states to use that organization or arrangement or to refrain from fishing in that region. Where a regional organization or arrangement does not exist, the convention calls upon states to establish one. Several such commissions now exist, to which the United States is a party, including the Northwest Atlantic Fisheries Organization (NAFO). Each year, NAFO establishes a total allowable catch for the high seas area of the Northwest Atlantic, which is then divided into quotas allocated to NAFO member states. The most recently established commission covers the last major area of the world's oceans that lacked a regional management regime—the Western and Central Pacific Ocean. *See* Convention on the Conservation and Management of Highly Migratory Fish Stocks in the Western and Central Pacific Ocean, Sept. 4, 2000, 40 I.L.M. 278 (2001). Two-thirds of the world's tuna catch comes from this region.

IV. DISPUTE SETTLEMENT

§ 10–13. LOSC dispute settlement. The LOSC promotes the settlement of disputes arising under the LOSC by peaceful means. In Section 1 of Part XV, the LOSC calls for an expeditious exchange of views between two parties whenever a dispute may arise, and for resolution of the dispute by whatever means agreed upon by the parties. If this is not possible, either party may request that the other party agree to use the conciliation procedure established by the convention (art. 284 & annex V). Under this procedure, each party chooses two conciliators (of which one may be its national) from a list established by the LOSC parties, and the four conciliators select a fifth to serve as their chairperson. The panel then issues a report in which it may make non-binding recommendations.

If the dispute is not capable of settlement under Section 1 of Part XV, either party may resort to the compulsory dispute settlement provisions contained in Section 2, so long as none of its exceptions apply. For example, most disputes concerning the exercise by a coastal state of its sovereign rights or jurisdiction within the EEZ are not subject to LOSC compulsory dispute settlement (art. 297; *see also* art. 298). Otherwise, disputes arising under the LOSC or its implementing agreements shall be resolved before one of four dispute resolution fora: (1) the International Tribunal for the Law of the Sea (ITLOS) established under LOSC Annex VI (discussed *supra* § 4–28); (2) the International Court of Justice; (3) a general arbitral tribunal established pursuant to LOSC Annex VII; or (4) an arbitral tribunal composed of specialists in certain areas (fisheries, environmental protection, marine scientific research, or navigation) established pursuant to LOSC Annex VIII.

When a state signs the LOSC, or at any point thereafter, it may indicate which of the four fora it selects for compulsory dispute settlement (if it fails to select a forum, it is deemed to have selected Annex VII arbitration). If two states have a dispute and have both selected the same forum, then that forum is used to resolve the dispute, unless the parties agree otherwise (art. 287(4)). If the two states have selected different fora, and cannot otherwise agree on a forum, then the dispute is submitted to Annex VII arbitration (art. 287(5)). Whichever fora hears the dispute, the forum applies LOSC rules and other rules of international law, and its decisions are final and binding on the parties (arts.

293, 296). In practice, many LOSC parties have not selected a forum, while others have accepted ITLOS (e.g., Argentina), the International Court of Justice (e.g., Germany), or Annex VII arbitration (e.g., the United States, although not yet an LOSC party, has indicated it will select this forum).

An example of LOSC dispute resolution is the *Southern Bluefin Tuna* case. In that case, Australia and New Zealand charged that Japan was violating its LOSC obligations by not sufficiently limiting its catch of southern bluefin tuna on the high seas. In July 1999, the two states notified Japan that they intended to institute LOSC Annex VII arbitration and to seek provisional measures of protection from ITLOS pending constitution of the arbitral tribunal, as is permitted under LOSC art. 290(5). In a decision rendered in August 1999, ITLOS found that the arbitral tribunal to be constituted would prima facie have jurisdiction over the dispute. Consequently, ITLOS imposed certain limitations on Japanese fishing pending the arbitral tribunal's decision. *Southern Bluefin Tuna Cases* (NZ v. Japan; Austl. v. Japan), 38 I.L.M. 1624 (ITLOS 1999).

Thereafter, an tribunal of five arbitrators was formed, presided over by former International Court of Justice President Stephen Schwebel. That tribunal, however, ultimately found that it had lacked jurisdiction over the dispute. *Award on Southern Bluefin Tuna* (NZ v. Japan; Austl. v. Japan), 39 I.L.M. 1359 (2000). The tribunal found that in Article 16 of the Convention for the Conservation of Southern Bluefin Tuna, May 10, 1993,

1819 U.N.T.S. 360, all three states had agreed that disputes arising under that convention would be resolved by binding third-party settlement only with the consent, in each case, of all the parties to the dispute. According to the tribunal, the effect of that agreement was to exclude compulsory dispute settlement under both that convention and the LOSC, since the LOSC was an "umbrella" or "framework" agreement designed to allow states to choose the means for resolving their disputes. Since it lacked jurisdiction over the merits of the dispute, the tribunal also revoked the provisional measures imposed by ITLOS. For a critique of this decision, taking the view that some form of *compulsory* dispute settlement is integral to the LOSC, see B. Oxman, *Complementary Agreements and Compulsory Jurisdiction*, 95 Am. J. Int'l L. 277 (2001).

CHAPTER 11

INTERNATIONAL ENVIRONMENTAL LAW

I. INTRODUCTION

International environmental law is a relatively recent branch of international law concerned with the preservation and enhancement of the global environment. To address transnational environmental problems, such as ozone depletion, climate change, and loss of biological diversity, states have developed a network of agreements and institutions, as well as certain legal principles and techniques, that are unique to this field of international law.

II. STRUCTURAL OVERVIEW

§ 11–1. **Historical background**. Beginning in the 19th century, states began concluding agreements regulating international fishing, protecting certain fauna (such as birds and seals), and protecting various plant species. For example, the treaty at issue in *Missouri v. Holland*, 252 U.S. 416 (1920) (discussed *supra* § 7–3) concerned the protection of birds migrating between the United States and Canada. In this early period, states also concluded agreements to regulate the use of water along boundaries, particularly to prevent pollution. An example of this for the United States and Canada is the U.S.-U.K. Treaty Relating to the Boundary Waters and Questions Arising Along the Boundary, Jan. 11, 1909, 36 Stat. 2448, 12 Bevans 319, which remains in force today.

Yet most contemporary international environmental law arose after the 1960's, when governments and the public at large became aware of the significant threats to the environment posed by rapid growth of population, industrial pollution, and human consumption of natural resources. In 1968, the U.N. General Assembly proposed the convening of a global conference on the human environment, to be held in Stockholm, Sweden. G.A. Res. 2398 (XXIII) (Dec. 3, 1968). The 1972 Stockholm Conference brought together for the first time representatives from 113 states, as well as representatives from hundreds of international and non-government organizations, to discuss all aspects of the global environment. Two key achievements occurred at Stockholm.

First, the conference adopted at its closing plenary session the Declaration on the Human Environment, 11 I.L.M. 1416 (1972). The Stockholm Declaration contained important preambular language and a series of politically-binding principles to be followed by governments and their peoples in preserving and improving the human environment for the benefit of all people and for their posterity. In general, the Stockholm Declaration advanced certain ethical and moral values in favor of preserving the human environment, while at the same time recognizing that economic and scientific realities would limit the steps that could be taken. *See* L. Sohn, *The Stockholm Declaration on the Human Environment*, 14 Harv. Int'l L.J. 423 (1973). For instance, Principle 2 of the Stockholm Declaration declared that:

> The natural resources of the earth including the air, water, land, flora and fauna and especially representative samples of natural ecosystems must be safeguarded for the benefit of present and future generations through careful planning or management, as appropriate.

While many of these principles were vague and conditional, they reflected commitments of states to the global environment that thereafter shaped the development of more specific international environmental agreements, national laws, and institutional initiatives.

Second, the Stockholm Conference adopted a politically-binding Action Plan containing 109 recommendations for future action in addressing international environmental problems. Special attention was paid to identifying and responding to environmental threats, but also to supporting such responses financially and institutionally (such as through education and training). In part as a result of the Action Plan, the U.N. General Assembly in 1972 created the U.N. Environment Programme (UNEP), based in Nairobi, Kenya (see next section).

In the twenty years after the Stockholm Conference, states moved rapidly to develop international environmental law across a range of sectors, as demonstrated by reference to some of the more important global agreements. With respect to the protection of endangered species, the 1973 Convention on International Trade in Endangered Species of Wild Fauna and Flora, Mar. 3, 1973, 27 U.S.T. 1087, 993 U.N.T.S. 243 (CITES), established a global system for strictly regulating trade in species threatened with extinction, and limiting trade in species that may become extinct or that are of concern to member states. To address atmospheric concerns, European and North American states in 1979 concluded a Convention on Long–Range Transboundary Air Pollution, Nov. 13, 1979, T.I.A.S. No. 10541, 1302 U.N.T.S. 217 (LRTAP Convention), which regulated emissions of sulfur dioxide, nitrous oxide, and other long-range pollutants through a series of protocols. Regarding the oceans, the U.N. Convention on the Law of the Sea (LOSC) was adopted in 1982 and entered into force in 1994 containing extensive and innovative provisions on the protection and preservation of the marine environment. *S. Treaty Doc.* 103–39 (1994); *see supra* ch. 10. With respect to land-based pollutants, the 1989 Basel Convention on the Control of Transboundary Movements of Hazardous Wastes and Their Disposal, Mar. 22, 1989, *S. Treaty Doc. No.* 102–5 (1991), 1673 U.N.T.S. 57, 28 I.L.M. 657 (1989), provided for environmentally sound management and disposal of hazardous wastes transported across borders principally through use of a notice-and-consent regime. With respect to areas outside the sovereignty of states, the Protocol on Environmental Protection to the Antarctic Treaty, Oct. 4, 1991, 30 I.L.M. 1461, provided an integrated approach to environmental protection of that fragile ecosystem. Although not adopted in treaty form, the U.N. General Assembly's 1982 World Charter for Nature contained twenty-four articles calling for the integration of nature conservation into the laws and practices of states. G.A. Res. 37/7 (Oct. 28, 1982). In addition to these global instruments, dozens of regional and bilateral international environment agreements were also adopted, such as the 1968 African Convention on the Conservation of Nature and Natural Resources, Sept. 15, 1968, 1001 U.N.T.S. 3. The European Community adopted several directives protective of the environment that are binding on its member states. *See, e.g.*, European Communities Council Directive 80/779 of 15 July 1980 on Air Quality Limit Values and Guide Values for Sulphur Dioxide and Suspended Particulates, 1980 O.J. (L229) 30. For further information on these instruments, see P. Birnie & A. Boyle, *International Law and the Environment* (2d ed. 2000); A. Kiss & D. Shelton, *International Environmental Law* (2d ed. 2000).

On the 20th anniversary of the Stockholm Conference, the U.N. General Assembly convened another conference, this time at Rio de Janeiro, Brazil. The 1992 U.N. Conference on Environment and Development (UNCED) involved representatives from 172 states, as well as thousands of representatives from international and non-governmental organizations. One important aspect of UNCED was the tension between the developed states and the developing states. The developed states desired stronger global environmental regulation. The developing states were unwilling to assume the burden of such regulation if doing so impeded their own ability to develop their economies. As a result, the means for blending environmental and developmental objectives pervaded the work of the conference. Ultimately, UNCED led to three key achievements.

First, important global conventions on climate change and on biological diversity (discussed *infra* §§ 11–6, 11–7) were opened for signature at the conference (the conference also adopted a politically-binding statement of principles on conservation and management of forests; *see* 31 I.L.M. 881 (1992)).

Second, UNCED adopted the Rio Declaration on Environment and Development, 31 I.L.M. 874 (1992), containing twenty-seven politically-binding principles that built upon the Stockholm Declaration, but with particular emphasis on integrating environmental protection with economic development ("sustainable development"). Thus, Rio Declaration Principle 4 provides: "In order to achieve sustainable development, environmental protection shall constitute an integral part of the development process and cannot be considered in isolation from it." Like the Stockholm Declaration, the Rio Declaration is not legally-binding, but is often referred to in negotiations or litigation as an authoritative statement of states' political commitments.

Third, UNCED adopted a politically-binding action program for the 21st century, called Agenda 21. U.N. Doc. A/CONF. 151/26 (vols. I, II, & III) (1992). Over the course of forty chapters, Agenda 21 provides extensive recommendations for addressing more than 100 topics relating to the international environment, such as changing consumption patterns (ch. 4), freshwater resources (ch. 18), and the role of indigenous peoples (ch. 26). Of particular relevance to the law, Agenda 21 contains chapters on international institutional arrangements (ch. 38) and on international legal instruments and mechanisms (ch. 39). Throughout Agenda 21, there is an emphasis on the development of national legislation and programs to implement its recommendations. UNCED called for the establishment of a high-level U.N. commission to monitor the implementation of Agenda 21, which led to the creation by the U.N. General Assembly of the U.N. Sustainable Development Commission (CSD), based in New York (*see infra* § 11–2).

In the decade following the UNCED conference, the global community continued to develop international environmental law through adoption of further agreements or protocols to existing agreements. Thus, in 1994, states adopted the U.N. Convention to Combat Desertification in Those Countries Experiencing Serious Drought and/or Desertification, Particularly in Africa, Oct. 14, 1994, 1954 U.N.T.S. 3, 33 I.L.M. 1328 (1994). In

2000, states adopted the Cartegena Protocol on Biosafety to the Convention on Biological Diversity, Jan. 29, 2000, 39 I.L.M. 1027 (2000), which, among other things, established a notice-and-consent regime for the export of living, genetically-modified organisms that are intended to be introduced into the environment of the importing state (e.g., genetically-modified seeds for planting). In 2001, states adopted the Stockholm Convention on Persistent Organic Pollutants, 40 I.L.M. 532 (2001) covering the production and trade in twelve uniquely hazardous chemicals that resist degradation and can travel long distances through air and water. That convention will enter into force after the fiftieth ratification or accession.

In addition to the development of new agreements, states have taken steps to implement Agenda 21 through the passage of national legislation and programs. Further, since the Rio Conference, other fields of international law—such as those of trade, human rights, and armed conflict—have become increasingly responsive to international environmental concerns. In an advisory opinion sought from the International Court of Justice on the legality of the threat or use of nuclear weapons, the Court declined to answer the question solely by reference to environmental agreements. The Court, however, declared that it:

> recognizes that the environment is not an abstraction but represents the living space, the quality of life and the very health of human beings, including generations unborn. The exis-

tence of the general obligation of States to ensure that activities within their jurisdiction and control respect the environment of other States or of areas beyond national control is now part of the corpus of international law relating to the environment.

Advisory Opinion on Legality of the Threat or Use of Nuclear Weapons, 1996 I.C.J. 226 at 241, para. 29 (July 8).

The following year, the International Court first confronted the difficulties of balancing environmental protection with economic development in *Gabčíkovo-Nagymaros Project* (Hung./Slov.), 1997 I.C.J. 7 (Sept. 25). That case involved a 1977 treaty between Hungary and Czechoslovakia (to which Slovakia succeeded) for constructing a system of locks and dams on the Danube River. As new evidence emerged regarding the environmental consequences of the project, Hungary suspended its part of the project. The Court found that Hungary breached the treaty and that the breach was not justified by "ecological necessity." At the same time, the Court found that Slovakia violated its obligations by proceeding on its own with a variant of the project. The Court concluded that the treaty remained in force and that the two parties should negotiate in good faith a resolution of their dispute. In doing so, the Court noted (at para. 140):

Throughout the ages, mankind has, for economic and other reasons, constantly interfered with nature. In the past, this was often done without consideration of the effects upon the environment. Owing to new scientific insights and to a growing awareness of the risks for mankind—for present and future generations—of pursuit of such interventions at an unconsidered and unabated pace, new norms and standards have been developed, set forth in a great number of instruments during the last two decades.... This need to reconcile economic development with protection of the environment is aptly expressed in the concept of sustainable development.

§ 11–2. International and non-governmental organizations. The Stockholm Declaration called upon states to "ensure that international organizations play a co-ordinated, efficient and dynamic role for the protection and improvement of the environment." Stockholm Declaration, princ. 25. The role of international institutions in this field of law is important for several reasons: (1) they allow states to pool their scientific knowledge about threats to the global environment; (2) they allow states to develop international rules and standards as a means of addressing those threats; (3) they provide a forum for resolving any ambiguities in the rules and standards, and for adapting the rules to address changing conditions; (4) they provide a means for monitoring adherence by states to rules and standards; and (5) they allow states to coordinate the provision of financial and other resources to states experiencing difficulty in complying with norms and standards. *See* A. Chayes & A. Chayes, *The New Sovereignty: Compliance with International Regulatory Agreements* 1–17 (1995).

The two most important international environmental institutions focused solely on international environmental problems are the U.N. Environment Program (UNEP) and the U.N. Sustainable Development Commission (CSD), both created by the U.N. General Assembly. *See generally* M. Soros, *Global Institutions and the Environment: An Evolutionary Perspective*, in *The Global Environment: Institutions, Law, and Policy* 27 (N. Vig & R. Axelrod eds., 1999).

UNEP, a special intergovernmental body within the U.N. system, was the first U.N. agency to be assigned an environmental agenda. The UNEP Governing Council consists of representatives from fifty-eight states elected by the U.N. General Assembly, who meet every two years to adopt decisions on UNEP environmental initiatives and programs. The UNEP High–Level Committee of Ministers and Officials, composed of representatives from thirty-six states, meets more regularly to prepare draft decisions for the Governing Council and to review the work of the Secretariat. The UNEP Executive Director, who is appointed by the U.N. Secretary–General, oversees the day-to-day operations of UNEP's Secretariat, which is largely based at UNEP's headquarters in Nairobi, Kenya (there are also regional offices worldwide). Finally, a Committee of Permanent Representatives, consisting of representatives from all U.N. member states, meets four times per year and serves as a communications link between UNEP and its member governments.

A key function of UNEP is to coordinate environmental initiatives and programs within the U.N. system and, when feasible, with institutions outside the U.N. system. For example, UNEP created a Global Environmental Monitoring System (GEMS), which pools information obtained from the monitoring of ecosystems by scientists worldwide. Another key function of UNEP is developing rules and standards in the field of the global environment. Since its inception, UNEP has sponsored more than forty multilateral environmental agreements at the global and regional levels, as well as numerous statements of principles that are not legally binding but provide important guidance for states. For further information, see <http://www.unep.org>.

The CSD is a functional commission of the U.N. Economic and Social Council (ECOSOC) and consists of representatives from fifty-three states elected by ECOSOC. The principal function of the CSD is to monitor and to make recommendations concerning the implementation of Agenda 21 (see prior section) at the international, regional, and national levels. Reflecting the emphasis of the 1992 UNCED, the CSD is concerned with integrating environmental objectives with developmental objectives, and to that end receives reports from other international institutions and from states. The CSD meets annually, but also establishes ad hoc expert groups to engage in work between its sessions. For further information, see <http://www.un.org/esa/sustdev/csd.htm>.

Many of the U.N. agencies, regional organizations, and supranational organizations referred to in Chapter 3 also play a role in the development of international environmental law, such as the Food and Agriculture Organization (FAO), the World Health Organization (WHO), the U.N. Development Programme (UNDP), and the World Bank group. Moreover, in 1991, UNEP, UNDP, and the World Bank jointly established a "Global Environment Facility" (GEF) to serve as a source of grant funds for incremental costs incurred by developing states in achieving global environmental benefits in four areas: ozone depletion, climate change, conservation of biological diversity, and protection of international waters. The GEF is the largest multilateral source of grant funds for environmental protection and operates as the financial mechanism for the Climate Change and Biological Diversity conventions (*see infra* §§ 11–6, 11–7). To scrutinize the World Bank's compliance, when issuing loans, with its environmental (and other) policies and procedures, an Inspection Panel was created in 1994 with the authority to receive claims of affected parties from the borrower's territory, to carry out independent investigations, and to make recommendations to the Bank's Board of Executive Directors. *See* I. Shihata, *The World Bank Inspection Panel* (1994).

Most contemporary global agreements relating to international environmental law establish a Conference of the Parties and a Secretariat (and sometimes a scientific commission). The Conference of the Parties typically meets annually or biennially to interpret and monitor compliance with the treaty and to adapt the treaty through adoption of adjustments, amendments, or protocols to the treaty. The Secretariat is an important standing institution typically charged with assisting the Conference of the Parties, coordinating the flow of information among the parties to the treaty, and assisting states in complying with the treaty through the facilitation of transfers of financial or other support, training and education programs, and the development of model national legislation. Rather than create a new Secretariat, some agreements call for an existing institution, such as UNEP, to serve as the Secretariat.

There are numerous international non-governmental organizations that play an important role in the development of international environmental law. These organizations help galvanize public support for environmental initiatives and channel that support to the governments of states and to negotiations of international instruments. Indeed, such organizations often participate in multilateral negotiating conferences as observers, which allows them to speak at the conference on issues under negotiation. The World Wildlife Fund (WWF) is an excellent example of such an organization. *See* <http://www.worldwildlife.org>; *see generally The International Politics of the Environment: Actors, Interests, and Institutions* (A. Hurrell & B. Kingsbury, eds., 1992).

§ **11–3. Key principles**. Agreements are the primary means by which states commit themselves to specific obligations to protect and enhance the global environment. In developing, interpreting, and implementing agreements, states often refer to certain key principles, which some states regard as having legal force while others view them as simply shaping legal obligations developed in agreements. The following are some of these principles.

Principles of Common Heritage and Common Concern of Humankind. The principle of the common heritage of humankind (or "mankind") maintains that all humans have a stake in resources located outside the territory of states, such as the high seas, the deep sea-bed, Antarctica, and outer space. As such, no one state should be able to exhaust the resources of these global commons and all are obliged to cooperate peacefully in managing them. *See, e.g.*, Treaty on Principles Governing the Activities of States in the Exploration and Use of Outer Space, Including the Moon and Other Celestial Bodies, Jan. 27, 1967, 610 U.N.T.S. 205, 18 U.S.T. 2410. The principle of the common concern of humankind, which is less widely adopted in agreements, speaks to a similar concept with respect to resources located *within* the territories of states. Thus, even though most biological diversity is located within states, the preamble of the Biological Diversity Convention asserts that "the conservation of biological diversity is a common concern of humankind." Convention on Biological Diversity, June 5, 1992, pmbl., 1760 U.N.T.S. 79, 31 I.L.M. 818 (1992) (Biological Diversity Convention)

Prevention of Environmental Harm Principle.
Stockholm Principle 21 provides that:

> States have, in accordance with the Charter of
> the United Nations and the principles of interna-
> tional law, the sovereign right to exploit their
> own resources pursuant to their own environmen-
> tal policies, and the responsibility to ensure that
> the activities within their jurisdiction or control
> do not cause damage to the environment of other
> States or of areas beyond the limits of national
> jurisdiction.

Rio Declaration Principle 2 (adopted twenty years
after the Stockholm Declaration) reiterated this language, but added the world "and developmental"
before the word "policies." This principle contains
two contrasting notions: one stressing the inherent
sovereignty of states; the other stressing that in
exercising such sovereignty states must ensure that
their activities (including activities by their nationals) do not harm the environment beyond their
territory. In practice, this principle is not viewed as
prohibiting *all* transboundary environmental harm;
indeed, pollution drifts across borders regularly
without claims that the polluting states are violating international law. Rather, the principle is usually interpreted as prohibiting significant (or at least
substantial) damage or, alternatively, as requiring a
state to exercise due diligence in seeking to prevent
such damage (thus imposing an obligation of conduct rather than an obligation of result). Cases
often cited in support of this principle are the *Trail
Smelter Arbitration* (1931–41), 3 R.I.A.A. 1905 (as-

serting a duty on the part of Canada to protect the United States from injurious transboundary air pollution generated by a Canadian smelter); and the *Lake Lanoux Arbitration* (1957), 12 R.I.A.A. 281 (holding that if France had adversely affected waters that flowed into Spain, France would have violated Spanish rights).

Precautionary principle. The precautionary principle, sometimes referred to as a "precautionary approach," generally provides that where there are threats of serious or irreversible damage, the lack of full scientific certainty that such threats will materialize should not be used as a reason for postponing cost effective measures to prevent the potential environmental degradation. *See* Rio Declaration, princ. 15. Some version of this principle appears in virtually all international environmental agreements adopted since 1990. Like the principle on prevention of environmental harm, the precautionary principle seeks to avoid environmental harm. Yet this principle is concerned with the difficulties in predicting with scientific certainty a future environmental harm, and calls upon states to tip the balance in favor of acting now even in the face of scientific uncertainty.

"Polluter pays" principle. The polluter pays principle provides that the polluter who creates an environmental harm generally should be forced to pay the costs of remedying that harm. The essential idea in this principle is to force polluters to internalize costs that would otherwise be imposed on others, so that polluters will consider environmen-

tal factors when making economically efficient decisions. *See* Rio Declaration, princ. 16.

Principle of non-discrimination. This principle provides that each state should ensure that its regime of environmental protection, when addressing pollution originating within the state, does not discriminate between pollution affecting the state and pollution affecting other states. An important example of this may be seen in multinational agreements on environmental impact assessments, which essentially require states to assess the extraterritorial environmental effects of projects within their jurisdiction in the same manner as they do the national effects of those projects. *See, e.g.*, Convention on Environmental Impact Assessment in a Transboundary Context, Feb. 25, 1991, 30 I.L.M. 800 (1991) (Espoo Convention).

Principle of Common but Differentiated Responsibilities. This principle recognizes that because developed states have contributed disproportionately to global environmental degradation, and because they command greater financial and technological resources, those states have a special responsibility in shouldering the burden of pursuing global sustainable development. *See* Rio Declaration, princ. 7. Some version of this principle also appears in virtually all global environmental agreements adopted since 1990.

Principle of Intergenerational Equity. This principle stresses that in making choices about meeting the needs of present generations, the needs of future generations should not be sacrificed. *See* Rio Declaration, princ. 3; E. Weiss, *In Fairness to Future Generations: International Law, Common Patrimony, and Intergenerational Equity* (1989).

§ **11–4. Techniques of legal regulation**. While all international environmental agreements seek in some way to protect or preserve the global environment, they employ a variety of techniques to regulate the behavior of states. In order to obtain reliable information on threats to the global environment, an agreement may contain provisions requiring a state to monitor and report on activities that may affect the quality of the environment. *See, e.g.*, LOSC, art. 204; Biological Diversity Convention, art. 7. With respect to specific development projects, an agreement may require the state to engage in an environmental impact assessment (EIA) so that the likely environmental consequences of the project are considered, as well as possible alternatives that are more environment-friendly. An entire agreement may be devoted to EIA, e.g., the Espoo Convention, or discrete provisions within agreements, e.g., Biological Diversity Convention, art. 14(1)(a).

Rather than simply monitor and assess adverse environmental effects, an agreement may require a state to apply the best available technology (BAT) or use the best practical means for avoiding such effects. *See* LRTAP Convention, art. 6. Whether a particular technology is BAT depends on various factors, such as its economic feasibility. An agreement may set standards regarding the manner in which products are produced (e.g., a ban on fishing with driftnets that sweep large quantities of non-targeted species into the net) or regarding the product itself (e.g., a regulation controlling the sulfur content of fuels). Many agreements establish limits on environmentally harmful emissions or discharges from a particular source, such as factories or oil tankers. *See, e.g.*, International Convention for the Prevention of Pollution from Ships, Nov. 2, 1973, 1340 U.N.T.S. 184, as amended Feb. 17, 1978, 1340 U.N.T.S. 61. If the risk of environmental harm is particularly high, an agreement may severely restrict or outright ban certain products or processes, such as a ban on the production of specified persistent organic pollutants. When establishing these regulations, the agreements may call for the state to impose a licensing or permitting system, a labeling system, or import/export restrictions as the means of regulation.

Yet rather than have the state impose specific restrictions, a few recent agreements call for or allow market-based measures that encourage efficiency in activities that pollute the environment. Such measures might involve taxing the polluter for emissions—a technique that does not bar pollution but creates an economic disincentive to pollute—or might involve a system of negotiable permits to pollute, so that the most economically productive entity can purchase rights to pollute from less economically productive entities, which would be "bought out" of their ability to pollute. *See* Kyoto Protocol, discussed *infra* § 11–6.

In certain limited circumstances, states have developed agreements that impose on private persons civil liability for the environmental damage they cause to other persons. The best developed of these regimes is the International Convention on Civil Liability for Oil Pollution Damage, Nov. 29, 1969, 973 U.N.T.S. 3, 9 I.L.M. 45 (1970), subsequently amended several times (CLC), and its associated Convention on the Establishment of an International Fund for Compensation for Oil Pollution Damage, Dec. 18, 1971, 1110 U.N.T.S. 57, 11 I.L.M. 284 (1972). The CLC provides that when damage occurs within a party's territory by discharges from ships carrying oil as cargo, the owner of the ship is liable, even without fault, in the local courts up to certain limits. The associated international fund pays compensation to claimants up to a certain limit when the shipowner is financially incapable of meeting its obligations or the damages exceed the shipowner's liability under the CLC. The fund is supported by pro rata contributions from entities within the parties' territories that receive large quantities of seaborne crude and heavy fuel oil. While several other civil liability conventions have also been concluded, they have experienced considerable difficulty in attracting widespread adherence. *See* G. Gauci, *Oil Pollution at Sea: Civil Liability and Compensation for Damage* (1997). A recent effort in this area is the Protocol on Liability and Compensation for Damage Resulting from the Transboundary Movement of Hazardous Wastes and Their Disposal, Dec.

10, 1999, U.N. Doc. UNEP–CHW.1–WG–1–9–2 (1999).

III.   REGULATION IN IMPORTANT SECTORS

§ **11–5. Ozone depletion**. The agreements designed to prevent the depletion of the stratospheric ozone layer are an excellent example of a sophisticated and successful international environmental regime. Beginning in the 1980's, scientists became convinced that certain widely used chemicals, when released into the air, were migrating up to the stratosphere where they would cause a chemical reaction that destroyed ozone molecules, allowing increased ultraviolet rays from the sun to pass through the ozone layer and harm human health and the environment on the earth. To address this problem, states adopted in 1985 the Vienna Convention for the Protection of the Ozone Layer, Mar. 22, 1985, T.I.A.S. 11097, 1513 U.N.T.S. 293 (Vienna Convention). Under that convention, the parties agreed to cooperate in monitoring and scientific assessment of stratospheric ozone depletion, and to take appropriate measures to prevent it from occurring. Vienna Convention, arts. 2–3. The Vienna Convention was a "framework convention," in the sense that it envisaged subsequent agreements on specific emissions obligations as scientific knowledge developed.

In 1987, the parties adopted the Montreal Protocol on Substances that Deplete the Ozone Layer, Sept. 16, 1987, *S. Treaty Doc. No.* 100–10 (1987), 1522 U.N.T.S. 3 (Montreal Protocol). The Montreal

Protocol provided for the progressive reduction by specified dates of the production of certain types of ozone-depleting chemicals—chlorofluorocarbons and halons—listed in annexes to the Protocol. Thereafter, further amendments to the Montreal Protocol have allowed additional chemicals or types of chemicals to be added to the control list (such as methyl chloroform, methyl bromide, and carbon tetrachloride), and further adjustments have been made by the Conference of the Parties so as to accelerate the reduction periods. An amendment in 1990 created a financial and technological assistance mechanism designed to help developing states meet incremental costs incurred in complying with the Montreal Protocol.

One important feature of the Montreal Protocol is the noncompliance procedure, called for in Montreal Protocol Article 8 and developed thereafter by decisions of the Conference of the Parties. Under this procedure, a party having difficulties in meeting its obligations, or a party with concerns about another party's fulfillment of its obligations, may report this to an implementation committee. The implementation committee gathers information, including on-site monitoring, and reports on the matter to the Conference of the Parties, which decides upon the steps necessary to bring the state into full compliance. Initially those steps might include providing assistance to the non-compliant state in the form of technology transfer, training, or financing. If a state remains non-compliant, a warning may be issued and ultimately a suspension of rights and privileges under the Protocol. For further information, see R. Benedick, *Ozone Diplomacy: New Directions in Safeguarding the Planet* (1998) (enlarged edition).

§ 11–6.   Global climate change. When coal, oil, wood, and natural gas are burned, they create gases (such as carbon dioxide) that rise into the atmosphere and create a screen comparable to tinted glass in a greenhouse. It is widely believed that by trapping solar heat in the earth's atmosphere, these "greenhouse gas" emissions are causing global warming, which over time may have dramatic effects on the global climate, causing polar ice to melt, ocean levels to rise, and worldwide temperatures and precipitation levels to change significantly. Under the U.N. Framework Convention on Climate Change (UNFCCC), May 9, 1992, *S. Treaty Doc. No.* 102–38 (1992), 1771 U.N.T.S. 107, states agreed to stabilize concentrations of all greenhouse gases in the atmosphere at a level that would prevent dangerous anthropogenic (i.e., human) interference with the climate system. UNFCCC, art. 2. The UNFCCC recognized the necessity of returning to earlier levels of emissions of greenhouse gases, but set no specific timetables and targets for doing so. UNFCCC, art. 4.

In December 1997, in Kyoto, Japan, a protocol to the UNFCCC was adopted accepting, in principle, that developed states should be bound to meet specific targets and timetables. If the standards set in the Kyoto Protocol, Dec. 10, 1997, 37 I.L.M. 22 (1998), were met, it was projected that by 2012 there would be an overall reduction in emissions levels to 5.2 percent below 1990 levels. Ratification of the Kyoto Protocol, however, was slowed by its failure to resolve a substantial number of issues about how it would operate.

In particular, difficult negotiations concerned: (1) the use of market-based approaches that would enable parties to engage in "emissions trading" and to employ other flexibility mechanisms in order to meet reduction requirements; (2) the means for counting carbon "sinks" (which remove greenhouse gases from the atmosphere) such as farmland, rangeland, and forests toward parties' reduction commitments; and (3) the means for determining and addressing a party's noncompliance. In 2001, before the Kyoto Protocol entered into force, the United States announced that it would not ratify the agreement on various grounds, including its view that the emissions targets were not scientifically based or environmentally effective, and that developing states should also be bound under any such protocol. Other developed states, notably Japan and the states of European Union, decided that they would go forward with ratification of the Kyoto Protocol, but since the United States was by far the largest emitter of global greenhouse gases, many states hoped that ultimately the United States would accept the Kyoto Protocol or a comparable agreement. For further information, see S. Oberthür & H. Ott, *The Kyoto Protocol: International Climate Policy for the 21st Century* (1999).

§ 11–7. Biological diversity. Contemporary concern with an integrated approach to the protection and preservation of global biological diversity is perhaps the logical outgrowth of the numerous early international instruments on nature conservation and protection of particular flora and fauna. The 1992 Biological Diversity Convention, cited *supra* § 11–3, defines biological diversity as:

> the variability among living organisms from all sources including, *inter alia*, terrestrial, marine and other aquatic ecosystems and the ecological complexes of which they are a part: this includes diversity within species, between species and of ecosystems.

Biological Diversity Convention, art. 2. Since the industrial revolution, pollution, urbanization, population growth, and the exploitation of natural resources has profoundly threatened biological diversity, leading to the extinction of many species worldwide at a rate far faster than would occur naturally.

The Biological Diversity Convention is a comprehensive umbrella instrument for protecting and preserving biological diversity. Recognizing that numerous other agreements address the protection of particular species, the Convention is directed principally at the rights and responsibilities of states at the national level with respect to biological diversity. Thus, the Convention requires states to identify important components of biological diversity within their jurisdiction, and to monitor activities that may have adverse impacts on that diversity. *See* Biological Diversity Convention, art. 7. Further, the Convention requires states to use this information to develop national strategies and plans for protecting and preserving biological diversity, thereby integrating concerns for biological diversity into national decision making. *Id.*, arts. 6 & 10. The Convention expresses a preference for *in-situ* conservation (in a natural habitat), but recognizes the complementary role of *ex situ* conservation (in a controlled environment, such as a "gene bank"). *Id.*, arts 8–9.

In the course of negotiating the Convention, the issue of the economic value of genetic resources could not be avoided. With respect to the ability to gain access to a genetic resource, the Convention states that decisions on such access rest with the national government where the resource is located. *Id.*, art. 15(1). At the same time, the Convention provides that states should facilitate access to such resources for environmentally sound uses and on mutually agreed terms. *Id.*, art. 15(2) & (3). Since a genetic resource can be used to develop a new biotechnology application (such as a new pharmaceutical), the Convention provides that states should take measures to share in a fair and equitable way the results of such biotechnology applications with the state providing the resource. *Id.* art. 19(2). For further information, see F. McConnell, *The Biodiversity Convention: A Negotiating History* (1996).

IV.   CROSS–SECTORAL ISSUES

§ 11–8.   Trade and environment. International environmental agreements may affect trade in various ways. They may impose trade sanctions as a means of encouraging non-parties to join the agreement or as a means of promoting compliance after a state has joined the agreement. They may directly restrict or prohibit trade in certain types of products as a means of fulfilling the purpose of the agreement. For instance, the Basel Convention on the Control of Transboundary Movements of Hazardous Wastes and Their Disposal, Mar. 22, 1989, 1673 U.N.T.S. 57, 28 I.L.M. 657 (1989), provides that a party may not export to, nor import from, a non-party any hazardous wastes, unless the party has a separate agreement with the non-party which is not less environmentally sound than the Basel Convention. *Id.*, arts. 4(5) & 11. Further, even as between parties, there may be no hazardous waste trade except pursuant to the notice-and-consent regime set forth in the Basel Convention, and a state wishing to prohibit such imports may do so. *Id.*, arts. 4 & 6.

Whenever international environmental agreements interfere with free trade, the values underlying both fields of international law can come into conflict. Further, there are often concerns stated that international trade obligations may be used to strike down national laws designed to protect the environment. The principal forum for adjudicating these conflicts has been the dispute settlement process before the World Trade Organization (WTO), which looks to trade agreements such as the General Agreement on Tariffs and Trade (GATT), Oct. 30, 1947, T.I.A.S. 1700, 55 U.N.T.S. 187, as amended, for its governing law. *See generally* F. Macmillan, *WTO and the Environment* (2001).

Under the GATT, trade restrictions are generally impermissible if they: (1) treat imports from one state less favorably than like products from another state (thus violating the most-favored-nation principle in GATT Article I); (2) treat imports less favorably than like local products (thus violating the national treatment principle in GATT Article III); or (3) constitute quantitative restrictions, such as quotas or bans (thus violating GATT Article XI). At the same time, GATT Article XX provides that impermissible trade restrictions may be justified if: (1) they are not applied in a manner which constitutes arbitrary or unjustifiable discrimination or a disguised restriction on trade; and (2) they constitute measures necessary to protect human, animal, or plant life or health, or constitute measures relating to the conservation of exhaustible natural resources (so long as those measures are made effective in conjunction with restrictions on national production or consumption).

An example of the use of these provisions before the WTO is the "shrimp-turtle case." Various states sued the United States over a U.S. law designed to protect endangered sea turtles by restricting imports of shrimp and shrimp products if they are caught without using "turtle excluder devices" (TEDs) or equally effective means of protecting turtles. *See* 16 U.S.C. § 1537 note (1994). In 1998, the WTO appellate body found that the U.S. import restrictions violated the GATT and that the Article XX exception could not be invoked because—while the law was designed to conserve sea turtles and while those turtles were an "exhaustible natural resource"—the *manner* in which the United States implemented its law constituted arbitrary and unjustifiable discrimination. Part of this discrimination derived from prohibiting imports of shrimp harvested by the commercial shrimp trawlers of certain states, even though those vessels were using turtle-excluder devices comparable to those considered acceptable for U.S. vessels. *See United States— Import Prohibition of Certain Shrimp and Shrimp Products*, WTO Doc. No. WT/DS58/AB/R (Oct. 12, 1998). Thereafter, rather than change or repeal the law, the United States pursued various steps to bring its implementation of the law into compliance with its GATT obligations, such as being more flexible in certifying foreign programs when comparable to U.S. programs. When Malaysia subsequently challenged the U.S. implementation of the appellate body report, the appellate body found the U.S. implementation to be GATT-compliant. *See United States—Import Prohibition of Certain Shrimp and Shrimp Products*, WTO Doc. No. WT/DS58/AB/RW (Oct. 22, 2001), *reprinted in* 41 I.L.M. 149 (2002); *see also EC Measures Affecting Asbestos and Asbestos–Containing Products*, WT/DS135/R (Sept. 18, 2000) (upholding under Article XX a 1996 French ban on imports of chrysotile asbestos from Canada).

The North American Free Trade Agreement, Dec. 17, 1992, Can.-Mex.-U.S., 32 I.L.M. 289 & 605 (1993) (NAFTA), contains some provisions on environmental protection. For instance, Article 1114(2) states that "it is inappropriate to encourage investment by relaxing domestic health, safety or environmental measures." Article 104 states that where there is a conflict between NAFTA and trade sanctions called for in certain international environmental agreements (such as the Montreal Protocol on ozone-depleting substances), the latter shall prevail. Further, NAFTA parties concluded a side agreement on environmental cooperation, 32 I.L.M. 1480 (1993), addressing government transparency and enforcement actions regarding environmental protection, and addressing private rights of action for violations of environmental laws and regulations. Various cases under NAFTA's investor-versus-state dispute resolution process have concerned environmental matters. For example, in *Metalclad Corp. v. United Mexican States*, 40 I.L.M. 36 (2001), a NAFTA arbitration panel found that Mexico expropriated the property interest of a U.S. investor when the Mexican federal government issued a permit allowing the U.S. investor to construct a hazardous waste disposal facility, but then failed to prevent Mexican local authorities from interfering with its operation purportedly on environmental grounds.

For further information on the trade and environment debate, see *Environment, Human Rights and International Trade* (F. Francioni ed., 2001); D. Esty, *Greening the GATT: Trade, Environment, and the Future* (1994).

§ 11–9. Extraterritorial application of environmental law. The shrimp-turtle case is an example of a national law being used as a means of regulating conduct outside U.S. territory. Yet not all U.S. environmental laws are regarded as applying extraterritorially. *Compare Amlon Metals, Inc. v. FMC Corp.*, 775 F.Supp. 668 (S.D.N.Y.1991) (finding that the Resource Conservation and Recovery Act did not provide a cause of action for damage in the United Kingdom from hazardous wastes shipped from the United States), *with Environmental Defense Fund v. Massey*, 986 F.2d 528 (D.C.Cir. 1993) (finding that the National Environmental Policy Act did require an environmental impact statement for major federal actions affecting the quality of the human environment in Antarctica).

Where U.S. environmental laws are viewed as applying extraterritorially, an issue arises regarding the propriety under international law of a state unilaterally using its law to control or influence activities occurring outside its borders. As discussed in Chapter 8, international law recognizes the ability of a state to prescribe legislation on the basis of certain principles, such as the territorial principle. National laws used to protect or preserve the foreign environment (such as turtles in foreign waters) do not fall neatly within those principles. Even if they did, the national laws must also be reasonable, taking into account factors such as the extent to which another state has an interest in regulating the affected activity.

CHAPTER 12

USE OF FORCE AND ARMS CONTROL

I. INTRODUCTION

The maintenance of international peace and security is a primary role of the United Nations under the U.N. Charter. Article 2(3) requires all members to "settle their international disputes by peaceful means in such a manner that international peace and security, and justice, are not endangered." Article 33(1) lists several peaceful dispute settlement mechanisms to serve as the first resort in lieu of force of arms (these processes are discussed in Chapter 4). Nevertheless, at times states resort to the use of military force against other states to resolve disputes, which implicates further Charter provisions and customary rules. This chapter addresses international norms regulating the use of force, as well as instruments in the field of arms control.

II. THE USE OF FORCE

§ 12–1. General prohibition on the use of force. The principle that the use of force is prohibited in international relations is embodied in Article 2(4) of the U.N. Charter. It provides:

All Members shall refrain in their international relations from the threat or use of force against the territorial integrity or political independence of any State, or in any other manner inconsistent with the Purposes of the United Nations.

The broad term "use of force" (rather than "war") reflects a desire to prohibit the resort to armed conflict generally, not just conflicts arising from a formal state of war. As such, many scholars interpret Article 2(4) as prohibiting all uses of force that were deemed permissible prior to enactment of the Charter, such as armed reprisal by a state to punish the unlawful act of another state.

By contrast, some scholars have argued that the phrase "against the territorial integrity and political independence of any state" should be read to limit the prohibition to uses of force that are above a threshold where territorial integrity or political independence of a state is impugned. Under this interpretation, a use of force to annex territory is prohibited, but not forcible action such as the protection of human rights, since the latter is not directed at altering territorial or political structures. Critics see this interpretation as eroding the strength of the overall prohibition on the use of force. They note that the quoted phrase was inserted in the text of Article 2(4) at the San Francisco conference in September 1945 as an effort to enhance the overall prohibition, not curtail it. *See* I. Brownlie, *International Law and the Use of Force by States* 265–68 (1963).

In the *Corfu Channel* case, the International Court of Justice was not sympathetic to the United Kingdom's claim that it could intervene in Albanian territorial waters to vindicate U.K. rights of innocent passage. The Court took the position that, regardless of the United Kingdom's good motive in clearing unlawful mines, the action was a violation of Albanian territorial integrity. Further, the Court was unmoved by arguments that unilateral action was necessary in the face of an inability or unwillingness of the Security Council to act:

> The Court can only regard the alleged right of intervention as the manifestation of a policy of force, such as has, in the past, given rise to most serious abuses and such as cannot, whatever be the present defects in international organization, find a place in international law.

Corfu Channel (U.K. v. Alb.), 1949 I.C.J. 4, 35 (Apr. 9).

§ 12–2. Inherent right of self-defense. The use of force in self-defense has always been recognized as legitimate in international law. Article 51 of the Charter makes this explicit by stating:

> Nothing in the present Charter shall impair the inherent right of individual or collective self-defence if an armed attack occurs against a Member of the United Nations, until the Security Council has taken measures necessary to maintain international peace and security. Measures taken by Members in the exercise of this right of self-

defence shall be immediately reported to the Security Council....

Article 51 does not grant a right of self defense but, rather, preserves a right that predated the U.N. Charter under customary international law. *See Military and Paramilitary Activities in and against Nicaragua* (Nicar. v. U.S.), 1986 I.C.J. 14, para. 176 (June 27). At the same time, Article 51 requires that there be an "armed attack" prior to the resort to self-defense; force or intervention below the level of an "armed attack" does not trigger a right of self-defense. *Id.*, para. 249.

The nature of the initial "armed attack" need not be conventional in the sense of military forces from one state invading another state to seize territory. On various occasions since 1945, when nationals of states have been threatened abroad, states have reacted by using armed force to conduct a rescue operation. In such instances, states usually characterize their actions as a lawful exercise of the right of self-defense, thereby implicitly viewing the threats to nationals abroad as an "armed attack." *See* N. Ronzitti, *Rescuing Nationals Abroad Through Military Coercion and Intervention on Grounds of Humanity* (1985).

Further, it does not appear that the initial "armed attack" needs to be made by a government. A terrorist organization based in Afghanistan, Al–Qaeda, orchestrated a series of airplane hijackings in the United States on September 11, 2001, which led to the collapse of the World Trade Center and extensive damage to the Pentagon. The United States first unsuccessfully demanded that the de facto government of Afghanistan (the Taliban) hand over the terrorists, but then exercised its right of self-defense by pursuing a military campaign in Afghanistan against both the terrorist organization and the Taliban. In its report to the Security Council explaining why it was exercising its right of self-defense, the United States asserted:

> The attacks on 11 September 2001 and the ongoing threat to the United States and its nationals posed by the Al–Qaeda organization have been made possible by the decision of the Taliban regime to allow the parts of Afghanistan that it controls to be used by this organization as a base of operation. Despite every effort by the United States and the international community, the Taliban regime has refused to change its policy. From the territory of Afghanistan, the Al–Qaeda organization continues to train and support agents of terror who attack innocent people throughout the world and target United States nationals and interests in the United States and abroad.

U.N. Doc. S/2001/946 (2001). The reaction of the global community to this resort to self-defense was largely supportive. The Security Council passed two resolutions prior to the U.S. military response declaring that the terrorist attacks threatened international peace and security, and expressly recognizing in this context the right of self-defense. S.C. Res. 1368 (2001); S.C. Res. 1373 (2001).

When a state resorts to self-defense, it remains a matter of debate whether an armed attack must have already occurred or can instead simply be imminent. In an age of weapons of mass destruction, some states and scholars assert that a right of "anticipatory" self-defense must exist since it is unreasonable to expect a state to refrain from responding to a potentially devastating, imminent attack. Others doubt the ability of a state to predict a future armed attack and view the concept of anticipatory defense as an undesirable erosion of the requirements of Article 51. *Compare* J. Stone, *Aggression and World Order: A Critique of United Nations Theories of Aggression* 100 (1958), *with* Q. Wright, *The Prevention of Aggression*, 50 Am. J. Int'l L. 514 (1956).

Article 51 recognizes an inherent right of individual *or collective* self-defense. Several regional defense agreements provide for collective self-defense, such as the North Atlantic Treaty, Apr. 4, 1949, 63 Stat. 2241, 34 U.N.T.S. 243, which is the charter for the North Atlantic Treaty Organization (NATO). NATO consists of seventeen European states, the United States, and Canada. Under Article 5 of the North Atlantic Treaty, the parties agree that an armed attack against one party in Europe or North America shall be considered an attack against all NATO parties, such that the other parties will assist the attacked party by taking such actions as they deem necessary. NATO's North Atlantic Council invoked Article 5 for the first time in the aftermath of the September 2001 terrorist incidents (discussed above).

An important rule of customary international law associated with the right of self-defense is that the defensive force must be necessary and proportionate to the armed attack that gave rise to the right. Reference in support of this proposition is typically made to the *Caroline* incident. In 1837, certain insurgents in Canada were receiving private support from within the United States. That support prompted British forces to attack and burn a vessel in a U.S. port, the *Caroline*, that was being used to support the insurgents. Britain claimed that the act was in self-defense, but U.S. Secretary of State Daniel Webster asserted that the action was neither necessary nor proportionate, as required under international law. *See* 29 Brit. & Foreign State Papers 1129, 1138 (1857). The continuing role of this requirement under the U.N. Charter was confirmed by the International Court of Justice in its *Advisory Opinion on Legality of the Threat or Use of Nuclear Weapons*, where it stated:

The submission of the exercise of the right of self-defence to the conditions of necessity and proportionality is a rule of customary international law. As the Court stated in the case concerning Military and Paramilitary Activities in and against Nicaragua (Nicaragua v. United States of America), there is a "specific rule whereby self-defence would warrant only measures which are proportional to the armed attack and necessary to respond to it, a rule well established in customary international law" (I.C.J. Reports 1986, p. 94, para. 176). This dual condition applies equally to Article 51 of the Charter, whatever the means of force employed.

1996 I.C.J. 226, para. 41 (July 8). In considering whether force is "necessary," the Court and scholars ask, among other things, whether there are peaceful alternatives to self-defense, such as pursuing diplomatic efforts. "Necessity" does not require the defender to limit itself to action that simply repels an attack; a state may also use force in self-defense to remove a continuing threat to future security. "Proportionality" does not require that the force be the mirror image of the initial attack, nor that the defensive actions be restricted to a particular geographic zone. Rather, proportionality will be assessed based on the result to be achieved by the defensive action, and not on the forms, substance and strength of the action itself.

§ 12–3. Peace enforcement by the Security Council. Under the U.N. Charter, the U.N. Security Council has primary responsibility for maintaining international peace and security. U.N. Charter, arts. 24 & 39. Under Chapter VII of the Charter, the Security Council has the authority to determine the existence of any "threat to the peace, breach of the peace, or act of aggression," and to decide upon either non-forcible or forcible measures to restore peace and security. U.N. Charter, arts. 39, 41 & 42. All member states are bound by such a decisions. U.N. Charter, art. 25. The Charter originally envisaged states entering into agreements with the United Nations so that armed forces could be quickly called up by the Security Council. U.N. Charter, arts. 43–46. Yet no such agreements were ever concluded. As a result, any Security Council measure authorizing a use of force typically leads to states deploying, on an ad hoc basis, national contingents under national command in support of the Security Council objective.

From 1945 to 1990, the Security Council rarely invoked its powers under Chapter VII because ideological conflicts between the East and West resulted in one or more of the permanent members of the Security Council vetoing such initiatives. During this period, the only Security Council authorization to use force against a "breach of the peace" was in response to North Korea's attack on South Korea in 1950 (at a time when the Soviet Union was boycotting the Security Council and was therefore unable to cast a veto). The Security Council recommended that states furnish "such assistance" to South Korea as necessary to repel the attack and "restore international peace and security in the area." S.C. Res. 82 (1950). Forces from various states deployed to Korea under overall U.S. command with the authority to use the U.N. flag in the course of its operations.

When the Soviet Union returned to the Security Council and blocked any further action, the General Assembly began to exercise some of the Council's power, relying to some extent on the so-called Uniting for Peace Resolution, see G.A. Res. 377 (1950), which provides in part:

[The General Assembly] *Resolves* that if the Security Council, because of lack of unanimity of the permanent members, fails to exercise its primary responsibility for the maintenance of international peace and security in any case where there appears to be a threat to the peace, breach of the peace or act of aggression, the General Assembly shall consider the matter immediately with a view to making appropriate recommendations to Members for collective measures, including in the case of a breach of the peace or act of aggression the use of armed force when necessary, to maintain or restore international peace and security.

The Uniting for Peace resolution, however, never became a significant means of conflict management, as the states best equipped to engage in "peace enforcement" actions were unwilling to assign to the General Assembly authority in this area. Rather, those states ultimately preferred to have authority in this area remain with the Security Council and, if the Security Council failed to authorize action, to proceed either unilaterally or under the authority of a regional organization.

Beginning in 1990, with the end of the Cold War and the decline of East–West tensions, the Security Council became much more active in authorizing the deployment of military force. After Iraq invaded Kuwait in August 1990, the Security Council imposed trade sanctions on Iraq and authorized a forcible maritime interception operation by states acting in defense of Kuwait. *See* S.C. Res. 665 (1990). Ultimately, the Security Council authorized states "to use all necessary means to uphold and implement" Security Council resolutions that demanded Iraq's immediate and unconditional withdrawal. *See* S.C. Res. 678 (1991). Under the authority of that resolution, a U.S.-led multinational coalition in January 1991 commenced an air campaign that concluded 42 days later after coalition ground forces swept through Kuwait and into southern Iraq, setting up a buffer zone between the two states. The Security Council then adopted a cease-fire resolution that, among other things, required Iraq to renounce its claims to Kuwait, accept a process for demarcation of the Iraq–Kuwait boundary, pay compensation for losses incurred during Iraq's invasion, and accept a U.N. inspection commission to oversee the elimination of Iraqi weapons of mass destruction. *See* S.C. Res. 687 (1991).

In the 1990's, the Security Council also began authorizing the deployment of military force to address widespread human rights violations, such as: the 1992 authorization for a U.S.-led coalition of states to intervene in Somalia to reopen food supply lines, *see* S.C. Res. 794 (1992); the 1993 authorization for NATO to use air power to protect six enclaves of Bosnian Muslims in Bosnia–Herzegovina, *see* S.C. Res. 836 (1993); the 1994 authorization for France to intervene in Rwanda to protect civilians from ethnic violence between Hutus and Tutsis, *see* S.C. Res. 929 (1994); and the 1994 authorization for a U.S.-led coalition to oust a military junta in Haiti and restore its democratically-elected

President, *see* S.C. Res. 940 (1994) (forcible intervention ultimately was not necessary as the military
junta then agreed step down).

Both the General Assembly and the Secretary–
General may bring to the attention of the Security
Council situations which are likely to endanger
international peace and security. *See* U.N. Charter,
arts. 11(3) and 99.

**§ 12–4. Peace enforcement by regional
organizations**. Chapter VIII of the U.N. Charter
encourages the use of regional organizations to
maintain international peace and security consistent with U.N. principles. U.N. Charter, art. 52.
Further, Chapter VIII envisages peace enforcement
by regional organizations, but only with Security
Council authorization. U.N. Charter, art. 53.

The most relevant regional organizations in this
regard are found in the Americas, Africa, and the
Middle East. In the Americas, the fundamental
agreements include the Inter–American Treaty of
Reciprocal Assistance, Sept. 2, 1947, 62 Stat. 1681,
21 U.N.T.S. 77 (the Rio Treaty), and the Charter of
the Organization of American States, Apr. 30, 1948,
2 U.S.T. 2394, 119 U.N.T.S. 3 (OAS Charter). The
OAS Charter expressly provides that "[w]ithin the
United Nations, the Organization of American
States is a regional agency." *Id.*, art. 1. Both the
Rio Treaty and the OAS Charter recognize the
territorial integrity and inviolability, sovereignty,
and political independence of the parties. Moreover,
they bind the parties not to use force against each
other and authorize the collective use of force for

the maintenance of peace and security on the continent. Of course, if an American state is attacked, that state may invoke the inherent right of self-defense under U.N. Charter Article 51, and these regional agreements recognize the principle of collective self-defense to meet such an attack. The charters of the African Union and the Arab League contain similar provisions.

The OAS "quarantine" of Cuba is the primary example of a use of force by a regional organization purportedly under the authority of Chapter VIII. In 1962, U.S. spy planes determined that the Soviet Union was equipping Cuba to launch long-range missiles. After the OAS recommended that states take all measures necessary to ensure that Cuba could not receive from Sino–Soviet powers missiles that might threaten the American continent, naval vessels from the United States and certain other American states turned back Soviet vessels headed to Cuba with arms. The United States argued that the action did not violate U.N. Charter Article 2(4) because it was permissible under Chapter VIII. Many doubted the validity of the legal justification given the absence of Security Council authorization. For subsequent reflections by the State Department's Legal Adviser, see A. Chayes, *The Cuban Missile Crisis* (1974).

A more recent example of peace enforcement by a sub-regional organization is the 1990 intervention in Liberia by states purportedly acting under the authority of the Economic Community of West African States (ECOWAS). When civil conflict broke out in Liberia, leading to extensive refugee flows to neighboring states, the sixteen states of ECOWAS decided to deploy military forces to Liberia to quell the fighting. Here, too, there was no advance authorization by the Security Council, and the intervention appeared outside the scope of ECOWAS's institutional authority, yet the international community tolerated the intervention, and after the fact the intervention was in effect endorsed by the Security Council. *See* U.N. Doc. S/22133 (1991); S.C. Res. 788 (1992).

§ **12–5. Mixed bases for the use of force**. When states engage in uses of force, they will sometimes use multiple arguments for why the force is justified, rather than just argue that an action constitutes self-defense. For instance, for the first time in its history, NATO in March 1999 used military force against a foreign state, the Federal Republic of Yugoslavia (FRY). As there was no Security Council resolution expressly authorizing the use of such force, the NATO states had to develop positions regarding why the action was lawful.

The U.S. position referred to various factors that, taken together, the United States believed justified the action: the commission by the FRY military and police of serious and widespread violations of international law in the FRY province of Kosovo against Kosovar Albanians; the threat that FRY actions in Kosovo could lead to a wider conflict in Europe; the FRY failure to comply with agreements with NATO and with the Organization for Security and Cooperation in Europe regarding FRY actions in Kosovo;

the FRY failure to comply with Security Council resolutions regarding FRY actions in Kosovo; the FRY failure to cooperate with the International Criminal Tribunal for the former Yugoslavia; and the FRY failure to abide by its own unilateral commitments.

For its part, the FRY viewed the NATO campaign as an unlawful use of force. Consequently, during the course of the bombing campaign, the FRY filed cases against ten NATO states before the International Court of Justice, along with a request for interim measures of protection. The Court denied that request and further dismissed the two cases brought against Spain and the United States on grounds that the jurisdictional grounds pled by the FRY were plainly untenable. The other eight cases remain pending as of mid–2002. For a discussion of the legality of NATO's intervention, see Symposium, *The International Legal Fallout from Kosovo*, 12 Eur. J. Int'l L. 391 (2001); *Editorial Comments*, 93 Am. J. Int'l L. 824 (1999).

§ 12–6. **U.N. peacekeeping**. Even during 1945–1990, when the United Nations was largely ineffective in engaging in "peace enforcement" activities, the United Nations had some success in dealing with hostilities through the use of multilateral "peacekeeping." Beginning as early as 1948, the Security Council has authorized on several occasions the deployment of military or police forces to maintain peace *when there was consent* from the states where the forces were to be deployed. In response to a request from the Secretary–General, states volunteer personnel, equipment, supplies or other support for a peacekeeping mission, and are then reimbursed from the mission budget at agreed rates. Peacekeepers remain members of their own national establishments, but are under the operational control of the United Nations.

These "peacekeeping" missions are not specifically provided for in the U.N. Charter, but can be based either on the Security Council's overall power in Chapter VI to recommend appropriate procedures or methods for resolving disputes peacefully, or its power in Chapter VII to issue binding decisions to restore international peace and security. The General Assembly's formal role in peacekeeping is small, being restricted principally to its function as a forum for public discussion of the issues, U.N. Charter, arts. 10–12, 14, although the I.C.J. has suggested that the Assembly's role may be somewhat greater than the language of the Charter suggests. *See Advisory Opinion on Certain Expenses of the United Nations*, 1962 I.C.J. 151 (July 20).

Different peacekeeping missions have served different functions, such as: assisting in a return to peace through mediation efforts; supervising a cease fire agreement; monitoring the disarmament of factions pursuant to a peace agreement; patrolling a buffer zone; and, more recently, monitoring elections and helping to rebuild failed states. While serving different functions, peacekeeping operations tend to share certain key elements. The presence of the peacekeepers is predicated on consent of the states in which they operate. The peacekeepers strive to maintain impartiality as between states or factions. Finally, the peacekeepers are lightly armed or unarmed and, as such, are neither equipped nor authorized to engage in military action other than as necessary to protect themselves. *See* H. McCoubrey & N. White, *The Blue Helmets: Legal Regulation of United Nations Military Operations* (1996). As of mid–2002, the United Nations had deployed since its inception fifty-four peacekeeping operations worldwide, with fifteen pending in places such as Bosnia–Herzegovina, the Congo, Cyprus, East Timor, Georgia, Kosovo, the Middle East, and Sierra Leone.

As is the case for U.N. authorization of peace enforcement, there can be significant difficulties in obtaining Security Council approval for a peacekeeping operation. Closely related to the political difficulties is the high cost of such operations. In the *Certain Expenses* case, the International Court of Justice found that expenses connected with the maintenance of peacekeeping forces in the Middle East and the Congo were properly expenses of the United Nations and could be assessed by the General Assembly. Consequently, the General Assembly apportions these costs to all U.N. members based on a special scale of assessments applicable to peacekeeping, taking into account the relative economic wealth of member states.

III. ARMS CONTROL

§ 12–7. Background. At the Hague Peace conferences of 1899 and 1907, states adopted various conventions codifying the rules of warfare. A basic rule laid down in Article 22 of the 1907 Hague Regulations on the laws and customs of war on land was that the "right of belligerents to adopt means of injuring the enemy is not unlimited." Convention Respecting the Laws and Customs of War on Land, Oct. 18, 1907, Annex, art. 22, 36 Stat. 2277, 205 Consol. T.S. 277, *reprinted in* A. Roberts & R. Guelff, *Documents on the Laws of War* 73, 77 (3d ed. 2000). This rule has animated subsequent agreements in which states have prohibited the use of certain kinds of weapons in warfare. Further, states have also found it in their interests to limit the level of armaments that states may have, with such limitations sometimes expressed in terms of ratios based on the size of the participating states. Finally, the United States and the Soviet Union engaged in important bilateral arms agreements, some of which remain important in the post-Soviet era.

§ 12–8. Conventional weapons. Perhaps the most important agreement in this area is the Treaty on Conventional Armed Forces in Europe, Nov. 19, 1990, *S. Treaty Doc. No.* 102–8 (1991), 30 I.L.M. 1. Under the CFE Treaty, North American and European states set specific limits for each party on a range of conventional weapons, such as tanks, artillery, aircraft, helicopters, and armored combat vehicles. Further, the CFE Treaty provided for extensive monitoring and verification procedures.

More recently, states worldwide have been concerned with the international small arms trade, particularly as it affects conflict-prone states in Africa and parts of Asia. In December 1999, the

U.N. General Assembly launched a conference to address this issue. Although some states sought a legally-binding agreement, other states (notably the United States) resisted any agreement that would constrain the legitimate weapons trade or that would infringe upon rights in national laws to own small arms. On July 21, 2001, the participating states adopted a voluntary, politically-binding program of action calling upon states to pursue a variety of national, regional, and global measures against the illicit international trade in small arms.

§ 12–9. Chemical and biological weapons. Three important multilateral agreements ban the use of chemical and biological weapons. The Geneva Protocol, June 17, 1925, 26 U.S.T. 571, 94 L.N.T.S. 65, bans the use in war of "asphyxiating, poisonous or other gases," as well as "bacteriological methods of warfare." The protocol does not, however, ban the production or possession of such weapons.

The Biological Weapons Convention, Apr. 10, 1972, 26 U.S.T. 583, 1015 U.N.T.S. 163, bans the development, production, stockpiling or acquisition of biological agents or toxins "of types and in quantities that have no justification for prophylactic, protective, and other peaceful purposes." The convention contains no inspection or verification provisions, but in 1994 the parties decided to establish a special conference of the parties to consider the creation of verification measures, including through adoption of a legally-binding protocol. Such a protocol was ultimately drafted, but in July 2001, the

United States announced that it could not support further negotiation of such a protocol since it did not believe that the mechanisms envisioned would provide useful, accurate and complete information on illicit activity, and might have adverse effects on legitimate commercial activities (e.g., by exposing lawful trade secrets).

The Chemical Weapons Convention (CWC), Jan. 13, 1993, *S. Treaty Doc. No.* 103–21 (1993), 32 I.L.M. 800, forbids parties from developing, producing, stockpiling, or using chemical weapons, and requires all parties to destroy existing chemical weapons within ten years after the convention's entry into force, which occurred in 1997. The CWC has two verification regimes designed to ensure compliance: one involving routine visits by teams of inspectors; and the other involving challenge inspections initiated by a member state against another member state when noncompliance is suspected. The CWC created the Organization for the Prohibition of Chemical Weapons (OPCW), which is based in The Hague, The Netherlands.

§ 12–10. Nuclear weapons. The Limited Test Ban Treaty, Aug. 5, 1963, 14 U.S.T. 1313, 480 U.N.T.S. 43, banned all nuclear explosions except for underground tests. While many nuclear weapon states (including the United States) currently follow a self-imposed moratorium on any underground nuclear tests, India and Pakistan both conducted such tests in 1998. In 1996, the U.N. General Assembly adopted a Comprehensive Test Ban Treaty (CTBT) that would prohibit states from conducting any nuclear tests, whether for purposes of weapons development or otherwise, and would establish a system for monitoring seismic incidents and on-site inspections. *See* G.A. Res. 50/245 (1996). Although the United States signed the convention in 1996, a Senate vote in October 1999 failed to achieve the requisite consent of two-thirds of the Senate (the vote was 51–48).

The Nuclear Nonproliferation Treaty, July 1, 1968, 21 U.S.T. 483, 729 U.N.T.S. 161, calls upon states to work toward nuclear disarmament and to share nuclear technology for peaceful purposes, while at the same time preserving the right of five (and only five) states to possess nuclear weapons (China, France, Russia, the United Kingdom, and the United States). However, other states with nuclear capability, such as India, Israel, and Pakistan, have not joined this treaty.

One of the most important nuclear arms control agreements was the Treaty on the Limitation of Anti–Ballistic Missile Systems (ABM Treaty), May 26, 1972, U.S.-U.S.S.R., 23 U.S.T. 3435. As further amended in 1973, the ABM Treaty provided that the United States and the Soviet Union each could have only one very restricted ABM deployment area, thus precluding either state from developing a nationwide ABM defense. Since each side would have the ability to retaliate against the other side, the ABM Treaty was thought to make it far less likely that either side would resort to a nuclear first strike. In December 2001, President George W. Bush announced that the United States was withdrawing from the ABM Treaty, so as to be able to develop and deploy a national missile defense system capable of stopping ballistic missiles that might be launched by "rogue" states, such as North Korea.

Various other agreements—the Strategic Arms Limitation Talks (SALT) agreements, the Strategic Arms Reduction Talks (START) agreements, and the Intermediate Nuclear Forces (INF) Treaty— were all designed to freeze, reduce, or eliminate different types of nuclear weapons during the period of the Cold War. Some of these agreements never actually entered into force, while others have been questioned in the post-Cold War era as no longer responding to contemporary needs. In May 2002, Russia and the United States built upon these treaties by concluding a Strategic Offensive Reductions Treaty, in which they agreed to reduce nuclear warheads on launchers to a range of 1,700 to 2,200 warheads. When signing the treaty, President Bush stated that "[t]his treaty liquidates the Cold War legacy of nuclear hostility between our countries."

CHAPTER 13

INTERNATIONAL LEGAL RESEARCH

I. INTRODUCTION

Chapter 2 dealt with the formal sources and evidence of international law. This chapter introduces specific textual and online sources that international lawyers employ when they search for specific authority on a given point of law. The presentation assumes that the reader has an understanding of the conceptual framework and sources of international law described in Chapter 2.

II. TREATISES AND OTHER SCHOLARLY MATERIAL

§ **13–1. Treatises**. Treatises are the most useful starting point for research in international law. These books, usually written by leading scholars in the field, provide an analytical exposition of the law and contain extensive citations to all relevant authorities. Such treatises exist in many languages and translations. The following are useful English-language treatises:

A. Aust, *Modern Treaty Law and Practice* (2000).

I. Brownlie, *Principles of Public International Law* (5th ed. 1998).

A. Cassese, *International Law* (2001).

L. Chen, *An Introduction to Contemporary International Law: A Policy–Oriented Perspective* (2d ed. 2000).

L. Henkin, *Foreign Affairs and the United States Constitution* (2d ed. 1996).

D. O'Connell, *International Law* (2d ed. 1970) (two vols.).

Oppenheim's International Law (R. Jennings & A. Watts, eds., 9th ed. 1992).

O. Schachter, *International Law in Theory and Practice* (1991).

M. Shaw, *International Law* (4th ed. 1997).

§ 13–2. Encyclopedias, dictionaries and restatements. Various encyclopedias, dictionaries, and restatements are available for research on specific topics or terms. The following are of particular value:

Encyclopedia of Public International Law (R. Bernhardt ed., 1994–2000) (four volumes containing hundreds of essays and bibliographies by leading scholars and practitioners from around the globe). This version reprints, updates, and supplements a twelve-volume series published in 1981–1990.

E. Osmanczyk, *The Encyclopedia of the United Nations and International Relations* (2d ed. 1990).

J. Fox, *Dictionary of International and Comparative Law* (2d ed. 1997).

Restatement (Third) on the Foreign Relations Law of the United States (1987) (two volumes) (supplemented annually).

Published by the American Law Institute (ALI), the *Restatement (Third)* is a highly valued international law research tool. U.S. courts generally view it as the most authoritative U.S. scholarly statement of contemporary international law. The *Restatement (Third)* deals with public international law and the relevant U.S. law bearing on the application of international law in and by the United States (including where U.S. law differs from international law). Each section consists of a statement of the "black letter law," followed by comments and reporters' notes. The latter are particularly useful because of their careful analysis of and citations to the relevant international law authorities. Unlike the comments, the reporters' notes state the views of the reporters only and their substance is not endorsed as such by the ALI.

The ALI adopted in 1965 the *Restatement (Second) on the Foreign Relations Law of the United States*. Although forming part of the *Restatement (Second)* series, no earlier official version was ever published.

§ 13–3. Casebooks. Casebooks are widely used in the United States for the study of law and can be useful reference tools for international law research. Besides reproducing the major international and national judicial decisions dealing with international law questions, casebooks usually also contain extensive notes, comments and valuable bibliographic information. A casebook is often accompanied by a supplementary volume of basic documents, containing the texts of major international agreements and other materials of importance. The supplements themselves are a useful source of sometimes hard to find information and documentation. The following are among the major U.S. casebooks:

C. Blakesley, E. Firmage, R. Scott & S. Williams, *The International Legal System: Cases and Materials* (5th ed. 2001).

B. Carter & P. Trimble, *International Law* (3d ed. 1999).

L. Damrosch, L. Henkin, R. Pugh, O. Schachter & H. Smit, *International Law: Cases and Materials* (4th ed. 2001).

M. Janis & J. Noyes, *International Law: Cases and Materials* (2d ed. 2001).

J. Dunoff, S. Ratner, & D. Wippman, *International Law: Understanding Process Through Problems* (2002).

H. Steiner, D. Vagts & H. Koh, *Transnational Legal Problems: Materials and Text* (4th ed. 1994).

B. Weston, R. Falk & H. Charlesworth, *International Law and World Order: A Problem Oriented Casebook* (3d. ed. 1997).

In addition to international law casebooks of a general type, more and more specialized casebooks are now also being published. These deal with a variety of subjects, including international organizations, human rights, national security law, law of the sea, international civil litigation, international criminal law, international environmental law, international business transactions, trade law, and European Union law.

§ 13–4. **Periodical literature**. For research involving contemporary international law issues, it is imperative to check the periodical literature on the subject. In the United States, there are some seventy student-edited and about seventeen peer-edited journals focusing on international or comparative law. *See* G. Crespi, *Ranking International and Comparative Law Journals: A Survey of Expert Opinion*, 31 Int'l Law. 869 (1997). Further, articles dealing with international topics appear not only in specialized international law journals published in the United States and abroad, but also in general law reviews. Articles published in U.S., U.K. and some Commonwealth law journals are indexed in the *Index to Legal Periodicals* (1886–) and the *Current Law Index* (1980–). Material on international law appearing in foreign journals and in a selected number of U.S. reviews are noted in the *Index to Foreign Legal Periodicals* (1960–). An even more comprehensive bibliographic guide, published by the Max Planck Institute for Comparative Public Law and International Law, is *Public International Law: A Current Bibliography of Articles* (1978–). It provides access to more than 1,000 journals and collected works from all parts of the world.

Some of the leading law journals in the field of public international law are:

American Journal of International Law (1907–) (the leading U.S. law review on this subject).

European Journal of International Law (1990–).

International and Comparative Law Quarterly (1952–).

International Lawyer (1966–) (a practice-oriented journal, published by the International Law Section of the American Bar Association).

Leiden Journal of International Law (1988–).

Indian Journal of International Law (1960–).

Recueil des Cours (1924–)(reprints of the course lectures, in English and French, offered each summer at the Hague Academy of International Law by leading international lawyers, usually containing extensive bibliographies).

Revue Générale de Droit International Public (1894–) (contains articles in French).

Zeitschrift für Ausländisches Öffentliches Recht und Völkerrecht (title in English is the *Heidelberg Journal of International Law*) (1929–) (contains articles in German and English).

Many foreign-language international law journals publish a significant number of articles in English. Hence, the mere fact that a citation to an article points to a Dutch, French or German international law review, for example, does not exclude the possibility that the piece appears in English. Where this is not the case, moreover, English summaries are at times provided. Foreign international law journals as a rule also reproduce or summarize decisions of national tribunals, legislation and governmental pronouncements of interest to international lawyers.

III. INTERNATIONAL AGREEMENTS

§ 13–5. International agreements generally. Article 102 of the U.N. Charter provides that every international agreement entered into by a U.N. member state shall be registered with and published by the U.N. Secretariat. Consequently, the principal source for the official texts of multilateral and bilateral agreements on a worldwide basis for the years 1946 forward is the *United Nations Treaty Series,* (UNTS)(1946–). U.N.T.S. presently contains more than 30,000 international agreements and related documents, and texts are provided in their official languages. Texts may also be accessed online from the U.N. treaty collection for a fee at <http://untreaty.un.org>.

For treaty texts not yet published in U.N.T.S., reference may be made to *International Legal Materials* (I.L.M.) (1962–). Published bimonthly by the American Society of International Law, the I.L.M. is a very current source for texts of significant international agreements. I.L.M. is available for full text searching on the *WESTLAW* electronic database, in the *ILM* file (1980–), and on the *LEXIS/NEXIS* electronic database, in the *INTLAW* library and the *ILMTY* file (1980–).

For treaties predating the United Nations, reference should be made to the *League of Nations*

Treaty Series (LNTS)(1920–45). As the predecessor treaty compilation to U.N.T.S., this set provides texts of treaties from 1920 to 1945. Index volumes are available with the set, but there is no cumulative index.

For treaties predating the League of Nations, reference should be made to *Consolidated Treaty Series 1648–1919* (1969–86). Edited by Clive Parry and published by Oceana Publications, this series is the major compilation of treaties on a worldwide basis from 1648 to 1919, without subject indexes, but with chronological and party indexes.

Some Internet sites seek to provide the texts of the most important international agreements, as well as links to sites containing other agreements. *See, e.g.*, <http://fletcher.tufts.edu/multilaterals.html>.

For indexes allowing you to determine the existence of a U.S. international agreement on a particular subject or with a particular state, the best place to start is the United Nations' *Multilateral Treaties Deposited with the Secretary–General* (1981–). This is an annual cumulative index to 486 major multilateral treaties deposited with the United Nations. Citations are given to U.N.T.S., if available, along with information on the date of entry into force and a list of the parties. This index also provides updates on treaty status and amendments. For an online version of this index, see <http://untreaty.un.org/English/bible/englishinternetbible/bible.asp>. For a cumulative index on CD–

Rom for all U.N.T.S. agreements, see William S. Hein & Company's *United Nations Master Treaty Index on CD–Rom* (1995–).

Another useful index is C. Wiktor, *Multilateral Treaty Calendar—Repertoire des Traités Multilateraux*, 1648–1995 (1998). The *Multilateral Treaty Calendar* contains a detailed subject index and chronological list of all multilateral treaties concluded between 1648–1995. For each treaty entry, citations to relevant print treaty compilations are included, along with information concerning treaty amendments, modifications, extensions and terminations.

§ 13–6. International agreements of the United States. There are various official sources that may be checked to locate an international agreement to which the United States is a party.

For international agreements that the United States concluded more than approximately eight years ago, reference can be made to the Department of State's series entitled *United States Treaties and Other International Agreements* (U.S.T.) (1950–). U.S.T. is the official bound publication of U.S. international agreements arranged chronologically. This series also includes relevant presidential proclamations, diplomatic correspondence, and conference documents. Once an agreement is concluded, however, it may take up to eight years before the agreement appears in a U.S.T. volume. The *US-TREATIES* library available in *WESTLAW* also provides access to treaties found in this source from June 1979 to the most recent volume.

For U.S. international agreements not in U.S.T., reference may be made to the individual pamphlets issued by the Department of State in the *Treaties and Other International Acts Series* (T.I.A.S.) (1946–). The individual pamphlets issued in this series are numbered chronologically, but these too lag behind the conclusion of an agreement by about five years. Once an international agreement is published in U.S.T. (see above), the U.S.T. contains a T.I.A.S. to U.S.T. conversion table. The predecessor series to T.I.A.S. was the Department of State's *Treaty Series* (T.S.) (1908–46).

For U.S. treaties not in one of the above sources, reference may be made to *Senate Treaty Documents* (1981–), published in both pamphlet and microfiche form. These documents, which are numbered sequentially within each Congress (*e.g.*, Treaty Doc. 99–1), contain the texts of treaties as submitted to the Senate for its advise and consent, as well as useful explanatory messages from the President and the Secretary of State. Once a treaty is submitted to the Senate, it retains the treaty document number through subsequent Congresses, until it is ratified, defeated, or withdrawn. Before 1981, such information was found in *Senate Executive Documents* (1895–1981), which were lettered sequentially within each session of Congress (*e.g.*, *S. Exec. Doc. A*). Researchers should also be aware of the *Senate Executive Reports,* issued by the Senate Foreign Relations Committee after its consideration of individual treaties, containing the committee's analysis of a treaty and its recommendation as to consent by the whole Senate.

For U.S. international agreements not in one of the above sources, reference may be made to unofficial sources, such as *International Legal Materials (I.L.M.)* (noted above) or *Hein's United States Treaties and Other International Agreements Current Service* (1990–). The latter is a microfiche set providing full-text reproductions of current U.S. international agreements that have not yet been assigned T.I.A.S. numbers.

For pre–1950 U.S. international agreements (predating the U.S.T. series), reference should be made to *United States Statutes at Large* (1789–). This source published all ratified U.S. treaties from 1776 to 1949 and all executive agreements from 1931 to 1951. Volume 64, Part 3, at B1107, conveniently indexes by state all international agreements published in *Statutes at Large* for the period 1776–1949. Volume 8 conveniently collects together all the texts of ratified U.S. treaties from 1776–1845. After 1949, U.S. international agreements were published in T.I.A.S. and U.S.T., not in *Statutes at Large*.

Another useful source of pre–1950 U.S. international agreements is *Treaties and Other International Agreements of the United States of America, 1776–1949* (1968–1976) (commonly known as "Bevans," since it was compiled by Charles I. Bevans of the U.S. Department of State). Volumes 1–4 are multilateral agreements arranged chronologically by date of signature, while volumes 5–12 are bilateral agreements arranged by state. Oceana Publications' *Unperfected Treaties of the United States of America, 1776–1976* (1976–1994), provides the texts of proposed U.S. treaties from 1776 to 1976 that never entered into force.

For indexes allowing you to determine the existence of a U.S. international agreement on a particular subject or with a particular state, the best place to start is the Department of State's *Treaties in Force: A List of Treaties and Other International Agreements of the United States in Force on [Year]* (1944–) (TIF). Published annually, TIF indexes only U.S. international agreements in force as of January 1 of each year of publication. International agreements are arranged by broad topics and by state, with citations to the U.S.T. or T.I.A.S. series as appropriate. To identify new international agreements that the United States has concluded since January 1, or to determine if any new parties have acceded to a particular multilateral agreement, reference may be made to the "Treaty Actions" section of the Department of State's monthly *Dispatch* publication, which can be found at <http://www.state.gov/www/publications/dispatch/index.html>.

Alternatively, reference may be made to William S. Hein & Company's *Guide to United States Treaties in Force* (I. Kavass ed., 1982–). This commercial publication expands on the indexing of TIF by including agreements entered into force after TIF's publication. It also includes non-binding and other unrecorded international agreements, as well as updates relating treaty status and amendments. Further, *Hein's U.S. Treaty Index on CD–Rom* (1991–), provides citations for international agreements from 1776 to the present, as well as information concerning subsequent history, including amendments and status updates.

§ 13–7. International agreements on electronic databases. For those with access to the *WESTLAW* and *LEXIS/NEXIS* electronic databases, international agreements are available in various libraries and files of those databases. For example, *U.S. Treaties and Other International Agreements* from June, 1979 to the present may be found in *WESTLAW: USTREATIES*. Likewise, basic documents of international economic law may be found in *LEXIS: INTLAW* library, *BDIEL* file.

IV. STATE AND INTERNATIONAL ORGANIZATION PRACTICE

§ 13–8. Contemporary practice of governments. Governmental pronouncements and official positions on questions of international law play a vital role in the creation of customary international law. *See supra* § 2–3. Evidence of this practice is, therefore, carefully collected by foreign offices and/or legal scholars in different states.

Both periodical journals (*see supra* § 13.4) and yearbooks on international law are an excellent source of information regarding a state's practice in the field of international law for a given year. Often they include cases from national courts interpreting international laws, reviews of the international practice of particular states or regions, essays by scholars on topics of contemporary importance, and excerpts from national statutes that touch upon international issues. Some significant yearbooks include:

African Yearbook of International Law—Annuaire Africain de Droit International (1993–).

Annuaire de l'Institut de Droit International (1877–).

Annuaire Français de Droit International (1955–).

Asian Yearbook of International Law (1991–).

British Yearbook of International Law (1921–).

Canadian Yearbook of International Law 1963–).

German Yearbook of International Law—Jahrbuch für Internationales Recht (1957–).

Max Planck Yearbook of United Nations Law (1997–).

Netherlands Yearbook of International Law (1970–).

§ 13–9. Contemporary practice of the United States. Researchers interested in obtaining information about the practice of the United States in international law should refer to the U.S. Department of State's Internet site at <http://www.state.gov>. Further, until 1999 the Department of State issued monthly the *Department of State Dispatch* (1990–99), which provided State Department news and policy documents. It is also available via *WESTLAW* in the *USDPTSDIS* library.

The predecessor to the *Department of State Dispatch* was the *Department of State Bulletin* (1939–89). The *Bulletin,* also published monthly, is a good source of information for historical materials and policy statements of the Department of State.

Each quarterly issue of the *American Journal of International Law* contains a section on *Contemporary Practice of the United States Relating to International Law*, which summarizes the U.S. position on recent developments in international law, with extracts of relevant documents and citations to further sources.

§ 13–10. Past practice of the United States. For past practice of the United States in matters relating to international law, the following volumes are useful.

S. Murphy, *United States Practice in International Law, 1999–2001* (2002). This volume is the first in a planned series of volumes providing a comprehensive overview of the United States' involvement in international law during the course of three-year periods. Unlike the other volumes listed below, these volumes are not prepared under the auspices of the U.S. government.

Digest of United States Practice in International Law, 2000 (S. Cummins & D. Stewart eds., 2001). This U.S. Department of State digest, the first in a planned series, reproduces without commentary extracts of State Department documents for the covered year, such as speeches and court pleadings.

Cumulative Digest of United States Practice in International Law (1993). This U.S. Department of State digest covers developments during 1981–88 and was published in two volumes.

Digest of United States Practice in International Law (1973–80). This U.S. Department of State digest covers developments from 1973 to 1980 and was published in seven volumes.

M. Whiteman, *Digest of International Law* (1963–73). This U.S. Department of State digest primarily covers developments from 1940 to 1960 and was published in fifteen volumes.

G. Hackworth, *Digest of International Law* (1940–44). This U.S. Department of State digest primarily covers developments from 1906 to 1939 and was published in eight volumes.

J. Moore, *A Digest of International Law* (2d ed. 1906). This U.S. Department of State digest covers developments from 1776 to 1906 and was published in eight volumes.

F. Wharton, ed., *A Digest of the International Law of the United States* (1886). This digest is considered the first true digest of U.S. practice in international law and was published in three volumes.

Digest of the Published Opinions of the Attorneys–General, and of the Leading Decisions of the Federal Courts with Reference to International Law,

Treaties, and Kindred Subjects [1877] (rev. ed. reprinted by William S. Hein & Company in 1998). The original edition, prepared by John L. Cadwalader, was the first subject compilation of official texts on U.S. practice in international law.

§ 13–11. Practice of the United Nations. The legally relevant practice of the United Nations is periodically recorded in the official multi-volume *Repertory of Practice of United Nations Organs* (1958–). This publication analyzes the practice by reference to individual provisions of the U.N. Charter. Another very useful research tool on the practice of the United Nations and its specialized agencies is the *United Nations Juridical Yearbook* (1962–). It reproduces, *inter alia,* important opinions rendered by the legal officers of the United Nations and the specialized agencies, summaries of the decisions of the U.N. and ILO Administrative Tribunals and of national tribunals bearing on the work of the United Nations, and selected resolutions and other legally significant information. Each volume also contains a useful systematic bibliography.

Although not designed for lawyers as such, the *Yearbook of the United Nations* (1947–), which chronicles the activities of the United Nations on an annual basis, is a useful research tool. It provides the reader with a thorough overview of the work of individual U.N. organs, together with often hard to find citations to the relevant documents bearing on the subject under consideration. The annual *Report of the Secretary–General on the Work of the Organi-*

zation performs a similar function by summarizing the activities of the different U.N. organs.

The resolutions of the U.N. General Assembly and the Security Council are issued in separate publications. The resolutions of the subsidiary organs of the U.N. can be found in the annual reports these bodies submit to their respective parent organs. These reports frequently contain much information of interest to the legal researcher.

The United Nations Internet site is very comprehensive and well organized. Many important U.N. documents, including Security Council and General Assembly resolutions, can be retrieved online at <http://www.un.org>. This site also contains a research guide to retrieve other U.N. documents. For a UN-oriented Internet site set up by Yale University, see <http://www.library.yale.edu/un/index.html>.

Useful recent treatises on the United Nations are:

The United Nations and International Law (C. Joyner ed., 1997).

The Charter of the United Nations: A Commentary (B. Simma ed., 1994).

La Charte des Nations Unies: Commentaire Article par Article (J. Cot & A. Pellet eds., 2d ed. 1991).

§ 13–12. International Law Commission. The activities of the International Law Commission of the United Nations (*see supra* §§ 2–7, 3–7) are described in three sources. First, the *Yearbook of*

the International Law Commission (1949–) reproduces records of meetings which took place in a
given year (vol. I) and the texts of major reports
produced during the year, including the annual
report to the General Assembly (vol. II). Many of
these studies are comprehensive legal monographs
of great practical and scholarly authority, and thus
are a valuable resource for international lawyers.
Second, *The Work of the International Law Commission* (5th ed. 1996) gives an overview of the
I.L.C.'s activities and reproduces the full text of
legal instruments drafted under its aegis. Third, the
*Analytical Guide to the Work of the International
Law Commission*, 1949–1997 (1998) describes the
work of the I.L.C. on legal issues falling within its
mandate with references to source materials. For
information   online   about   the   I.L.C.,   see
<http://www.un.org/law/ilc/index.htm>.

V.   JUDICIAL AND ARBITRAL DECISIONS

§ **13–13.   General sources for judicial and
arbitral decisions**. The best general source for
finding recent international judicial and arbitral
decisions, as well as some national court decisions
dealing with international law issues, is *International Law Reports* (1950–). Each volume includes a
digest of cases, a table of treaties, and a subject
index. A cumulative index exists for volumes 1–80.
The predecessors to this series were *Annual Digest
and Reports of International Law Cases* (1933–49)
and *Annual Digest of International Law Cases*
(1919–32).

The most comprehensive collection of international arbitral decisions is the United Nations publica-

tion *Reports of International Arbitral Awards* (1948–), where selected decisions rendered since the 1890's are reproduced. Other early collections are J. Scott, *Hague Court Reports* (ser. 1, 1916) (ser. 2, 1932) and J. Moore, *International Arbitrations* (1898).

International Legal Materials often reprints important decisions of international judicial and arbitral decisions, as well as U.S. and foreign court decisions relating to international law. Each quarterly issue of the *American Journal of International Law* summarizes important decisions of such tribunals, as do several of the other journals listed *supra* § 13–4. Other specialized law reviews follow a similar practice in their field. Thus, *Human Rights Law Journal,* reproduces major decisions of the European and Inter–American human rights tribunals and of other international human rights bodies. Important national court decisions are also reported in the various national yearbooks listed *supra* § 13–8.

§ **13–14. I.C.J. decisions**. The International Court of Justice publishes decisions in volumes entitled *Reports of Judgments, Advisory Opinions and Orders* (1947–). Other materials relating to International Court proceedings are issued in *Pleadings, Oral Arguments and Documents* (1948–). The United Nations has published *Summaries of Judgments, Advisory Opinions, and Orders of the International Court of Justice, 1948–1991* (1992). The Max Planck Institute has published many of the Court's decisions in an analytical format. *See Digest of the Decisions of the International Court of Justice, 1976–1985* (1990); *Digest of the Decisions of the*

International Court of Justice, 1959–1975 (1978). Further information relating to the work of the International Court and its jurisdiction can be found in the annual *Yearbook of the International Court of Justice* (1947–) or online at <http://www.icj-cij.org>. The Permanent Court of International Justice followed an official publication practice similar to that of the International Court.

§ **13–15. EC court decisions**. Decisions of the Court of Justice of the European Community are found in the official *Reports of Cases before the Court of Justice and the Court of First Instance* (1991–) and predecessor series on cases before the Court. Unofficial commercial collections published in the United Kingdom (*Common Market Law Reports*) and in the United States (*CCH Common Market Reports*) are also available. Information may also be found online at <http://www.europa.eu.int/cj/index.htm>.

The European Court of Human Rights publishes *Publications of the European Court of Human Rights: Series A, Judgments and Decisions* (1960–) and *European Court of Human Rights: Series B, Pleadings, Oral Arguments and Documents* (1960–). These materials are also available online at <http://www.echr.coe.int>. Decisions of the European Court of Human Rights and the European Commission of Human Rights are also reproduced in the *Yearbook of the European Convention of Human Rights* (1960–). The *Yearbook*, however, does not always reprint material in full.

§ **13–16. Inter–American Court of Human Rights decisions**. From 1982 to 1987, the Inter–

American Court of Human Rights used a two-series approach similar to that of its European counterpart; namely, *Series A, Judgments and Opinions* and *Series B, Pleadings, Oral Arguments and Documents.* In 1987 it added a third series, entitled *Series C: Decisions and Judgments.* Decisions of the Inter–American Court and Commission of Human Rights are also published in their separate *Annual Reports to the OAS General Assembly.* These materials are also available online at <http://www.corteidh.or.cr>. For an annual yearbook reporting on the Court, see *Anuario Interamericano de Derechos Humanos* (1968–).

§ 13–17. International criminal tribunal decisions. For a multi-volume collection containing decisions of the International Criminal Tribunal for the former Yugoslavia (ICTY) and the International Criminal Tribunal for Rwanda (ICTR), see *Global War Crimes Tribunal Collection* (J. Oppenheim & W. van der Wolf eds., 2001). Other useful sources are *Substantive and Procedural Aspects of International Criminal Law: The Experience of International and National Courts* (G. McDonald & O. Swaak–Goldman eds., 2000) (containing commentary in volume one and documents and cases in volume two); J. Jones, *The Practice of the International Criminal Tribunals for the former Yugoslavia and Rwanda* (2d ed. 2000). ICTY and ICTR decisions can also be found online at <http://www.un.org/icty/index.html> and <http://www.ictr.org>. Information on the permanent International Criminal Court may be found at <http://www.un.org/law/icc/index.html>.

§ 13–18. ITLOS decisions. The Tribunal publishes decisions in volumes entitled *Reports of Judgments, Advisory Opinions and Orders* (1997–) and its proceedings in volumes entitled *Pleadings, Minutes of Public Sittings and Documents* (1997–). Some of these materials may be found online at <http://www.itlos.org/>. For background on the Tribunal, see G. Eiriksson, *The International Tribunal for the Law of the Sea* (2000).

§ 13–19. WTO decisions. The World Trade Organization (WTO) and Cambridge University Press are jointly publishing WTO panel, appellate body, and arbitrator decisions in *Dispute Settlement Reports* (1996–), and have jointly published the WTO agreements themselves in *The Legal Texts: Results of the Uruguay Round of Multilateral Trade Negotiations* (1999). Decisions and legal texts may also be found online at <http://www.wto.org>.

§ 13–20. NAFTA dispute settlement decisions. For a collection of computer disks that include all the cases decided under the Canada–Mexico–United States North American Free Trade Agreement (NAFTA), see R. Folsom, M. Gordon & J. Spanogle, *Handbook of NAFTA Dispute Settlement* (1998). NAFTA dispute settlement decisions can also be found at <www.naftaclaims.com>.

VI. INTERNET RESEARCH

§ 13–21. Internet sources. There is an extraordinary array of information on international law available on the Internet, although the researcher needs to be discriminating in seeking out sites containing accurate and current information.

See generally ASIL Guide to Electronic Resources for International Law (M. Hoffman & J. Watson eds., 2d ed. 2002), *at* <http://www.asil.org/resource/home.htm>. The following Internet sites contain extensive information regarding international law and/or extensive links to relevant Internet sites.

<http://www.un.org>. The United Nations Internet site has links to U.N. created tribunals and courts, including the International Court of Justice, the Tribunal for the Law of the Sea, the International Criminal Court, the International Criminal Tribunal for the former Yugoslavia and the International Criminal Tribunal for Rwanda. The site also contains treaty information, committee information and extensive documents (such as maps and photographs) covering both U.N. history and current events relating to international law.

<http://www.state.gov>. The U.S. Department of State Internet site contains extensive information relating to U.S. involvement in international law and institutions , as well as many related links to Internet sites. For example, the Internet sites of the World Trade Organization, North American Free Trade Agreement, Free Trade of the Americas, and Asian–Pacific Economic Cooperation can all be accessed by links from the "Trade Policy and Programs" page on the State Department Internet site.

<http://www.asil.org>. The American Society of International Law Internet site provides links to

publications and activities of the American Society of International Law, as well as "Insights" papers on topics of current interest.

Several academic institutions worldwide have created Internet sites designed to provide extensive links to other Internet sites relating to international law or institutions, such as:

<http://www.library.northwestern.edu/govpub/resource/internat/igo.html> (maintained by Northwestern University).

<http://www.law.ecel.uwa.edu.au/intlaw/> (maintained by the University of Western Australia).

VII.   FURTHER REFERENCE WORKS

§ 13–22.   Additional help. Most U.S. guides to legal research also contain sections on international law. For works specifically addressing international law research, see *Guide to International Legal Research* (3d ed. 1998) (compiled by the editors and staff of the George Washington Journal of International Law and Economics); J. Rehberg & R. Popa, *Accidental Tourist on the New Frontier: An Introductory Guide to Global Legal Research* (1998); E. Schaffer & R. Snyder, *Contemporary Practice of Public International Law* (1997); C. Germain, *Germain's Transnational Law Research* (1991–).

SUBJECT INDEX

References are to Pages

*

AUTHOR INDEX

383

†